History Lessons

Teaching, Learning, and Testing in U.S. High School Classrooms

ჼ   ჽ

History Lessons

Teaching, Learning, and Testing in U.S. High School Classrooms

ဆ   ભ

S. G. Grant
University at Buffalo,
State University of New York

2003

LAWRENCE ERLBAUM ASSOCIATES, PUBLISHERS
Mahwah, New Jersey   London

Lawrence Erlbaum Associates, Inc., Publishers
10 Industrial Avenue
Mahwah, New Jersey 07430

Cover design by Kathryn Houghtaling Lacey

Library of Congress Cataloging-in-Publication Data

Grant, S. G.
History lessons : teaching, learning, and testing in U.S. High school
    classrooms / S. G. Grant.
        p.cm.
Includes bibliographical references and index.
ISBN 0-8058-4502-X (cloth : alk. Paper)
ISBN 0-8058-4503-8 (pbk. : alk.
    paper)
1. History—Study and teaching (Secondary)—United States.
    I. Title.
D16.3.G73 2003
907'.1'273—dc21

                                                        2002192833
                                                             CIP

Books published by Lawrence Erlbaum Associates are printed on acid-free paper, and their bindings are chosen for strength and durability.

Printed in the United States of America
10 9 8 7 6 5 4 3 2 1

To
Pat Ames,
a teacher of teachers

Contents

Part IV   Influences on and Prospects for Ambitious Teaching

Preface

The buzz around educational standards is nearing its second decade. Since the report *A Nation at Risk* (National Commission on Excellence in Education, 1983), state and national policymakers have offered a range of reform-minded policies with the ostensible purpose of promoting ambitious teaching and learning. Preliminary reports from New York, Kentucky, Texas, and Massachusetts are inconclusive, and it may be some time before a firm assessment of these efforts can be made.

In the meantime, the talk about standards has largely obscured the fact that little is known about what rich teaching and learning look like. Educational researchers have probed many aspects of schooling and we know a fair bit about "typical" classrooms. Lee Shulman (1987) notes, however, that "richly developed portrayals of expertise in teaching are rare" (p. 1). Especially important, Shulman argues, are cases that explore "the management of *ideas* within classroom discourse" (p. 1). Given that policymakers' efforts to reform school curriculum, standardized tests, and the like are presumably encourage more powerful teaching and learning, research that inquires deeply into the classroom lives of teachers and students is key.

The need for rich description and analyses of teachers' practices is particularly evident in the field of social studies. Long-running battles over social studies versus history and over competing visions of the "good" citizen have dominated the professional literature. Since the late 1980s, however, a small but important body of empirical work has developed, chiefly in the subject area of history. Digging deeply into teachers' knowledge, assumptions, and instructional decisions and students' approaches to and understandings of historical ideas, researchers such as Keith Barton, Ronald Evans, Stuart Foster, Linda Levstik, Peter Seixas, Stephen Thornton, Bruce VanSledright, Sam Wineburg, Suzanne Wilson, and Elizabeth Yeager examine how U.S. students make sense of history and how teachers construct their classroom practices.[1]

It is into this context that I offer *History Lessons: Teaching, Learning, and Testing in U.S. High School Classrooms*. In this book, I combine extended case studies of two New York teachers and their students with the extant research literature to explore issues central to understanding life in secondary school history classrooms.

---

[1]These researchers have both benefitted from and extended the work of a small group of British researchers, who have been closely examining students' understandings of history for almost 20 years. I draw on some of the British work, but given the U.S. focus of this book and the different contexts of schools, curriculum, and testing, my use of that research base is limited.

Rich cases of practice are especially useful for teachers and teacher educators trying to understand the possibilities for classroom practice. The cases of the two veteran teachers I profile, George Blair and Linda Strait, well serve that purpose, for although these teachers share several similarities, the teaching practices they construct could not be more different. The two teachers come to teaching from different paths, but Blair, a European American male in his early 50s, and Strait, an African American woman in her mid 40s, work in the same upper-middle-class school, have similar working-class and academic backgrounds, express similar attitudes about the importance of teaching history, and prepare their students under the same state curriculum to take the same mandated Regents examination. Moreover, neither teacher embodies the textbook–worksheet–recitation approach that characterizes so much of what passes for social studies instruction. These are teachers who demand a lot from their students, and state test scores suggest that they get results. Yet the decisions Strait and Blair make around what and how to teach differ dramatically.

To explore those differences, I ask what their teaching practices look like, how their instruction influences their students' understandings of history, and what role the state Regents exams play in their classroom decisions. In chapter 1, "Teaching History," I describe and analyze how each teacher planned and taught a unit on the civil rights era in the United States. Chapter 3, "Learning History," focuses on the students. Here, I use interview data from seven of Blair's and Strait's students to examine similarities and differences in the ways each group of students makes sense of the history they were taught. And in chapter 5, "Testing History," I examine the influence of the New York Regents' exam on each teacher's instruction.

Although cases of teachers and students can be illuminating, I take the analysis of history teaching, learning, and testing a step further in this book. Linda Strait and George Blair do not stand for all teachers in general or for all history teachers in particular. Neither do their students represent the great mass of children in American schools. To broaden the scope of teaching, learning, and testing, then, I pair each of the three empirical or "data" chapters just described with an essay review chapter in which I explore more broadly the corresponding phenomenon. These essay chapters are intended to help readers analyze the cases of Blair, Strait, and their students by looking at them in the context of the current research literature. For example, chapter 1 on how Blair and Strait teach their respective civil rights units is followed in chapter 2 by an essay in which I examine the research around issues related to teaching history, such as whether teachers should be knowledge givers or facilitators and whether they need to be content or pedagogical specialists. Following the chapter in which I describe Blair's and Strait's students' understandings of history is chapter 4, in which I appraise the broader issue of student learning by using the current research to understand the influences on student learning, the historical understandings they hold, and the dispositions of teachers who promote powerful learning. Finally, I pair the chapter where I portray the role of Regents exams in Blair's and Strait's classrooms with chapter 6, in which I use research to address issues related to the purposes of tests, the relationship between teaching and testing, and the impact of increasing the stakes of test performance on teachers and students.

These paired chapters form the bulk of *History Lessons*. In the last section are two chapters intended to extend the previous cases and analyses. In chapter 7, "The Influences on Teachers' Classroom Decision," I look at how and why history teachers like George Blair and Linda Strait construct their individual teaching practices. Drawing on the relevant research literature, I analyze the teachers' thinking and practice in terms of three distinct, but interacting sets of influences: personal, organizational, and policy factors. In the final chapter, I look at the prospects for promoting ambitious teaching and learning. *Ambitious teaching and learning* develops (a) when teachers know well their subject matter and see within it the potential to enrich their students' lives; (b) when teachers know their students well, which includes understanding the kinds of lives they lead, how they think about and perceive the world, and that they are capable of far more than they and most others believe; and (c) when teachers know how to create the necessary space for themselves and their students in environments that may not appreciate the efforts of either. Policymakers place great faith in new curriculum standards and tests, restructured schools, and improved professional development as means to richer teaching and learning. The research on such reforms undercuts a good deal of that faith, but not all. Ambitious teaching and learning develop when smart teachers, curious students, and powerful ideas come together. Policymakers many assume that standards-based reforms support the efforts of ambitious teachers, but until we better understand how these teachers, and the students in their classes, think and act, that assumption is hollow at best.

ACKNOWLEDGMENTS

This has been a satisfying, if challenging, book to write. Researching in the classrooms of Linda Strait and George Blair, and then writing about them and their students in conference papers and journal articles, provided an opportunity to think hard about a whole raft of issues. Returning to those issues and expanding them by contextualizing them within the larger research literature has added a whole other layer of richness. There is much that all of us interested in more ambitious teaching and learning can learn from the efforts of Blair, Strait, their students, and the teachers and students described in the extant research. I begin and I end this book by acknowledging my debt to all the teachers and students into whose classrooms I and other researchers have walked.

As I began to write about teachers and students and the issues of teaching, learning, and testing, I found great support, encouragement, and advice from practicing teachers, university colleagues, and my students. Alison Derme-Insinna, Lynn Pullano, and Kathryn Tzetzo, practicing teachers of great skill and insight, were particularly helpful in keeping the manuscript jargon free and relevant to the needs of preservice and practicing teachers. Sandra Cimbricz, Catherine Cornbleth, Terrie Epstein, Cecil Robinson, and Bruce VanSledright, colleagues at the University at Buffalo and across the country, read and responded to numerous drafts with patient questions and gentle nudges. And students, Jill Gradwell, Ann Marie Lauricella, and Martha Sanfillipo pushed me to think about how ambitious teaching and learning might be described to the widest audience. I especially want to thank Kathy Tzetzo, Linda Levstik, and Keith Barton—for although those just named read portions of these chapters and my earlier papers, Kathy, Linda, and Keith consented to read the entire manuscript. As an author, it is easy enough to lose one's way in a 25-page journal article; writing a 250-page book grossly compounds that tendency. These reviewers read and responded both broadly and deeply, and so saved me much embarrassment. A writer can ask for little more.

Finally, I can only begin to acknowledge the debt to my family. Anne and our children, Alexander and Claire, are the reason my smile brightened when I came downstairs from my computer. And it was their encouraging words that sent me back there the next day, even when those words were, "When are you ever going to finish that book, dad?"

—S. G. Grant
University at Buffalo

PART I
Teaching History

Teaching History: Linda Strait and George Blair Teach About the U.S. Civil Rights Movement

Good or bad, we remember our schooling. Memories of the way the locker room smelled, the first time we were sent to the principal's office, and the classes we liked and hated lie close to our consciousness. We remember the people we encountered—our friends, teachers, coaches. We remember the experiences we had with these people—the friend who stuck with us when we goofed up, the fourth-grade teacher who taught us read a map, the coach who embarrassed us when we make a mistake. These memories form powerful images of the best and worst of schooling, and as such, they shape much of how we think about education.

I am reminded of this truism each year when I interview students for admission to the teacher education program at the University at Buffalo. I ask about their experiences in social studies[1] classrooms and they tell me about the teachers they liked and those they didn't. The reasons they give vary, but most fall into predictable categories. Favorite teachers are those who cared about them personally, who pushed them to do more than they expected they could, who entertained the class with interesting anecdotes, or who encouraged them to think for themselves. Less favorite teachers are those who were boring, insensitive, or cruel.

These recalled memories can seem very powerful to the student sitting across from me. But they also can seem partial, for when I ask about the recalled teacher's classroom practices, the students hesitate. They recall listening to lectures or working on a project or taking lots of tests. Rarely,

---

[1]When talking about classroom practices, I follow the convention of using the terms "social studies" and "history" interchangeably. See Jenness (1990) for a useful description and analysis of the confusion between these two labels.

however, do they remember much beyond these surface-level distinctions. These students have seen a lot of teaching, but they know little about what makes good teaching different from bad, and they have even less understanding of how to do the former rather than the latter.

School classrooms can and should be places of vibrant teaching and learning. Two hundred or more years of something less notwithstanding, I find unconvincing those arguments that what has been must always be. But like any early spring seedling, ambitious teaching and learning demand careful support and attention, and fertile ground in which to grow. The students who sit in my office say they do not want to replicate the lousy instruction they endured. None wants children to fail, to feel bored, or to think education is a waste of time. All want more for their students than they experienced themselves. Yet few cite concrete actions that can enable these goals.

Lots of things can help these prospective teachers mature into smart, thoughtful, and considerate teachers. Good teachers know their subject matter well, have good resources, and possess a wide streak of patient understanding. Teachers flower when they work with supportive colleagues and administrators, and in schools and communities where the norms support academics as much as they do athletics. And state and national policies can encourage responsible experimentation in terms of curriculum, instruction, and assessment.

The several chapters in this book speak to these issues. But rather than an abstract discussion or one that draws only on the available theory and research, I want to center my arguments in the classroom lives of two teachers and their students. These teachers, Linda Strait and George Blair, are neither representative of all teachers nor are they isolated cases at one end or another of the pedagogical spectrum. Looking closely at the teaching, learning, and testing that occur in their classrooms, however, provides grounded insights into the complex world of teachers and learners, and offers some possibilities for thinking about educational change.

In this chapter, I introduce the teachers, Linda Strait and George Blair, and the context in which they teach. I describe how each prepares and delivers instruction around the topic of the U.S. civil rights movement. I follow these descriptions with an analysis that focuses on the distinctive features of each teacher's practice.

SETTING THE CONTEXT: LINDA STRAIT, GEORGE BLAIR, AND WESTWOOD HIGH

Linda Strait and George Blair teach in the same suburban high school. The Westwood[2] school district is located in a middle- to upper-middle-class, predominately White, suburban area in New York state. Westwood is me-

---

[2]As with the teachers and students, all proper names connected with the setting are pseudonyms.

dium-sized high school with just under 1000 students and 70 faculty. One of three high schools in the district, Westwood High is large, boxy, brick building surrounded by athletic fields and large, well-kept homes.

Walking inside the building, one is struck by its openness. Constructed on an open design, the school features a cafeteria and a large, tiered gathering area on the first floor; students congregate here before and after school and during study halls. The classrooms, library, and administrative offices are upstairs. Bookshelves, movable room dividers, and desks define the usable spaces. A couple of walled-in classrooms exist on each floor, but most teaching spaces are open on at least one side. Strait and Blair dislike this set-up, and Blair refuses to teach in the open classrooms.

Most students at Westwood High go on to post-secondary education, and many attend elite, private colleges and universities.[3] Blair and Strait are hard-working teachers, but they and their colleagues benefit from the cultural capital their students hold. That capital includes a fierce belief in the status, if not the power, of a good education, a wide range of cultural knowledge and experiences, the language of standard English, and a host of material comforts. The students at Westwood High are not without their problems. They deal with divorced and absorbed parents, alcohol and drugs, unwanted pregnancy and sexually transmitted diseases, and the general anxieties and ennui that haunt all adolescents. That said, the real advantages Westwood students hold are only dreams to their urban peers.

THE TEACHERS

Linda Strait and George Blair were born and raised in the area, but neither grew up in the Westwood district. Strait is an African American woman in her mid 40s. Raised in a lower-middle-income family that valued education, she holds bachelor's and master's degrees in U.S. history from a medium-sized public university in Michigan. Finding no job opportunities as a historian, Strait returned to New York state, married, and worked briefly in an area post office.

Soon discontented, Strait pursued a degree in library studies and, once finished, began an 8 year career as a librarian in a large county system. "I hated every minute of it," she said, "but once you get involved in things and then you start to make bills, I was sort of trapped staying there to help the family income."

In her eighth year, however, Strait took a leave of absence when she and her husband adopted a Korean infant. During that leave, Strait decided to leave the library system and pursue a teaching career. Her husband is a teacher, and Strait realized that some of the coursework she had done during her undergraduate program would count toward her state teacher cer-

---

[3]Over 80% of Westwood grads typically go on to a 4-year college with another 10% or so attending a 2-year college. Those few students who do not go on to postsecondary education go into the military or to work.

tification. Originally intending to become a mathematics teacher, Strait took the required mathematics and education courses at a local state college. Her student teaching placements, however, were in social studies rather than mathematics classrooms. With two degrees in history, Strait felt comfortable teaching the assigned U.S. history courses in the two schools in which she was placed.

Completing her student teaching with high praise, Strait was offered jobs at the sites of her two placements, a city magnet school and Westwood. The decision was difficult. "I made a list of all the positive and negative aspects of both positions," she said, "and in the long run, more positives to me came from making this selection [Westwood]." Several factors played into her decision: The city teachers were without a contract, she lived in the Westwood school district and her son attended a local school, and the salary offered by Westwood was substantially higher than that of the city school. One other factor also emerged: Westwood students seldom see African American teachers:

> I felt that students in this area need to see that there are Blacks who are successful. They have no Black teachers in this school. They need to see that, yes, there are some who are very successful, and they need to learn from that. So I said maybe it's a good idea that this is the place I should be. So I made the choice.

Westwood has not always been an easy choice. Strait is an avowed political liberal in an area well known to be conservative, and she has sometimes "gotten into trouble" with the building principal for expressing her views. She is not sanguine about this situation, but neither is she willing to abandon her ideas:

> People kept saying, "You're not tenured. Why are you doing this? Why are you saying that?" I said, "I made a promise to myself. I hated being a librarian for eight years, and I promised that if I'm going to teach, I'm going to teach the way I want to teach. And if they want to fire me, if they don't like it, then they'll just have to fire me because I'm not going to be unhappy."

Students and their parents occasionally complain. Strait provides convincing rationales for her actions, however, and her principal, who sometimes questions her approaches, nevertheless continues to back her up.

At the time of my data collection,[4] Strait had been teaching at Westwood for 5 years. She teaches three sections of U.S. History to juniors and two sections of Participation in Government to seniors.

George Blair is a European American male in his early 50s. Also from a lower-middle-income family, he joined the Air Force after graduating from

---

[4]I observed and interviewed Linda Strait over a 2-year period beginning in the 1994–1995 school year. The data on which this chapter is built came from the following year, 1995–1996.

an area high school. Blair spent part of his 4-year hitch in Vietnam, but he cites the time he spent teaching English in Japan as most important. Returning home, Blair enrolled in the local university where he completed bachelor's and master's degrees in U.S. history while becoming certified to teach social studies. Later, he completed a second masters degree in social studies education.

Blair's motivation to teach came in part from his Air Force experience, but the roots also lie in his adverse experience as a high school student:

> I had such negative experiences when I was in high school. I didn't do a lot of work in high school and I got called dumb so often I kind of started believing it. And then [I] realized some errors, such as I think I have to go there and change a little bit of that and try to make [school] a little more positive.

The "errors," Blair asserts, were those teachers, "real screwballs" in his mind, who were quick to dismiss him, and who wielded their classroom authority with little thought about how it affected students' lives. Blair resolved to be "positive in the classroom" and to teach students not only about U.S. history, but about "humanity and understanding" as well. "I make a lot of mistakes," he said, "[but] those are things that I try to accomplish."

Once certified to teach, Blair took at position at a middle school in the Westwood district, where he taught U.S. history for 13 years. Sensing that he was getting in a rut, he accepted a high school social studies position. "I decided to switch levels just to try something new," he explained. After an awkward first year, he reports quickly settling in and enjoying his work at Westwood High. He teaches four sections of the required junior U.S. History course and a senior history elective.[5]

TEACHING THE U.S. CIVIL RIGHTS MOVEMENT

George Blair and Linda Strait work in the same school, have similar working-class and academic backgrounds, express similar attitudes about the importance of teaching about civil rights, and prepare their students under the same state curriculum to take the same state-required Regents examination.[6] Neither teacher relies on textbook-worksheet-recitation approach

---

[5] I interviewed George Blair and observed his classroom practices during the 1995–1996 school year.

[6] The NYS Regents examination plays a prominent role in later chapters. A bit of background now, however, may be useful. Regents' tests are administered in all academic subjects. Social studies students take the Global Studies Regents test in 10th grade and the U.S. History and Government Regents test in 11th grade.

The high school level Regents' test in U.S. History combines multiple-choice questions with essays. Passing this test has been long considered an indication of quality education. A less rigorous test, the Regents Competency Test (RCT), was created in the 1980s for students who sought a local diploma instead of a Regents diploma. The RCT is being phased out and the Regents' exam has been revised in the latest round of state educational reform.

characteristic of social studies instruction (Goodlad, 1984). They work hard at their craft, demand a lot from their students, and they get results.

And yet the decisions Strait and Blair make around what and how to teach about the civil rights movement differ radically. Some hints about *why* they teach as they do surface in the accounts that follow; I deal explicitly with that question in chapter 7. Before dealing with explanations, let's look at each teacher's civil rights unit.

FRAMING A MASTER NARRATIVE: THE CASE OF GEORGE BLAIR

Five minutes into a typical George Blair class, one is struck with conflicting images. On the one hand, this looks like a stereotypical social studies class—a teacher standing and talking at the front of the room, an overhead projector displaying an outline of the textbook content, students silently copying notes. So familiar is this image that it seems almost a caricature. Listening to Blair talk confounds that image, however, for he neither parrots the textbook nor does he reduce the content of history to a parade of facts and dates. Instead, he crafts a master narrative and a series of stories based in fact, but developed as part of a story grammar, a narrative framework that includes complex characters, interesting plots, rising and falling action, and resolutions.

A Vietnam-era veteran, Blair is a self-described "old protester from the sixties." With two degrees in history, Blair knows well the subject matter he teaches. From his master's degree in social studies education, Blair learned about a number of instructional approaches. He rejects them, however, in favor of the lecture. "I use the lecture method," he said, "I use it the best. I've become fairly good at it." Blair disdains talk about instructional variety, small-group projects, performance assessments, and the like. He knows that he is a masterful storyteller, that his students generally do well on the state Regents' test, and that educational fads come and go.

Teaching Civil Rights in the Context of the Times and the Textbook

When I asked George Blair if I could observe his unit on the civil rights movement, he explained that he does not do "a unit as such." Instead, he addresses civil rights issues and events as they occur in the chronological order his textbook presents.[7] He invited me to sit in on his Eisenhower unit because civil rights would play a part in his lecture. I later learned that he picks up threads of the civil rights movement as it surfaces in subsequent textbook chapters.

---

[7]The textbook Blair uses is *A History of the United States* (Boorstin & Kelley, 1994).

After welcoming the students[8] and briefly reviewing the previous chapter test, Blair begins the new unit by comparing Dwight Eisenhower and his opponent in the 1952 and 1956 presidential elections, Adlai Stevenson. Eisenhower was "the hero of World War II.... He was loved by the GIs and the American public."[9] Stevenson, by contrast, "was considered an egghead ... you call them nerds today.... Also Stevenson was divorced and in the 1950s that was not as socially acceptable as it is today." Blair adds, "Stevenson was very nice. I liked him." Quickly concluding that the two elections were "essentially the same race.... Stevenson doesn't stand a snowball's chance in hell," Blair offers a glimpse into the master or framing narrative of this unit: Dwight Eisenhower's negotiation of dilemmas in both foreign and domestic policy:

> Eisenhower was conservative.... But it will blow up in his face.... He made several appointments to the Supreme Court, but one at least is very liberal ... and [emphatically] that shocks the hell out of Eisenhower.... Remember there was tremendous pressure ... very serious things happen and early on in Eisenhower's presidency.... He's hit in the face with the Brown decision.... Eisenhower disagrees, but he has to enforce it and he does ... and there is a serious confrontation in the South....

> Eisenhower also confronts the Soviets.... [dramatically]. We hate the Soviet Union, we fear the Soviet Union.... We've got the H-bomb, but we're scared as hell. So the foreign policy John Foster Dulles comes up with ... [is] a sad state of affairs.... It's called massive retaliation ... [and it means] any aggression by the Communists and we would retaliate with everything we have, massively, with everything we have.

After foreshadowing Eisenhower's domestic and foreign dilemmas, Blair begins his lecture on U.S. foreign policy:

> Now the book doesn't tell you this.... In the 1956 Hungarian Revolution ... the Hungarians ask for our help and we don't give it to them.... [incredulously; loudly] Massive retaliation? We aren't going to retaliate at all! It's just sword rattling and it doesn't make any sense. We're not going to blow up the world. Who're we trying to kid?.... Massive retaliation; but we can't do that.... Massive retaliation ... what sense does that make? [quietly] But it shows how afraid we really are....

> John Foster Dulles uses the idea of brinkmanship ... pushing the Soviets to the brink of war.... But how far can you push?.... The Soviets do the same thing.... Much of the Cold War, we push and push and push ... as far as we possibly can and there's tension, and stress, and anxiety. There's not a lot of fighting, but there's a helluva lot of tension, stress, and anxiety. [A student, David, asks, "Were any shots fired?"] Yes ... Korea, Vietnam ... between the U.S. and the U.S.S.R.? No ... they never attack one another directly.

---

[8]Of the 24 students, 16 are male; 8 are female. Other than 3 Asian American students, most appear to be European Americans.

[9]I follow the convention here of using ellipses to indicate places where the informants' words were not recorded and/or used in the material quoted. I use brackets [ ] to indicate words I have added in order to clarify a quote.

In these passages, we see several elements of Blair's narrative instructional style. The story he constructs is rooted in standard historical fare: personalities (Dwight Eisenhower, John Foster Dulles), policies (massive retaliation, brinkmanship), and events (Cold War, Hungarian Revolution). He occasionally refers to a point listed on the overhead notes and his stories always contain factual elements represented in those notes. Blair does not simply reiterate these ideas. Instead, he focuses on individuals' actions, and he uses various oratorical means (e.g., vocal inflection, emotion, personal reaction, rhetorical questions) as he builds a dramatic story of tension and fear between the United States and the U.S.S.R. And like most storytellers, Blair delivers the Cold War as a 45-minute monologue, punctuated only once by a student question.[10]

It is hard to tell what sense students are making of all this as they copy the outline notes displayed on the overhead projector. Few ever look up at Blair or respond overtly to his lecture. Blair's narrative has the elements of a good story, but whether his students perceive it this way is unclear.

Day two of the Eisenhower unit begins with Blair talking briefly about U.S. and U.S.S.R. summits. He then shifts to domestic policy. Following the overhead notes, he quickly reviews government policies toward farming such as the Agricultural Act of 1954, which encouraged farmers to produce less, and, because he has apparently talked about this before, the McCarthy hearings. Blair then announces that the class will go on to "some more interesting things"—civil rights:

> Now we move on to some more interesting things.... I remember a lot of this ... this is the beginning of the serious civil rights.... Now you remember Plessy v. Ferguson of 1896. We did that. Plessy v. Ferguson sets up the idea that the South can segregate Blacks and Whites as long as the facilities are equal.... I told you this even though the book doesn't.... In economic terms the South couldn't afford two systems.... It was too costly....

> The issue is going to come up again.... Several decisions will be made [around] equal rights for the Black population.... In 1953, Eisenhower appoints a new chief justice ... and it was not a popular choice.... Earl Warren was not a great jurist.... He was a politician in California, not an academic in constitutional law. When he goes to Washington, he was ignored by some of FDR's appointees [to the Supreme Court].... [He was] ignored, snubbed ... [dramatically] and he will change the court to this very day. Warren has a philosophical idea called judicial activism ... the process of allowing the Supreme Court to make decisions to help out social issues.... This is the first time the court ever did this and [solemnly] it will change the court forever.... Warren is a liberal and he will make several major decisions ... [for example] the 1954 Topeka, Kansas ... Brown v. the Board of Education....

> Topeka ... had separate Black and White schools as all the South did. The Browns wanted to send their daughter to the White school.... They can't ... so they go to court. The NAACP supported them.... The case was presented to the Supreme Court by a lawyer, Thurgood Marshall ... [who asks himself]

---

[10]In fact, David's question is the only substantive question I have witnessed in the many times I have observed Blair's classroom.

what kind of case can we come up with to stop segregation in schools? Now I've mentioned this before.... After much planning, Marshall puts together a defense based on social and psychological evidence. He argued that segregation was hurting black kids.... He puts the case together [so that it was] not an issue of constitutionality though Marshall cited the 14th amendment. But the evidence was psychological and social, not legal.... And the Supreme Court accepts the argument.... The Brown decision overturns Plessy.... Brown says that schools, when they segregate, do harm to the black population and segregation must end ... [voice rising] and it starts the major movement toward civil rights in the south that continues to today....

After that decision, the South refuses to integrate schools.... Little Rock in 1957 is the test.... [dramatically] God, I remember this on TV, too, kids.... Seven to eight Black children try to integrate Central High School.... They're prevented.... [incredulously] Orval Faubus, the Governor, refuses to allow the Black kids into the school.... He sends in the National Guard to prevent them.... Eisenhower notified Faubus of the Brown decision.... And even though Eisenhower doesn't like the Brown decision ... he thought the court overstepped their bounds ... he knows he must enforce the decision.... So he sends in the paratroopers, active military ... there were more soldiers than students.... And they escort the students to class for two years....

[Quietly] One of the young ladies recently published a book ... and she talks about the threats on her life.... The threats to her life were unbelievable.... [She talked about how] the Black community took the kids away every summer and put them with Black families around the country.... This woman lived with a doctor in Los Angeles.... She told stories of kids kicking her and pushing her down stairs.... [Softly] And when I read this, tears came to my eyes.... Man's inhumanity to man.

Here, Blair pauses, walks over to the overhead projector, puts up the next set of notes, and then walks back to the righthand corner of the room. He continues in more matter-of-fact tone, but as before, his voice gradually grows louder and his tone more insistent:

I don't think we need to spend a lot of time on Rosa Parks.... Civil rights just gets going and going and going.... Rosa Parks was just a plain, simple lady.... She refused to give her seat up to a White man.... When the buses were busy, Blacks had to move to the back of the bus .... Rosa Parks refuses and when push comes to shove, she's arrested.... The ultimate threat to Blacks was "Don't you know your place?" [Sadly] I know you don't identify with this and I'm glad you can't.... [There were so many] gutsy folks ... moving toward civil rights ... and I hope some day we'll have true civil rights....

[Loudly] What happens? A Baptist minister by the name of Martin Luther King comes to Alabama.... He goes on TV [and] says the city will desegregate mass transit or Blacks will use their most important weapon, the boycott. They will boycott until integration.... In just less than a year, representatives from the bus system and the government negotiate with Blacks and the buses will be desegregated.... Blacks will no longer ride in the back of the bus.... Blacks were poor so they had to use mass transit.... When they didn't use the buses, the companies ran in the red....

[Softly] As I say these things, things go through my mind.... Very big things. This was a very painful time for both the Black and White population.... This was not trite, it was earth-shattering.... I know I'm going through these things quickly, but they are not trite.

That said, Blair ends the focus on civil rights and returns briefly to foreign policy (i.e., more talk about John Foster Dulles and massive retaliation, the Hungarian Revolution—the bloody putdown is compared with Tiananmen Square, and the creation of Israel and tensions in the Middle East).

As he describes the beginnings of the civil rights movement, Blair uses the same elements of storytelling that surfaced in his earlier account of the Cold War. His story is faithful to the facts (e.g., the Brown v. Board of Education decision, the confrontation at Little Rock, Rosa Parks's action, Martin Luther King, Jr., and the bus boycott) and to a focus on individuals' actions and experiences, including his own. Again, facts serve as the threads with which he weaves a dramatic account of Black and White tensions, resolutions, and more tensions. He uses his considerable rhetorical skills to convey both the anxiety of the times and the struggles of individual actors.

In one sense, Blair is doing what many social studies educators advocate, teaching ideas—in this case, civil rights—in the context of the times. This makes sense as no era is ultimately reducible to a single focus. Civil rights is an important piece of understanding the 1950s, but so too is understanding the relationship between the United States and the U.S.S.R. So although some may argue that civil rights gets lost in Blair's master narrative about the Eisenhower era, others may argue with equal conviction that he is serving the goal of a more comprehensive history. By highlighting the Eisenhower presidency, Blair chooses a frame into which he links each of the ideas and issues discussed. One might question his choice to focus on Eisenhower rather than on any of several big issues, civil rights among them. Nevertheless, Blair's construction of a master narrative seems like a reasonable instructional approach.

Examining George Blair's Instructional Practice

Three features seem to define George Blair's narrative teaching approach. First, Blair weaves the U.S. civil rights movement together with U.S. foreign policy. Civil rights is important, but it is understood to be part of bigger picture rather than a stand-alone topic. Second, Blair highlights stories of individuals' actions and experiences. Dates, places, and events are prominent, but they serve primarily as the backdrop for stories of individual uncertainty, folly, courage, and determination. Finally, Blair's students play a passive role. Stories demand a storyteller and an audience, and there is no role confusion in Blair's classroom. As the narrator, Blair crafts the stories and delivers them without interruption. As the audience, students listen, take notes, and remain silent. Blair delivers a powerful performance, but it is a solo effort.

Weaving Civil Rights into a Larger Narrative

George Blair worries about the state of race relations in the United States and the growing intolerance he senses in his students and in the larger public. His response is to weave civil rights into a larger historical fabric rather than treating it as separate unit.

The "problem [of race relations] seems to be getting worse, not better," Blair said, "it scares the hell out of me." Like many of his generation, he once thought that the situation was improving. He is no longer sure. "The rift seems to be even greater," Blair said, "I mean, we're really in some serious trouble here. Very, very serious trouble."

Blair talks about race and civil rights with passion and conviction. As a set of important issues and events, he would no sooner ignore civil rights than he would the Declaration of Independence. But, as with the Declaration of Independence, Blair believes civil rights must be presented in a broader historical context. The U.S. civil rights movement was and continues be significant, but its importance can not be understood apart from a larger narrative of the times. Blair crafts that narrative around the dilemmas Dwight Eisenhower faced. One dilemma surfaces in the Supreme Court decision in Brown v. Board of Education, a decision with which Eisenhower disagrees, but enforces vigorously nevertheless. The drama of that story becomes a key moment in Blair's retelling. It is only one moment, however, for in Blair's master narrative Eisenhower faces other problematic moments in foreign policy, such as the Hungarian revolt. The view of history that emerges, then, is one where individuals and events are woven together into a master narrative and a series of dramatic stories.[11]

If weaving civil rights into a larger narrative reflects Blair's view of subject matter, so too is it part and parcel of his view of students. In short, he believes his 11th graders need to see the "big picture." Blair's students have already had 3 years of U.S. history: a year-long course in fifth grade, and a two-year sequence in seventh and eighth grades. He heavily discounts those experiences, however:

> When they [students] come here they don't have the faintest idea. People have said there's carryover from seventh and eighth grade…. [But] whoever says that doesn't have the foggiest idea of what goes on in a classroom…. To say there's carryover, that's absolutely asinine.

Blair senses his students arrive with a fragmented knowledge of history. By weaving individuals and events into a larger narrative, he believes he is helping students make sense of and remember the material.

---

[11]As noted earlier, Blair takes a narrative approach to each of the units he teaches. Listen to how he frames his unit on Reconstruction:

> I introduced Reconstruction in the Civil War as one of the lowest periods from a morale point of view, one of the lowest periods of U.S. history. I compare it to the '60s in Vietnam for the antiwar kind of thing. I said you have to remember it from that point of view, that we were really, from a morale point of view anyway, were very, very low, and I think that has a lot to do with some of the ideas that we had.

Focusing on Individuals

Weaving civil rights into a master narrative helps George Blair teach his students to have both "humanity and understanding." Central to that effort are stories of individual actors.

History in Blair's classroom is the story of great individuals. He may recognize the importance of social movements and structures, but these are not prominent in his view of history. Instead he focuses on individual belief and behavior, such that the 1950s become a study of key figures—Eisenhower, Dulles, Marshall, King—and the events they participated in—Hungarian Revolution, Cold War, Brown v. Board of Education, the Montgomery bus boycott. Most are the big names of U.S. history textbooks, but not all. Melba Beals (1994), the "young lady" who wrote a book about her experiences in integrating Central High School in Little Rock, receives as much attention as do Thurgood Marshall and John Foster Dulles. This does not mean that Blair emphasizes social history or the "lives of ordinary people in all their richness" (Appleby, Hunt, & Jacob, 1994, p. 84). The history he teaches is primarily political and economic, and it features those individuals who rise to the top. Nevertheless, Blair's interest in individual experiences and his narrative approach provide space for stories of the lesser known as well as the prominent.

Blair's narration of individual's lives and experiences also seems consistent with his concern for nurturing his students' humanity. His stories about the dilemmas Eisenhower faces and the struggles the student from Central High endures seem designed to emphasize the human dimension of history—to show real people in real situations that have real consequences. This is not unproblematic because Blair is not sure what effect his stories have. "You just put the question in their mind and then walk away from it and let them deal with it," he said, "I think a lot of them forget it. But at least they've been exposed to those kinds of ideas." Moreover, some observers may worry that Blair's emphasis on the great person view of history undercuts the possibility that students will see value in collective action. Blair's stories carry the potential for helping students make sense of history and of their own lives. Whether they do or not is less clear.

Teaching as Monologue

One last feature of George Blair's teaching is his use of monologue. Blair holds no truck with "new" teaching methods. In his view, small-group work, student presentations, and nontraditional assessments are simply fads. "Does learning go on?" he asks, "is the maturity level there for these students to truly understand what they're doing?"

Blair's lectures suggest that, although he genuinely appears to like his students, he holds a dim view of their capabilities. For example, he does not believe students glean much from the assigned textbook readings: "I want them to pick up the major points that are in the book, that are in the subject.... But I don't think they have the historical background to understand what the important points are in the chapter and what are not important." He also dismisses simulations and other experiential activities as games, doubting that they have any real or lasting effect: "I'd say I don't think the kid can make the generalization from this game to an historical event, or general ideas of life, or flow of society, or the flow of history, or the flow of psychology, the flow of people, the flow of culture." Blair assigns a research paper, but reports, "I don't expect much."

If Blair's monologues develop, in part, because he doubts students' capabilities, another reason comes from his felt need to prepare them for college studies. "I view the course also as preparation for college," he said, "They have to learn to study well.... They've got to get a ... physical tolerance for sitting down for three hours and studying and talking notes and that kind of thing."

Blair's practice of outlining the textbook chapter and displaying those notes on an overhead projector also underscores a sense that his students need more teacher direction rather than less. When he began teaching high school, Blair assigned textbook readings and assumed the students had digested them. Test scores and "the feel that you have for the class" suggested otherwise. "I would give an assignment in reading and then I would go through those points," he said, "[and] they didn't have the foggiest idea of what I was talking about.... So I said I'm going have to give them, probably have to give them something else to hold on to." Blair's solution: "I give them my notes in my class, which is literally an outline of the course."

George Blair believes he faces a simple reality: He must cover the entire history of the United States, "Colonialism to Clinton," with students whose historical knowledge is weak at best. "I gotta get through the material," he said, "we're content oriented." Given less content and more time, Blair said there are issues, such as civil rights, that "I might deal with differently." The press to cover the material is strong, however, so Blair's decision to streamline his instruction through a master narrative and overhead notes makes some sense: Teaching through narratives is far more efficient, timewise, than other methods such as class discussion. Using a narrative style also makes sense given Blair's view of his students. Sensing that they come to him with little knowledge of and no frameworks for thinking about history, Blair provides both. Some observers question the overuse of narrative in teaching history, arguing that it is but one way of making sense of history (e.g., Levstik, 1995). In Blair's hands, however, one could argue that it is a reasonable choice.

USING ACTIVITIES AND EXPERIENCES TO PUSH STUDENTS' THOUGHT AND FEELINGS: THE CASE OF LINDA STRAIT

Although Linda Strait and George Blair have much in common, a few minutes in each teacher's classroom reveal startling differences. Where Blair is a master storyteller, Strait is a purposeful provocateur. Rather than create and deliver a narrative in which civil rights plays only a part, Strait constructs a separate civil rights unit, which she expresses through a range of lectures, small- and whole-group activities, readings, and assignments. Rather than focus on individuals' actions, Strait weaves together attention to individual actors and to larger social forces. And rather than hold center stage, Strait frequently steps aside to push her students[12] to active engagement with the ideas and emotions.

One other difference between these teachers is worth note: Blair, a 25-year veteran teacher, already believes he is doing his best. In her sixth year, Strait acknowledges that she is "constantly tinkering" with her instructional planning and practice. "Any methods I come up with," she said, "I'm devising on my own, I'm making up as I go along."

It is the differences between these two teachers, then, that stand out, and those differences are most obvious in the instruction each offers.

Teaching Civil Rights
Through Activities and Experiences

Linda Strait crafts all of her teaching into topical units. Earlier in the year, I observed her unit on immigration, and in the previous year I saw units on Reconstruction and World War II. In each case, Strait focuses on a big topic rather than on a chronological era. From there she crafts a unit of study that draws on various sources: her college notes, the New York state 11th-grade social studies syllabus, various curriculum materials, and her own reading. The textbook[13] figures into this mixture; she reviews it for key ideas and assigns sections for students to read, but it drives neither her planning nor her instruction. Each of her units is a complex whole with various instructional activities and experiences designed to provide multiple opportunities for students to engage the ideas and emotions of the times.

Strait designed her civil rights unit to last eight class periods. In summary form, the instruction maps out this way:

- Day 1: Videotape from the Southern Poverty Law Center entitled "The Shadow of Hate," which describes majority discrimination against several religious (Quakers, Baptists, Jews), racial (Native, African, and Asian Americans), and ethnic groups (Irish Catholics, Mexican Americans). Following the videotape, Strait solicits written reactions from the class.

---

[12]Of the 29 students in Strait's class, 19 female and 7 males are European American. Two additional females are Asian American and one male is East Indian American.

[13]Strait uses Scott Foresman's high school U.S. history textbook, *American Voices* (Berkin et al., 1995).

- Day 2: Small-group activity where students discuss and list their reactions to the videotape on large pieces of chart paper. Strait later displays each chart on the back wall. At the end of the period, she distributes a feature article on school desegregation from *Time* magazine (April 18, 1995).

- Day 3: An ungraded quiz, based on the previous night's reading, asks students to categorize nine statements as either an instance of civil rights or civil liberties.[14] Strait then reviews part one of the notes she prepares and distributes for each unit.[15]

- Day 4: Videotape from the Southern Poverty Law Center, "A Time for Justice," which chronicles the civil rights movement for African Americans. At the end of the video, Strait poses four questions for discussion the next day. The questions are: (a) What were the goals of the movement? (b) What were the strategies of movement participants? (c) Why did the movement succeed? (d) Given the chance to participate in any of the events of this movement, which events would you participate in and why?

- Day 5: Roundtable discussion of the four questions posed the previous day. Strait then introduces an activity that takes up the rest of this class and all the next day's. The assignment calls for students to imagine that they were living in the early 1950s and that a local skating rink owner refused to admit minority customers. In small groups, students must create a strategy for winning access to the rink by listing their reasons, methods, and arguments on a worksheet Strait supplies.

- Day 6: Simulation where Strait portrays the skating rink operator and responds as students, in their groups, make their cases.

- Day 7: Review of part two of the notes[16] and a practice session devoted to writing essays culled from previous 11th-grade Regents tests.[17]

- Day 8: Review of the practice essays. Strait then rearranges student desks into a large circle and leads the class in a public reading of a handout entitled "Forty Lives for Freedom," a list of individuals who lost their lives to the cause of civil rights. Each student reads one person's name and the

---

[14]Statements included "a nine year old girl is not allowed to play on the school basketball team" and "you are arrested for burning the U.S. flag." As Strait explains, the first is an example of civil rights in that it applies to conditions of race, gender, or age, whereas the second is an example of civil liberties in that it refers to conditions intended by the Bill of Rights.

[15]This set of notes (another set is distributed and discussed on day 7) consists of the following elements: (a) definitions of "civil rights" and "civil liberties," and (b) a chronology of the civil rights movement with special attention to Harry Truman's efforts and the Brown v. the Board of Education decision. Also attached are additional readings on the Brown decision, equal opportunity, and the Swann v. Charlotte-Mecklenburg Board of Education decision in 1971, which allowed the use of forced busing to end patterns of discrimination.

[16]These notes include sections on the early philosophy of the civil rights movement, early leaders and activists, civil rights presidents, later philosophies, more "radical" leaders, assassinations, other civil rights movements (e.g., Women, Native Americans, Mexican Americans, and Handicapped/Disabled Persons), and Supreme Court cases.

circumstances of his or her death.[18] Strait then distributes and reviews a handout entitled "Hate Crimes (Summer, 1991)," a list of 13 crimes committed against individuals between June 4 and August 31, 1991.[19] Class ends with a slide/tape show Strait developed several years ago on Martin Luther King, Jr.[20]

Several notable features surface in this free-standing unit. First, Strait constructs a distinct unit that spans time, circumstances, and groups. She emphasizes African American experiences, but more as a case in point than as the definitive civil rights group. Second, Strait employs a wide variety of activities in an instructional tour de force. Multiple learning opportunities arise—reading, writing, viewing, role playing—each of which illuminates

---

[17]The prompts are these:

Essay #1: During various time periods in U.S. history, groups of people have been excluded from full participation in American society.

Groups
Native American Indians (1790–1890)
Latinos (1900–1970)
Japanese Americans (1900–1970)
Women (1940–1990)
African Americans (1945–1970)

a. Select *three* of the groups listed. For *each* one selected, discuss a specific example of how the group was excluded from full participation in American society during the time period indicated.

b. For *one* of the groups you selected in answer to a, discuss a specific action taken by the Federal Govt. *or* an organization *during* or *after* the time period indicated to help this group achieve full participation in American society.

Essay #2: Since 1865, agents of change have acted to advance the cause of civil rights and civil liberties in the United States.

Agents of Change
Government
A nongovernmental group
An individual

For *each* of the agents of change listed:

a. Explain one action taken by that agent of change to help advance civil rights or civil liberties in the U.S.

b. Describe the historical circumstances that led to that action.

[18]For example: Rev. George Lee—killed for leading voter registration drive (Belzoni, Mississippi, 1955); Willie Edwards—killed by the Klan (Montgomery, Alabama, 1957); Paul Guihard—European reporter killed during the Ole Miss riot (Oxford, Mississippi, 1962); and Virgil Lamar Ware—youth killed during wave of racist violence (Birmingham, Alabama, 1963).

[19]For example: Albuquerque, New Mexico (June 4, 1991)—A cross was burned on the lawn of a racially mixed family, Woodbridge, New Jersey (June 28, 1991)—Thirteen people were arrested for assaulting and harassing Asian Indians, Fullerton, California (July 7, 1991)—A Chinese American teenager was beaten unconscious by skinheads.

Strait adapted the "Forty Lives" and "Hate Crimes" lists from materials she received from the Southern Poverty Law Center.

[20]Strait had to be absent from school the next day. She prepared a 12-question, multiple-choice quiz to be administered that day. The questions ranged from definitional (e.g., Which action is the best example of civil disobedience?) to generalization (Which is the most valid conclusion to be drawn from the study of the civil rights movement in the U.S. since 1954?) to interpretive (e.g., students were presented with the quotation, "We will match your capacity to inflict suffering with our capacity to endure suffering …. We will not hate you, but we cannot obey your unjust laws," and were asked who was the most likely author—Booker T. Washington, Martin Luther King, Jr., W. E. B. Du Bois, or Malcolm X).

and complexifies the civil rights movement. Third, Strait expands the role of teacher. She plays the traditional roles of knowledge giver (when she reviews unit notes) and knowledge evaluator (when she scores the end-of-unit quizzes). Strait plays less traditional roles when she organizes students into small groups as a means of eliciting reactions to a videotape and when she organizes the skating-rink activity. Strait is not an "invisible" teacher who directs class from the sidelines (Wineburg & Wilson, 1991), but she pushes beyond the traditional parameters of "teacher." Finally, Strait promotes an expansive view of the subject matter. She gives attention to the major actors and events of the civil rights movement. She also gives significant attention to less known people (the "Forty Lives for Freedom" list) and events (the "Hate Crimes" list). The two videotapes and the skating-rink simulation seem especially designed to bring the civil rights movement down to a recognizable and empathic level. So although Strait covers much of the standard political and economic history curriculum, her unit delves far into the ordinary lives that represent an emphasis on social history.

For their part, students were often actively engaged, and there were several instances of powerful teaching and learning. Consider two examples. The first is the skating-rink simulation; the second is the roundtable discussion.

The Skating-Rink Simulation

During the class period before the simulation, Linda Strait assigns students to five groups. She allows them 10 minutes to brainstorm reasons, methods, and arguments in order to persuade a White skating-rink operator during the 1950s to rethink her policy of prohibiting entry to minority customers. While students begin the task, Strait circulates, alternately listening to and commenting on their deliberations. Just before the bell, she informs students that they will have 6 minutes to convince her, as the skating-rink operator, to change the policy during the simulation the next day.

Students arrive the following day to see one chair in the middle of the classroom and the remaining desks arranged around the room in five groups. After taking roll, Strait sits in the single chair and announces it is time to start. A pattern develops where each group, in turn, walks over to Strait (who plays the rink operator role with passion and spirit), makes its pitch, responds to Strait's questions and barbs, and then sits down. After the last group, Strait comments on the groups' various efforts. What follows are the interactions as two groups present their arguments, and then Strait's closing comments:

> The first group [Jerry, Sue, Linda, Rachel, and Terry—all White students] sheepishly approach Strait. She immediately launches her character. "How did you folks get in here?" she demands:
>
> Sue: "We want to skate."
>
> Strait: "Sorry, Whites only."

Jerry: "What's the difference?"

Strait: "That's the policy, that's always been the policy ... in this town."

Jerry: " ... that isn't fair ... "

Linda: "You're going to lose customers."

Strait: " ... no problem so far.... *You* [pointing to Jerry; presuming he is White and the others are minorities] can skate, but they have to go."

Jerry: "We have no choice but to protest."

Rachel: "And we'll encourage our friends not to come."

Strait: " ... I'm not too concerned.... As you can see, it's busy tonight."

Jerry asks if the students can regroup and come back. Strait, still in character, asks him what he's talking about. He tries to explain that he's talking to Strait, the teacher:

Strait: "I own a skating rink. I don't know any teacher. [to Jerry and the others] He can skate, but the rest of you got to get out of here."

Rachel: "If you don't let us skate, we're going to block the door."

Strait: "Well, that's fine. I'll just have you arrested.... I suggest you leave or I'm going to call to get you removed from the premises."

As Jerry's group leaves, Ned, a member of the audience, calls out, "Man, this is impossible!" Back in their seats, the group huddles and returns for a second try. Jerry says, "We have to emphasize that this is a racist facility." Strait shrugs: "It's no different from any other in this town."

The other groups follow. Most echo the arguments about fairness and the loss of business, and issue threats of ensuing protests. Some try to broker special times for minority skaters; others appeal to Strait's courage in breaking with tradition. The last group uses some of these appeals and adds one new one:

The final group [two White boys—Ben and Steve; two White girls—Melanie and Anna; and one Chinese American girl—Kim] approaches Strait. She ignores them. Finally, Melanie says, "Excuse me." Strait looks up.

Ben: "We'd like to skate in your rink."

Strait: "*You* can skate, but the rest of you have to get out of here."

Ben: "What you're doing is unconstitutional."

Strait: "I know my constitution."

Steve: "If you're going to segregate ... "

Strait: "Look, I'm not a lawyer, I'm a businesswoman.... But there's no law in this town that says I can't just have Whites."

Steve: "But if you kick us out, where can we go?"

Strait: " ... not my problem. Find another place."

Anna: "It's our right to skate.... Think of all the money you're losing."

Strait: "Well, it's about closing time.... [This is a] teen curfew violation [Ned calls out: "There was no teen curfew in the rules!"].... I need to be getting home.... There's no law that says I have to let you in."

Kim: "Where are we supposed to go?"

Strait: "Go somewhere else."

Melanie: "If the movie theater let us in, would you let us in?"

Strait: "That's an interesting question."

Ben: " ... are you thinking about it?"

Strait: " ... but ... [if I did that, then others would be] ready to lynch me."

Steve: " ... the minorities would stand up for you."

Kim: " ... think about it, you're a female.... How do you know that others wouldn't follow you?"

With that, Strait announces "Time's up." Jerry calls out, "That's the closest [to being convincing]." In the last few minutes, Strait thanks the students for their efforts and talks through some of the arguments made. "I do believe that two of you convinced me," she said, " ... but I continued saying no.... Two of you convinced me to think about changing my ways." The class explodes as students call for Strait to reveal which groups succeeded. After a pause, she extracts a promise that they will not tell succeeding classes, and then describes her thinking:

> The last group.... Being a woman hit my feminist side even though there wasn't a strong woman's movement in the '50s.... The woman's movement picks up in the '60s.... But it appealed to me even though there wasn't a feminist movement. I hadn't expected that. And Mary's group convinced me ... [Mary had announced that she had skated before and that, unbeknownst to the operator, was of mixed race background]. [Her background] was an interesting twist. It threw me off. The others were just making me mad.... I didn't like the personal attacks ... but you continued pressing [and that was good].

Jerry calls out, "We came back." "Yeah," said Strait, "but telling me I was losing business ... wouldn't convince me.... " Strait then adds a final comment on playing her role: "I didn't like the feeling of being a racist," she said. " ... I was out of my element.... But I realized I was doing pretty good [at rebutting the students' arguments] and that didn't make me feel very good either!" Several students nod in response.

This vignette illustrates several dimensions of Linda Strait's approach to teaching. First, it demonstrates Strait's impulse to go beyond traditional instructional methods. Students learn about arguments against segregation and methods of fighting it through videotapes, their textbook readings, and the unit notes. Here, however, not only must they apply what they learned, but they must do so in a very different context. Second, Strait provides opportunities for her students to feel the emotions of an era as well as to learn facts and concepts. Although she knows that many of her students sympathize with the experiences of African Americans during this period, she also knows that few truly understand those experiences. She wants students to have an intellectual grasp of the era, but she wants them to have an experiential grasp as well. Third, Strait knows that there is power in students working together on challenging problems. There are no right answers in this exercise, and Strait understands that students will struggle together even more than they would if they participated in the activity as individuals.

Finally, Strait illustrates her willingness to step outside the traditional teacher role. She is still at the center of the class. Yet, in assuming the skating-rink operator role she takes on a different persona, even to the extent that she ignores Jerry's effort to talk to her as a teacher. Strait can and does deliver instruction through traditional means, but she also constructs activities where she can expand her role.

The Roundtable Discussion

The skating-rink simulation was a powerful activity. Students seemed engaged from the moment the activity started, and their small victories and many defeats at the hands of Linda Strait's skilled acting registered on their faces and in their public and private comments. Other activities during the civil rights unit, although also powerful, were slower to develop. The roundtable discussion exemplifies an activity that, despite an uncertain start, develops into a richly complex lesson.

The roundtable discussion builds on the four questions Strait posed the previous day. The questions are:

1. What were the goals of the movement?
2. What were the strategies of movement participants?
3. Why did the movement succeed?
4. Given the chance to participate in any of the events of this movement, which events would you participate in and why?

On the day of the discussion, students take seats in a large circle that Strait arranged ahead of time. In her brief introduction, Strait explains that the discussion will be a graded assignment, which means she keeps track of which students speak and how often. Then she asks the first question.

The discussion begins slowly. A few students volunteer brief responses; most look around nervously, anticipating who will speak next. Some of the awkwardness disappears when a boy calls out, "I agree!" after another student's response. Strait and the students laugh, especially when he adds, "Does that count [as a graded response]?" Strait assures him that it does not, but the number, length, and substance of student responses pick up afterward.

The second question (i.e., strategies of the movement) generates more and more expansive talk than the first, but the third (why the movement succeeded) falls flat. Apart from a couple of provocative claims about the role White interest played in the movement for Black rights, the discussion flags.

When Strait pushes on to the fourth question (i.e., if and how students might have participated), the discussion explodes. Most students sit forward in their seats, several who have been silent offer their views, and the length and quality of the responses expand:

> Strait: "Okay, number four is, 'Given the chance to participate in any of the events of this movement, which events would you participate in and why?'"
>
> Jerry: "The problem is, one, after you get your butt kicked, you'd quit.... You wouldn't know the first time [you protested], but if you found out you could be killed, I don't think many people would go again."
>
> Tom: "I would have gone on marches going to see the governor ... that was an important one."
>
> Sarah: "I would have participated in the march to the governor also.... Go to the source."
>
> Anna: "After seeing all that stuff, I started to feel bad. But I would be afraid others would think it was wrong [to participate in marches]."
>
> James: "I would want to participate too. The trouble is I don't think others would agree and you could get killed."
>
> Jerry: "Should we assume we are White or Black?"
>
> Strait: "As Whites. Whites were also active throughout. The NAACP had both Black and White members."
>
> Melanie: "If I was living then, I would feel like I had to do something. I've done protests before."
>
> Strait: "Do you think if you were Black it would make a difference?"
>
> Melanie: "If I was Black, then I'd be involved from the beginning. If I was White, I would have had to learn and then I would have participated."
>
> Jerry: "If I was Black, then the whole struggle is a Black thing really, so I'd be more anxious to get involved. [pause] I guess it was also a White problem, but it was more of a Black problem.... It was easier for Whites to stay out.... As a Black, I would feel more pressure to get involved."
>
> Katrina: "I would participate in the bussing [boycott]. I don't see why they had to sit in the back of the bus. Everybody's the same."
>
> Lori: "White or Black, I would have participated if I wanted, if I believed it was wrong, I would have participated. [some snickers] I would have!"
>
> Strait: "The bus boycott lasted over a year. What if you needed the bus for work?"
>
> Linda: "During the boycott, it was giving Whites what they wanted. They didn't want Black people there so the boycott was not the best [strategy]."

Sue: "I agree, but it lasted so long that it worked." [cacophony of student voices talking to one another and to Strait]

Strait: [quieting the class] "Interesting.... I put this question to myself, would I have participated? I don't think so if I was in elementary school, but if I had been older, I would have participated.... Idealistically yes, but realistically ... I still think I would have done so. I participated in protests over the Vietnam war. I wore a black armband and went to campus demonstrations ... and we took over the administration building.... But it was a kind college. They didn't call the police, they just wanted us out ... [lots of student chatter at this revelation].... But it's hard to think about giving up your life for that."[21]

In this vignette, we see the power of a good question. For whatever reason, Strait's first three questions fail to engage the students' active interest and attention. Those who respond do so in desultory fashion; most just sit quietly. The fourth question strikes harder, as something closer to a real discussion or conversation (Wilen & White, 1991) develops. More and different students participate, their responses seem more thoughtful and textured, and they seem to be listening to and talking with one another. Make no mistake; this is brief moment—something less than 10 minutes—and, one could argue that many of the students' responses seem thinly developed. Yet in this short time, we see students thinking hard and expressing their nascent ideas about a issue of some importance to them.

Not all of Strait's activities are successful. Students' engagement ebbs and flows, and sometimes, most often at the end of class, it fades into idleness and social chat. Those times stand out in large part, however, because they contrast with the more frequent instances where students are actively interested and involved.

Understanding Linda Strait's Instructional Practice

Three features define Linda Strait's teaching. One is that she constructs a separate unit on the civil rights movement rather than teach it in a textbook context. Doing so, in effect, allows her to recontextualize civil rights for African Americans by including other groups who also experienced discrimination. A second feature of Strait's practice is the broad range of activities and assessments she creates. These lessons offer opportunities to understand the era both intellectually and emotionally. Finally, Strait is trying to negotiate a different role for herself. She is seldom offstage for long, but she constructs opportunities where she can expand the role of teacher.

---

[21]Like George Blair, Linda Strait often uses personal stories to illustrate points she wants to make. Throughout the civil rights unit, Strait added glimpses into her past. For example, as part of her wrap-up of the simulation, she told a story about a bus strike that hindered her getting to a summer-school class.

Constructing a Distinct Unit

Linda Strait shares her colleague's concern that the mostly White West-wood students need to think hard about the civil rights movement histori-cally and about race relations today. Toward that end, she creates a distinct unit that both features the struggle of African Americans and gives attention to other minority groups.

W. E. B. Du Bois (1903/1989) nominated the "problem of the color line" as the most enduring of American problems. Strait agrees. Her first goal is to help students understand that "[racism] is really still happening today." "I think it's pushed in the back of the memory of people that they don't seem to see that this is still a really awful problem," she said, "I see it and I have always seen it as the biggest problem in America today ... how the races get along."

Strait contends that students today are more tolerant than those she had five years ago. That tolerance, however, seems limited to religious differ-ences. Racial differences are another matter. "It seems like, on the sur-face, superficially, that they might be more tolerant in terms of religion," she said, " ... you [get] more heated, close-minded debates about the race issue as opposed to the religion issue."

Strait's second goal is broader; it underscores the view that history is more than politics and economics, and more than a record of the victorious:

> What I try to convey is that America is multifaceted. That there—it's not *just* White America anymore. I don't know if it ever was *just* that, but that's how it was always taught in the history books. So, I'm trying to let them see that there's another side, and it's ever increasing, that other side of the diversity in America, and we have got to see it, recognize it, and start working together.

Strait sees clear implications for this goal. "I'm not necessarily trying to tell ev-eryone that you gotta love everybody," she said, "but you have to accept them and you can't, you shouldn't just hate them because of the differences."

In addition to these substantive goals, Strait creates a distinct and ex-pansive civil rights unit because she has faced what she perceives as ugly reactions from students when she raises racial issues alone. "So of-ten, it seems they feel that when you bring up civil rights, anything about racial issues, that you're attacking them because they are White," Strait said, "So I wanted to approach it from a different [angle]." One of those angles is to make it clear that Strait does not blame her White students for the sins of their forefathers and -mothers. "I wanted to bring out the point that I didn't hold them responsible for what happened," she said, "It's the fault of our forefathers. I do hold them responsible for today if they allow things like that to continue." The other angle Strait pursues is one that presents civil rights as more than an issue for African Ameri-cans alone:

Because I wanted everything that I taught to touch on ... all of the different people that are in the United States today, I try to be inclusive of all groups, and to bring out ... all the other groups.... That's why I like those—the civil rights films—because it is all of the groups. Not just the blacks—the Japanese, Latinos, everybody.

Given her broad purposes, it is no surprise that Strait would construct a distinct civil rights unit. That decision makes even more sense when one realizes that Strait's purposes push beyond the borders of any one textbook chapter.

Developing a Broad Range of Activities and Assessments

Constructing a distinct unit is one way Linda Strait tries to elevate the importance of civil rights. Another is through a broad range of activities and assessments designed to give students multiple opportunities to think about and express their ideas.

Strait knows that civil rights is a thorny subject, and that her mostly White students feel uncertain and uncomfortable talking about it. She also knows that many teachers shy away from the issues. She will not, but she recognizes that students need a variety of experiences—both cognitive and affective—to catch hold of the big ideas. "I wanted knowledge about what happened," she said, "and I wanted feelings.... I wanted to appeal to them on an emotional level. And in the process, to learn about other history. Not just White man's history."

To address her interest in students' knowledge, Strait develops a range of activities. She uses videotapes, textbook and other readings, and unit notes to convey the facts and themes central to understanding the civil rights movement. She assesses students' cognitive understanding through the reactions students list after seeing the first videotape, the strategies worksheet they complete for the skating-rink simulation, the ideas they contribute to the roundtable discussion, the ideas they express in their practice essays, and their answers to the quiz she developed. Strait uses multiple activities and assessments because she believes all students can learn. She knows, however, that not all students learn in the same ways and that different learning experiences will engage different students. "I am of the belief that all students can learn," she said, "just in different ways, and different styles."

Strait also varies her instructional approaches in order to explore her students' affective responses. Although all her activities have an academic element, Strait expands most of them to promote her affective purposes. For example, students' written reactions to the first videotape take on additional meaning when Strait asks students to talk about their reactions with classmates. Similarly, the strategies that students brainstorm in the skating rink exercise become a means of involving them in a firsthand experience with discrimination. Strait knows that much rides on her students' performance on the state Regents test. She wants them to do well, and to that end she pushes her students academically. At the same time, Strait wants her students to feel something of the life lived by people in the past. "I would like students to be more empathetic with other people," she said, "Try and just imagine if you were in their shoes. Even if they can never be your best friend, you know, try and understand others."

The range of instructional activity evident in Strait's civil rights unit owes much to her sense that students need to master a considerable amount of subject matter knowledge and to experience something of the passion of the times. Knowledge is important, she asserts, but without empathy, it is hollow.

Redefining the Teacher's Role

The third feature of Linda Strait's instructional practice is her reconstructed role of teacher. Strait can play the traditional role of knowledge giver and knowledge evaluator, but she strives to take herself off center stage and push more of the responsibility for learning on her students.

"I try to throw in as many activities and projects," she said, "but I still feel that I am too heavily the center of it." From her reading of documents like the New York State *New Compact for Learning* (New York State Education Department, 1991), Strait believes that her teaching should be less teacher centered. Evidence of that belief surfaces in activities like the skating-rink simulation and the round table discussion. True, Strait is not far away. But in both of these activities, Strait's role is more facilitative than directive, and the emphasis is on how students make sense of the ideas and contexts rather than on right answers.

In expanding the role of teacher, Strait is also redefining the role of student. Put simply, the kinds of activities she constructs push students to be more actively engaged and more responsible for their own learning. The open-ended nature of activities like the roundtable discussion and the skating-rink simulation encourages students to interpret the meaning of these experiences both academically and affectively. To be sure, some students fail to do the assigned readings, some sit out class discussions, and some goof off during the small-group sessions. Too, one could argue that Strait's preparation and coverage of unit notes spoon-feeds rather than challenges students. Considered in the context of the entire unit, however, these elements are far more the exception than the rule. Students can refuse to participate and they can duck their responsibility to understand the import of classroom activities. But in contrast with more traditional classroom settings (Goodlad, 1984; Shermis & Barth, 1982), Strait urges her students to expand their sense of themselves as students.

Strait's efforts to redefine the roles of teacher and student come with a price, however. She worries, for example, that as she moves away from the role of knowledge giver, her students may not learn all that they need to in order to pass the Regents test. "Knowing what the exams are like," she said, "I see so much content there, so I don't know how to get them to learn that content without me being the center and everything for them." Strait straddles an uncomfortable dilemma here: The view of teaching she advocates may be more meaningful to students, but it is also more complex and takes more time than direct instruction approaches do. Strait seems committed to rethinking her teaching practice. The pressures to do otherwise, however, are there.

CONCLUSION

Two teachers, two radically different approaches to teaching. George Blair and Linda Strait hold similar academic credentials, hold virtually identical views on the importance of teaching the civil rights movement, and hold teaching positions in the same school, with the same kinds of kids, with the same school norms, and with same pressures of a state exam. And yet the classroom pedagogy each constructs pushes in a fundamentally different direction.

What explains the different route each teacher takes? Influences like the teachers' subject matter knowledge, their views of students, and their sense of the state tests bubble up throughout the cases. But how important are these factors, and are there others that may be just as important? I take up these questions in chapter 7. Before that, however, I want to stretch my initial understanding of Blair's and Strait's practices by comparing them with the practices of other teachers. I do so, in chapter 2, by examining their instruction in the context of the extant research on teaching history.

Teaching History:
The Nature of Pedagogy
in History Classrooms

By popular conception, high school history teachers fit a common mold: They lecture, they assign textbook readings, they pass out and collect worksheets with end-of-chapters questions, and they use a lot of multiple-choice, short-answer, and true–false questions on their exams. That conception presents a reality that researchers and students know all too well. Time and again, observers (Cusick, 1983; Goodlad, 1984; McNeil, 1988) have chronicled the dulling stereotype of teachers who aim no higher than a stack of completed worksheets. Far too many students, current and former, roll their eyes and sigh in response to the history teaching they have experienced.

The stereotypical history teacher still exists. Yet, the accounts of teachers like Linda Strait and George Blair in chapter 1, and those in the recent research literature, suggest that history teaching may be more complex, nuanced, and engaging than presumed. These accounts of ambitious teaching enrich our understanding of teachers' practices because they highlight both the pressures toward the pedantic and the agency of teachers who resist those pressures. Certainly teachers can choose to fit the stereotype, but that they are *choosing* to do so can not be denied. Steve Thornton (1991) calls this ability to choose, "gatekeeping," by which he means that teachers make the kinds of long and short term decisions about what students will learn and how. Teachers do not make these decisions in a vacuum (Cornbleth, 2002), but they do exercise considerable autonomy over the kinds of learning experiences their students have.

I conceptualize this chapter around three big and enduring questions: Can teachers be both knowledge givers and knowledge facilitators? Should teachers be content or pedagogical specialists? What instructional approaches should teachers use? This questions present a thorny set of issues, largely because the empirical literature addressing such matters is small and generates mixed results. That said, the available research offers both useful directions and necessary cautions as teachers negotiate the uncertain terrain that is teaching history. In light of those directions and cautions, I conclude this chapter by exploring the active role teachers can play as pedagogical gatekeepers.

WHAT SHOULD BE THE TEACHER'S ROLE IN THE CLASSROOM?

Let's start with the distinction developed in chapter 1, where I framed the difference between George Blair and Linda Strait as one of the teacher's role as knowledge giver v. knowledge facilitator.

Other researchers use alternate frames. For example, Ron Evans (1989, 1990) identifies five approaches to teaching history: storyteller, scientific historian, relativist/reformer, cosmic philosopher, and eclectic. Evans describes each of these orientations in terms of the teachers' view of history, their classroom practices, and their political ideologies. Less concerned with ideology, Sam Wineburg and Suzanne Wilson (1991) focus on teachers' subject-matter knowledge and its relationship to the content of their instruction. The *visible* teacher in their study explicitly directs the flow of classroom ideas and conversation whereas the *invisible* teacher guides students' interactions with ideas and each other through rich instructional activities. Finally, Christine Bennett and Elizabeth Spaulding (1992) identify seven perspectives teachers may hold: inculcator, friendly scholar, scholar psychologist, facilitator, nurturer, empowerer, and friendly pedagogue. The authors divide these perspectives into two major camps: those who promote the transmission of knowledge (inculcator, friendly scholar, and scholar psychologist) and those who promote the construction of knowledge (facilitator, nurturer, empowerer, friendly pedagogue).

Each of these frames plays a part in what I conceive of as a continuum between knowledge giving and facilitation. I prefer this framework as it allows me to portray the three factors that seem most relevant to an understanding of George Blair's and Linda Strait's teaching practice. Those factors emphasize each teacher's collective views of knowledge, students, and teaching. Although Evans (1989, 1990), Wineburg and Wilson (1991), and Bennett and Spaulding (1992) give more or less attention to these concerns and others, I believe these factors interact in ways that clearly define each teacher's choice of instructional venue.

Teachers as Knowledge Givers

The stereotype invariably portrays teachers as knowledge givers. These teachers stand in front of the class, deliver ready-made lectures, and assign textbook and workbook pages. In doing so, such teachers embody a particular stance toward knowledge, learning, and teaching: Typically they believe that knowledge consists of facts, objectively derived from past sources. They believe that students come to them either knowing few of these facts or knowing them in confused ways. Independent thought, they assert, is dependent on the mass accumulation of factual information. Finally, they believe that teaching consists of passing on historical information. George Blair epitomizes the knowledge giving teacher when he asserts, "I want them to pick up the major points that are in the book, that are in the subject.... But I don't think they have the historical background to understand what the important points are in the chapter and what are not important."

The image of teachers as knowledge givers has a long history. Cohen (1988) observes that this image reflects "an old inheritance," and reflects the notion of teaching as telling:

> In this inheritance, teachers are active; they are the tellers of truth who inculcate knowledge in students. Learners are relatively passive; students are accumulators of material who listen, read, and perform prescribed exercises. And knowledge is objective and stable. It consists of facts, laws, and procedures that are true, independent of those who learn, and entirely authoritative. (p. 39)

Paulo Freire (1972) makes much the same point through his notion of the "banking concept of education," where knowledge is "a gift bestowed by those who consider themselves knowledgeable upon those whom they consider to know nothing" (p. 58).[1]

Decried by reformers, the role of knowledge giver has proven tenacious (Bickmore, 1993; Goodlad, 1984; McNeil, 1988; VanSledright, 1996a; Yeager & Davis, 1996). And why not? National surveys show American students are distinctly unaware of their past; state curriculum makers and textbook publishers add pages of new content with every revision; standardized assessments promote the notion that it's the facts that matter; the organization of the typical high school day into 45-minute time blocks undercuts the potential for extended discussion; and some students (and their parents), conditioned to passive learning, balk if they asked to take a more active role in their education.[2]

Proponents cite these realities as justification for knowledge giving (e.g., Hirsch, 1987; Leming, 1994). If students do not demonstrate command of tested facts, the argument goes, then give them more facts and give all the ideas taught more emphasis. If state leaders expect more content to be taught and yet allow no more time during the school day, then teach in the

---

[1] Thanks to Sandra Cimbricz for pointing this quote out to me.

[2] I have more to say on this point later. For now, I simply remind the reader that Dewey's (1902/1969) explanation for why children comply with pedantic instruction includes the notion that "familiarity breeds contempt, but it also breeds something like affection. We get used to the chains we wear, and miss them when they are removed" (p. 28).

most efficient ways possible: lectures and worksheets. And if students and their parents expect history to be taught as it has been in the past, why buck this expectation?

Although studies of knowledge-giving teachers percolate throughout the research literature (Bennett & Spaulding, 1992; Evans, 1989, 1990; McNeil, 1988; Thornton, 1988; VanSledright, 1996a), Elizabeth Yeager and O. L. Davis, Jr. (1996), presented a particularly clear example in their case of Jordan, a 25-year veteran urban teacher. Jordan's view of knowledge revolves around the centrality of facts. Historical interpretations and "bizarre theories" do not interest him; Jordan asserts that history is the search for accurate facts. Consistent with this view of historical knowledge is Jordan's view of students: "If it's not cut-and-dried, I've lost them. I try to embroider, but I know that when it really comes down to what I need them to know, it had better be the cut-and-dried version" (p. 160). Students are incapable of analyzing historical documents and constructing interpretations on their own, Jordan asserts, so it falls to him to give them both the facts and the proper interpretation of those facts. It is no surprise, then, that Jordan's view of teaching emphasizes the transmission of knowledge, or teaching as telling.

Too much content, too little time, and too many tests lead many teachers to conclude that giving students knowledge in bite-sized bits is the only reasonable approach. Reformers may carp about what students "understand" through such instruction, but to teachers like Jordan and George Blair, the belief prevails that unless history comes from them or from the textbook, students cannot possibly know it. This view may seem old-fashioned, even parochial, but in many respects it is the normal practice.

Teachers as Knowledge Facilitators

Normal practice does not mean exclusive practice, however. The image of teachers as knowledge facilitators may not predominate, but recent research suggests that teachers like Linda Strait are more common than one might expect. That said, portraying such teachers is tricky. For although the portrait of a knowledge-giving teacher is fairly standard, knowledge facilitating teachers may adopt any number of classroom stances. Different in manifestation, these teachers nevertheless exhibit common threads in their views of knowledge, students, and teaching.

Knowledge facilitating teachers generally believe that historical knowledge is a human construction. Advocates of this view (Becker, 1932; Carr, 1961; Holt, 1990; Novick, 1988; White, 1987) hold that rather than a set of secure, immutable ideas, what we know about the past is complex, uncertain, revisable, and always interpreted. Historians of this ilk do not abandon the notion of factual knowledge,[3] but they do assume that history is more than

---

[3]Historian R. G. Collingwood and others do, however. As Collingwood (1947) notes, "I am now driven to confess that there are for historical thought no fixed points thus given: In other words, that in history, just as there are properly no authorities, so there are properly speaking do data" (p. 243).

what Carr calls "mere facts." Becker (1932) notes, "To establish the facts is always in order, and is indeed the first duty of the historian; but to suppose that the facts, once established in all their fullness, will 'speak for themselves' is an illusion" (p. 232). Facts do not speak for themselves, historians do. And they do so through the interpretations they construct:

> [History is] but an imaginative reconstruction of vanished events.... It is thus not the undiscriminated fact, but the perceiving mind of the historian that speaks: the special meaning which the facts are made to convey emerges from the substance-form which the historian employs to recreate imaginatively a series of events not present to perception. (Becker, 1932, pp. 233–234)

These "imaginative reconstructions" or interpretations represent the precipitate of historians' energies, the ways they make sense of historical phenomena. Historians understand, however, that as much as they would like to have the last word, their interpretations are likely to be challenged, revised, and/or discounted. There is no "revisionist" history, there is only history that is continually revised:

> However accurately we may determine the "facts" of history, the facts themselves and our interpretations of them, and our interpretation of our own interpretations, will be seen in a different perspective or a less vivid light as mankind moves into the unknown future. (Becker, 1932, p. 236)

The notion of historical knowledge as a human construction resonates with a constructivist view of learning (Bruner, 1990; Vygotsky, 1978; Wells, 1986). Advocates of this stance challenge traditional notions of learning that emphasize rote memorization and drill. Like the knowledge studied, learning is a complex, uncertain, interpretative activity that becomes embodied in the understandings that learners construct. Constructivists do not pretend that memory and memorization do not exist, but they do assert that how memories are formed is strongly influenced by learners' prior knowledge, beliefs, and experiences and by the environments in which learners interact. These influences, individual and social, combine in myriad ways such that the ways learners make sense of ideas are as likely to be different as they are the same. Students, then, are active meaning makers, building understandings from their experiences and employing those understandings to refine and construct new understandings.[4]

Consistent with constructivist notions of knowledge and learning is a view of teaching as facilitating knowledge (Bickmore, 1993; Leinhardt, 1994; Rossi, 1995; Rossi & Pace, 1998; Thornton, 1988; Wineburg & Wilson, 1991; Yeager & Davis, 1996). This view can look very different across teachers' classrooms, but common to these settings are instructional strategies

---

[4]I return to and expand on the notion of constructivist learning in chapter 4.

that encourage student meaning making. Characteristic of these strate-gies are learning activities that present challenging tasks, that demand ac-tive student participation, and that presume students' may come to differing conclusions.

Portraits of the kind of ambitious teaching represented by knowl-edge-facilitating teachers are emerging in the research literature. The two teachers Wineburg and Wilson (1991) profile illustrate the practice of fa-cilitating knowledge; they also illustrate the very different paths teachers may take in doing so. Elizabeth Jensen, the *invisible* teacher, teaches stu-dents about the American Revolution through a 7-day unit that combines student research with an extended debate over the following resolution: The British government possesses the legitimate authority to tax the American colonies. During the unit, Jensen does little explicit teaching: "She does not lecture; she does not present information; she did not write on the blackboard; she did not intercede when students became confused; she did not hand out a worksheet, a quiz, or a test" (p. 314). In-stead, Jensen begins by organizing students into three groups—rebels, loyalists, and judges—and assigns readings selected to help them form their arguments for the upcoming debate. During this activity, Jensen cir-culates throughout the room, acknowledging, but not always answering directly, her students' queries. "Never ... is information delivered ready-made," Wineburg and Wilson observe, but instead it comes through sug-gestions or questions (p. 315). Jensen's nonintrusive role continues dur-ing the debate, which lasts for 3 days. In that time, the student judges conduct the debate while Jensen sits on a side of the room taking notes. Between the opening and closing arguments, points and counterpoints fly between loyalists and rebels, as do shouts when factual errors are de-tected. The activity is moderated exclusively by the judges, and Jensen intercedes only once when the cacophony of 32 voices press over the lead judge's gavel.

In the end, the judges' verdict shocks class: The loyalists' case prevails. Where Jensen's call for volunteers to take up the loyalist cause was initially ignored, students had come to see reason and intelligence in a perspec-tive they had been taught to disdain. More important than the actual ver-dict, however, is affirmation of Jensen's twin pedagogical aims. One is students' understanding that "the making of history is a dynamic process in which people face real choices and rarely are those choices as simple as those presented in textbooks" (Wineburg & Wilson, 1991, p. 316). In Jensen's words:

> I want them to understand that there were two points of view, that there was legitimacy to both sides—to understand the specifics of the mercantile sys-tem, the specifics of home rule, the problems of internal and external reac-tion.... Basically we're not asking whether [the Americans] should've fought the war, or whether they should've won the war. We're asking about legiti-mate authority to tax. (p. 316)

Jensen's second aim is foster students' responsibility for their own learning, or as Wineburg and Wilson observe, "knowing that the success of the
activity is up to them" (p. 315). Jensen describes the tension between facilitating and giving students' knowledge:

> If I make substantive comments [students] are going to look to me for the
> substance. Until I help them debrief and get the issues out—if I enter with
> anything more than regulations to prevent it from becoming a shouting
> match ... then they're going to look to me for all of it. (p. 315)

Taken together, these twin goals describe a teacher whose instruction
supports a view of history as a construction and of learning as a
constructivist activity.

Elizabeth Jensen might seem a portrait of the prototypical knowl-
edge-facilitating teacher. Wineburg and Wilson (1991) complicate that
image, however, with their description of John Price, the *visible* teacher in
their study.

On quick inspection, Price seems to be one more example of a knowledge-giving teacher: He directs the class activities and his voice dominates in the classroom conversation, a "sage on the stage." Consider this
bit of dialogue during a lesson on rebel propaganda during the American
Revolution:

> Price: See how carefully this is written to create a mood? And so, how would
> *you* respond then to the third question here? How could this story influence
> the Revolution? Who was going to read it?
>
> Mark: It could make them all hyped up.
>
> Price: It was going to hype people up. It's adding gasoline to the fire. It's mak-
> ing it worse. Can you imagine that this guy was maybe the friend of someone
> or himself was a member of the Sons of Liberty? Trying to sway those people
> who were sitting on the fence and don't want to get involved? (Wineburg &
> Wilson, 1991, p. 324)

This passage sounds like a traditional teacher in his element, but consider
how Price extends his unit on the Revolution:

> I decided to have my U.S. history class utilize three different textbooks. I have
> a group of people and they did research on the authors and found out as
> much about them as they could. Then, when we look at the Boston Massa-
> cre, I'll say, "Alright, I want a brief report from you people, you Boorstein peo-
> ple. What does he have to say about it? What happened there at the Boston
> Massacre? Then we'll look at what Jordan says. Then we'll look at another
> and compare. I think it's important for them to understand that history is not
> what is between the covers of those books.... The nice thing about having
> the three textbooks, and having me give my version, is that we have this
> better grasp of what history really is. Where did he get his evidence for that I
> wonder? And how come this version is so different from this one? And then

you get into the values of the author. What are their experiences? What are their ages? (Wineburg & Wilson, 1991, p. 329)

Price wants his students to know the "facts" of the American Revolution, but knowledge of the event is but one of his goals. The other is to explore for themselves how historical knowledge is constructed:

> My mission ... is to really get them excited about some of the characters along the way so that they have some interest in the past. Second, for them to realize that there is a real excitement in how this information was discovered.... Those are the things I constantly have in mind. (Wineburg & Wilson, 1991, p. 329)

In Wineburg and Wilson's view, the pairing of these goals means that Price pushes well beyond the traditional role of knowledge giver. While he is a gifted storyteller, they argue that "the stories Price tells are not finished; they are not closed books with beginnings, middles, and ends.... Instead, history is an anthology of stories, told by people with differing values and commitments, many of whom cannot even agree on the story line" (p. 330).

Ambitious teachers like Jensen and Price facilitate rather than give students knowledge. Their instructional approaches may differ radically,[5] but they share a commitment to a view of history as a human construction and to constructivist ideas about learning. Teachers who hold these views and act on them in ways similar to Jensen and Price work in the same schools, with the same students, and under the same social and institutional constraints that their knowledge giving peers do. And yet they construct teaching practices that look worlds apart.

The Choice Between Giving and Facilitating Knowledge

The picture of history teaching is complex—images of the traditional and the unconventional, giving knowledge and facilitating knowledge. Rather than isolated poles, however, it makes sense to see teaching on a continuum. Teachers like George Blair and Linda Strait may well define the outer reaches of that continuum, but there is common ground as well as distance between them.

Two implications ensue. One is that teachers have considerable room in which to craft their teaching practices; teaching practice is not monolithic. Knowledge giving in the form of George Blair's and Jordan's practices may continue to define the norm, but the cases of Linda Strait, Elizabeth

---

[5]It is important to add that Jensen and Price also share teaching practices, for although Wineburg and Wilson (1991) highlight the teachers' differences in their approaches to the American Revolution, they note that each teacher displayed elements of the visible and invisible role over the course of the school year.

Jensen, and John Price illustrate the potential for facilitating knowledge as a viable pedagogy. The second implication is that teachers choose the knowledge stance that they enact. Both knowledge-facilitating and knowledge-giving teachers can be found in exactly the same school environments; in fact, as the cases of Blair and Strait suggest, they may be teaching in adjoining classrooms. So although knowledge giving is the default teaching stance, it still represents a *choice* rather than an obligation, a compulsion, or a reflex. George Blair chooses to give his students the knowledge he believes they need. Linda Strait chooses differently. The influences and constraints on these teachers' pedagogical stances and on the rationales they construct to support those practices are real and important. But as teachers interpret the influences and constraints on their practices, they make choices that can offer very different classroom experiences for their students.

SHOULD TEACHERS BE CONTENT
OR PEDAGOGICAL SPECIALISTS?

We turn now to a second question of teaching. The debate over whether teachers ought to be content or pedagogical specialists has great currency in the social studies. Although the wealth of content to be taught suggests the need for subject matter specialists, critics of history teaching have long descried its pedantic nature, arguing instead for a dynamic pedagogy (Hertzberg, 1988; Whelan, 1997).

The argument for history teachers as content specialists draws largely on enormous body of extant knowledge: Consider that the 1-year, 11th-grade U.S. history and geography curriculum in New York (New York State Education Department, 1999) features 33 single-spaced pages of fact after concept after topic.[6] The daunting scope of this and other social studies courses promotes the view that teachers must be foremost experts in their subject matters (Bradley Commission, 1989; Leming, 1994; Seixas, 1993b, 1999).

Knowing the subject matter is important, but those who propose pedagogy as primary assert that content is not the whole picture. The rationale behind the move from a straight history curriculum to "social studies" in the early 1900s included the hope that teachers would embrace different forms of teaching. Jenness (1990) notes that the originators of the social studies curriculum "fulminated against the mere imposition, the enforced memorization, of facts" (p. 72). Early reformers offered new curriculum proposals, but they combined those proposals with suggested

---

[6]By odd contrast, the New York state Global History and Geography curriculum, which covers two school years and considerably more history (i.e.,. the first humans to the 21st century), is but 27 single-spaced pages.

instructional methods that emphasized group work, projects, and the use of documents.

Like the debate over teachers as knowledge givers and knowledge facilitators, I argue that the quarrel over content and pedagogy is better represented as a continuum than as a dichotomy. Unlike the earlier discussion, however, I believe teachers need to find a common ground where their classroom goals can be best realized. That common ground, expressed by Lee Shulman (1987) as *pedagogical content knowledge*, melds concerns for rigorous subject matter with ambitious teaching methods.

Teachers as Content Specialists

The argument for history teachers as content specialists seems commonsensical: The teacher–student relationship is predicated on the notion that the former has more knowledge than the latter. Concurrent with the view of teachers as knowledge givers is the long-standing image of teachers as experts in their fields. Socrates' confessions of ignorance aside, teachers in Europe and the United States have historically accepted the mantle of content expert. Cohen (1988) notes, "Teachers were persons of authority. They had special knowledge. Their task was to pass this knowledge on, intact, to students" (p. 42).

The central assumption in the teachers as content specialists view can be plainly stated: Once one gains sufficient command of the relevant content, then the teaching of that content falls out naturally. This assumption has two parts, both of which are worth investigating.

The first part of the assumption concerns the subject matter knowledge a teacher holds. Questions continually arise over what and how much knowledge teachers need. Some reformers (Bradley Commission, 1989) call for all social studies teachers to have at least the equivalent of a major in college-level history coursework. Counting courses is one way of measuring a teacher's subject matter knowledge, but it is no guarantee of deep understanding. A better approach is understanding the kind of knowledge teachers hold. Suzanne Wilson and Gary Sykes (1989) provide a useful characterization of teachers' historical knowledge. One element of their scheme is *differentiation*, or the notion that a teacher "perceives and understands the several dimensions of a particular topic in history" (p. 271). By this, Wilson and Sykes mean that teachers hold considered, nuanced, and multiple understandings of historical actors and events. *Elaboration* represents "the complexity of problems historians wrestle with, those subtle distinctions that make the obvious not so obvious" (p. 272). This idea refers to deep and detailed understanding that "goes beyond skeletal pieces associated with differentiated knowledge of subject matter" (p. 271). Wilson and Sykes's third category, *qualification*, speaks to the provisional nature of historical knowledge, which is "often qualified and tentative" (p. 272). Rather than a fixed and unchanging body of facts, historical knowledge represents the current, collective views from the field. Those views may be more or less agreed on at any time (Novick, 1988), but the nature of historical inquiry demands that all knowledge is qualified. The last of Wilson and Sykes's categories is *integration,* or the "need to know how one event is tied to another, both causally and thematically, in order to make events and ideas meaningful" (p. 272). Here, the emphasis is on meaning making and the idea that meanings can reflect causal and/or thematic relationships. Wilson and Sykes leave unanswered *how* one might assess preservice and practicing teachers' knowledge of these elements, but in offering them, they ratchet up the importance of knowing one's content.[7]

What teachers know about history is key. The assumption behind teachers as content specialists has a second part, however: Teaching history demands no special pedagogical knowledge. The idea here is that history consists primarily of stories, and that the principal vehicle for teaching stories is lecture and recitation (Evans, 1992). Although some (Barton, 1997a, 1997b; Levstik, 1989, 1993b, 1995; VanSledright & Brophy, 1992) question the reduction of history to stories, the perception continues that good history teachers are those who can captivate their students with a story well told (Bradley Commission, 1989; California Board of Education, 1988). If true, this view undercuts any need for pedagogical variety: What carries a good lesson is the content rather than the method. In fact, some observers suggest that attention to pedagogy or "process" actually interferes with student learning. "The culprit is 'process'—the belief that we can teach our children *how* to think without troubling them to learn anything work thinking about" (Cheney, 1987, as cited in Jenness, 1990, p. 366).

Teachers like George Blair would agree. Although he has studied various instructional methods, they do not impress him as useful. "I use the lecture method," he said. "I use it the best. I've become fairly good at it." With content coverage paramount—"Colonialism to Clinton"—Blair sees a direct path between history and his students, and he sees his lectures as the most efficient means of constructing that path.

Teachers as Pedagogical Specialists

The notion of teachers as content specialists, although long held, has also been long criticized. The dulling effects of knowledgeable, but pedantic teachers are well chronicled (McNeil, 1988; Powell, Farrar, & Cohen, 1985). Criticism of such teaching was central to the reforms initiated as part of the 1916 birth of "social studies" (Jenness, 1990). A major piece of those reforms dealt with the content taught, especially the move to curricula with a more contemporary foci. Concurrently, reformers attacked the "serious pedagogical weakness" (p. 72) of instruction rooted in lecture and recitation. Determined not to continue a failing tradition, reformers

---

[7]See Wilson and Wineburg (1993) on the use of performance assessments to understand teachers' knowledge of history.

promoted pedagogical diversity as a means of making how students learned as important as what they learned.[8]

The efforts to diversify teaching methods attracted some adherents, but failed to become the classroom norm (Cuban, 1984; Goodlad, 1984). As the nation's focus on education developed during the 1980s, however, reformers revisited pedagogy as a "cure" for the problems of education. Now termed "effective teaching," advocates built the case for a generic view of teaching predicated on psychological research. That research focused on the characteristics of teachers whose students performed well on standardized assessments (Brophy & Good, 1986; Gage, 1986; Rosenshine & Stevens, 1986). The ensuing prescriptions highlighted general principles of teaching that could be applied across all teaching contexts. Factors such as the subject matter, the students' prior knowledge and experience, the teachers' goals, and the like were discounted. Good teachers were those who mastered a wide range of instructional strategies which could be brought to bear regardless of the subject taught (Bedwell, Hunt, Touzel, & Wiseman, 1984; Hunter, 1976).

What counts as good pedagogy? Madeline Hunter (1976) and others argue that strategies as simple as informing students of the lesson's objective at the beginning of class pay off. Additional practices such as using pacing guides for lessons, breaking content into small bits, demanding lots of practice, asking direct rather than open-ended questions, and offering lots of praise are cited as exemplary strategies. Also encouraged are direct teaching methods. These methods include lecture, recitation, and drill-and-practice activities. Some effective teaching advocates argue for more pedagogical diversity. Bruce Joyce and Marsha Weil (1986), for example, propose that numerous "models of teaching," which include reports, oral presentations, and group projects, can be used effectively as long as students' performance on standardized assessments is not compromised.

Linda Strait's practice fits some of the tenets of effective teaching. She employs a wide range of teaching strategies, including lecture, group work, simulation, and individual seatwork. She praises students' individual and collective efforts. And she assigns practice activities—such as the essays tied to the Regents exam—that underscore the importance of standardized assessments.

In other ways, however, Strait's classroom actions push beyond the effective teaching model. She does not always preview the day's lesson, preferring instead to let it unfold. She uses no explicit pacing guide, relying instead on her teacher's intuition about how the class is proceeding. She asks some direct questions, but in the main, her questions push students beyond easy, yes/no answers. Finally, although she breaks some of the content into smaller chunks (e.g., the difference between civil rights and

---

[8]Jenness (1990) rightly points out, however, the flaw in the early reformers' actions, that is, that teachers' dependence on lecture and recitation would not disappear "by virtue of being denounced" (p. 72).

civil liberties, a chronology of major civil rights era events), more often she seems to promote bigger, more expansive understandings. Many of those understandings are content centered. Strait wants her students to be able to identify civil rights leaders and events, to know which groups were affected (and how) by civil rights era legislation, and to understand what options civil rights groups employed. At the same time, Strait wants her students to experience something of the times, to understand affectively as well as cognitively. "I wanted knowledge about what happened," she said, "and I wanted feelings ... I wanted to appeal to them on an emotional level." Exposing the emotions of the time as well as the facts, Strait believes, offers students more opportunities to understand the relevant ideas. She measures herself, in part, by students' performance on the Regents exam, but her goals reach far beyond a set of test scores. "I would like students to be more empathetic with other people," she said, "try and just imagine if you were in their shoes. Even if they can never be your best friend, you know, try and understand others."

Linda Strait's pedagogy challenges the dictates of effective teaching in two important ways. One is that subject matter counts. Strait employs multiple teaching strategies, but always with an eye on how those strategies promote the particular understandings she desires. And those understandings represent the second way that Strait's practice diverges from the standard view of effective teaching. She is not content with superficial learning, as in the right answers to standardized test questions. She is after bigger, more powerful understandings of the forces that move men and women during challenging times. Moreover, she is after understandings that are affective as well as cognitive. Advocates of effective teaching shy away from the affective, largely because it is difficult to measure. Strait sees the cognitive and affective as mutually supportive; what students *know* about the civil rights era depends, in part, on what they *feel*. Neither alone is sufficient; both are necessary for what Strait sees as her principal objective, helping her students see the "other side of the diversity in America, and we have got to see it, recognize it, and start working together."

Pedagogical Content Knowledge

Linda Strait's pedagogy tests the distinction between teachers as content or pedagogical specialists. Pedagogy matters to her more than it does to her colleague, George Blair, but does content matter any less? Is there another way of thinking about the relationship between content and pedagogy?

Lee Shulman and several of his former Stanford University students think so. Although not ignoring the work on effective teaching, Shulman and others argue that powerful teaching includes more than a generic list of teaching behaviors. And a big part of that "more" is subject matter. Drawing on the work of John Dewey (1902/1969) and Joseph Schwab (1978), Shulman (1987) outlines a long list of knowledge good teachers possess: content knowledge, general pedagogical knowledge (e.g., classroom management principles), curriculum knowledge (e.g., materials and programs), knowledge of learners and their characteristics, knowledge of educational contexts, and knowledge of educational ends, purposes, and values. Shulman adds to this list *pedagogical content knowledge*, which he describes as "that special amalgam of content and pedagogy that is uniquely the province of teachers" (p. 8). That amalgam, Shulman notes, "represents the blending of content and pedagogy into an understanding of how particular topics, problems, or issues are organized, represented, and adapted to the diverse interests and abilities of learners, and presented for instruction." (p. 8). It is this knowledge that represents a nexus between content and pedagogy, a place where teachers can pull from a palette of teaching strategies those which they believe will help and encourage their students to engage the particular ideas at hand.

This is no mean feat. Dozens of instructional strategies beckon and a teacher's time is always tight. Students vary in their individual and collective responses to ideas and activities; every classroom teacher knows the experience of the strategy that worked brilliantly with one class only to bomb with the next. Building subject matter knowledge is a never-ending process because new interpretations continually appear. And knowing deeply the material to teach all of U.S. history is a daunting task. The notion of pedagogical content knowledge offers a useful way of understanding teachers' classroom practices, an alternative to the view of teachers as content or pedagogical specialists. But it offers no easy prescriptions.

Content *and* Pedagogy

A casual observer might conclude that the split between content and pedagogical specialists is alive and well in the classrooms of George Blair and Linda Strait. From that vantage, the division is clear—Blair represents the primacy of content, Strait the ascendance of pedagogy. Introducing the notion of pedagogical content knowledge complicates this neat division because it suggests that teachers meld content and pedagogy in ways responsive to the students they teach.

Linda Strait blends content and pedagogy, and in that sense she exemplifies Shulman's (1987) notion of pedagogical content knowledge. But so too does George Blair. They do it differently.

Like Strait, George Blair has distinctive views of history and of pedagogy. History is a series of narratives, organized chronologically, that highlight the dramatic tension among people, places, and events. Facts abound in this view, but not as isolated bits of information to be rehearsed and spit back. Instead, history is a series of stories, often morality plays, meant to offer something about the human condition. Reflecting his view of the subject matter, Blair constructs a coherent pedagogy: He organizes the facts into master narratives, which he delivers in a storytelling fashion. And like most storytellers, Blair works alone. His lectures are monologues; students participate to the extent that they listen and take notes. We can argue about the relative merits of Blair's and Strait's ped‹ knowledge, but both find ways to blend content and in that reflect their ideas about teaching and learning.

WHAT INSTRUCTIONAL APPROACHES
SHOULD TEACHERS USE?

Seeking the one best approach to engage and sustain students' attention is endless. Numerous strategies have been nominated: cooperative learning, role playing and simulations, differentiated instruction, peer teaching, computer drills, decision-making models. At the same time, advocacy for some practices, such as lecture and worksheet activities, rises, falls, and rises again. Educators' efforts to construct the one best practice may be genuine, but they seem misguided. Just as there is no one best approach to building a car, social enterprises seem hard ground on which to build universal support for one model of action. Think about it: Psychology, government, economics, and the like are characterized by multiple stances. Freudians, Marxists, and Keynesians may believe that their respective models best represent human nature in their fields. Stepping outside those beliefs, however, one is quickly impressed with the number and range of viable alternatives. Some dispute the value of multiple approaches in these areas, but many observers (King & Brownell, 1966; Kuhn, 1970; Schwab, 1978) conclude that knowledge growth in a field corresponds to the energy with which its members argue.

Giving up on the search for a single best instructional approach is more opportunity than defeat, for doing so prompts teachers to focus on a more useful pursuit: Which of the many teaching practices available best meet one's instructional goals? This is no simple question, but if we take seriously the notion of pedagogical content knowledge, then the pursuit of this question puts teachers in an instructionally useful position.

In this section, I want to make three points. First, teachers like George Blair and Linda Strait can draw from a wide range of pedagogical options. Second, those options often support some kinds of teaching goals better than others. Finally, teachers' instructional choices need to reflect the subject matter and learners at hand.

A Palette of Teaching Practices and Materials

One way to understand the range of teaching practices available to teachers like Linda Strait and George Blair is to focus on how students are grouped for instruction. In this way, we can talk about practices that emphasize individual student learning, opportunities for small group learning, and whole group instruction. Concurrent with decisions about appropriate teaching practices are decisions about curriculum materials. Again, a wide variety is available. In this section, I highlight three types of materials: textbooks, priɪnary source documents, and computer programs. Whether choosing a teaching practice or material, two points surface. One is the realization that any method or source can be used well or poorly: A lousy cooperative learning lesson is no substitute for a good lecture, and a diary entry may better serve than a flashy computer simulation. The second point is that there is no valor in instructional purity: Not every lesson need be small group based, employ primary sources, or involve discussion. Each of these approaches can be useful, but only if they serve the purpose of the lesson intended.

Teaching Strategies for Individual Instruction

Individual learning is a staple of U.S. classroom lessons (Goodlad, 1984). Assignments can take a number of forms, but common to all is the notion that students draw on their own resources as they work alone on a task.

In history classes, individual learning most often takes the shape of reading and/or writing assignments. Students read textbook chapters or public speeches. They analyze political cartoons or graphs of consumer confidence. They write answers to worksheet questions, essays, journal entries, or letters to public officials.[9] The assignments may be routine or challenging, they may be short or long term, they may be done for a grade, for practice, or for use as fodder for a future lesson. Key to any of these tasks is the individual student's effort.

Individual learning activities (other than copying notes from the overhead) play little role in George Blair's classroom; his practice revolves exclusively around whole-group lectures. Linda Strait, by contrast, assigns individual learning tasks along with small- and whole-group activities. Examples of individual assignments occur when she asks students to write their reactions to the "Shadow of Hate" videotape and when she assigns practice essays based on a previous Regents exam. Strait later comes back to these tasks in small- and whole-group sessions, where she asks students to share their work. Making the individual assignments, then, serves the purpose of pushing each student to do the necessary preparatory work.

Teaching Strategies for Small-Group Instruction

Once almost unheard of in social studies classes, small-group learning activities are increasingly used as teachers perceive value in students' efforts at working together. Small group work need not employ the particular structures of cooperative learning, as popularized by David and Roger Johnson (1991; Johnson, Johnson, & Holubec, 1993), such as the assign-

---

[9]Astute readers will recognize that I am blurring the distinction between instruction and assessment. That is, assigning an essay can be considered alternately an instructional or an assessment. And that's key, for good instruction generally includes some form of assessment (Rogers & Stevenson, 1988; Wiggins, 1993, 1995).

ment of specific group member roles. Nevertheless, small-group learning activities typically emphasize the cognitive and social gains students make when, in a group, they confront a challenging task (Slavin, 1993, 1996).

Brainstorming is a common small-group assignment. For example, a teacher may ask groups to construct T-charts which separate the pros and cons of supporting the Vietnam war or the advantages and disadvantages of U.S. dependence on foreign oil. Another common small-group activity is jigsawing. Here, a teacher assigns different aspects of a lesson to different groups. After each group has explored its assigned dimension, the teacher reorganizes the groups such that each constitutes one member from each of the original groups. The task then calls for each student to share the results of his or her initial group's investigations. For example, a teacher might teach about the diverse perspectives on American slavery by assigning to each of five groups a role inherent during the antebellum period. Those roles could include African slaves, Southern slave owners, Northern freedmen, Western farmers, and New England factory workers. By design, a jigsaw activity offers students both the opportunity for deep consideration of each of these roles as well as a broader consideration of the many facets of the historical era.

Teachers may also assign to students, in small groups, tasks normally done individually. For example, groups might be given photographs to analyze or a simulated newspaper story to compose. One reason for assigning such tasks to groups is that they promote students' social development (i.e., through discussion) as well as their understanding of the ideas embedded in the task. A second reason for this assignment is opportunity to present more challenging tasks. Realizing that not all students bring forth the same abilities, teachers can use the power of group thinking to engage all students in more complex activities than they might handle as individuals. Reflecting these two motives, advocates of small-group work routinely cite the salutary effects, both cognitive and social, of students working on a common task (Johnson & Johnson, 1991; Johnson, et al., 1993; Slavin, 1993, 1996). Moreover, researchers consistently report positive gains for students of all ability levels. In other words, small-group work *works* for all kids.[10]

George Blair rejects such research findings. In his view, students gain little from group activities because they lack the requisite knowledge. "The blind leading the blind," he observes. Linda Strait disagrees. She believes that students benefit both academically and socially, so she often uses a group work format. Recall that she asked students to share and record their individual responses to the "Shadow of Hate" videotape in small groups and that she assigned students to groups during the skating-rink simulation. Notice the difference in these tasks, however. In the first, she hopes only to alert students to the diversity and range of their peers' reactions. The second activity is far more complex. First, students had to

[10]No set of research findings are ever without doubt. Jacobs (1999) argues that the research on cooperative learning presents "a mixed picture of successes, failures, and missed opportunities" (p. xi).

strategize, arguing over and coming to agreement on a set of arguments to present to Strait as skating rink operator. They then had to employ those arguments (or revise them) during the simulation. The social dimension of this activity is clear: Students had to negotiate a common strategy, and they did so with various degrees of skill. Equally apparent is the cognitive challenge of the task: Students would be unlikely, as individuals, to generate the full range of possible strategies on their own. As we see in the vignette, assigning the task to groups did not guarantee a winning strategy. Several groups seemed confident in their preparations only to fall apart during the confrontation with their teacher. Strait might have done more to push students' thinking about the strengths and weaknesses of group efforts during her recap of the activity. That said, it is hard to imagine students not taking away powerful lessons about the central issue of prejudice and protest.

Teaching Strategies for Whole-Group Instruction

Like individual lessons, whole-group learning is a fixture in social studies classrooms. Although lecture and recitation dominate, discussion, brainstorming, role playing, and simulation also work within whole-group settings. Just as the form of whole-class instruction varies, so too do the potential benefits.

Lecture and recitation, although often reviled by students, offer clear advantages (Leming, 1994). One of those advantages is efficiency. Content-heavy courses like history make huge demands on classroom time, so teachers who lecture can cover large amounts of material quickly. As state and local curricula continue to expand, the ability to teach efficiently is no small virtue. Lectures also offer a second advantage, particularly when demonstrated by teachers like George Blair. Blair and other good lecturers use that method to construct narratives that can help students make sense of historical events. The aimless quality of many teachers' lectures (Goodlad, 1984) contrasts sharply with Blair's more focused approach.

Like many teachers, George Blair leads whole-class recitations before exams. This practice serves very different purposes than either lectures or most other whole-group methods. The function of a recitation is to check students' ability to remember course material. Recitations can take various forms—question and answer, games like Jeopardy, and variations on the spelling bee. In each case, though, the idea is to review the taught content and to quickly assess students' recall.

Recitations encourage the convergence of students' knowledge toward right answers. Whole-group methods such as class discussion and brainstorming also may lead to some convergence of ideas. The main purpose of these practices, however, is for students to generate and examine multiple ideas (Larson, 2000). Students may agree on common themes as a result, but they may also agree to disagree.

Role-playing and simulations offer opportunities to promote academic goals like the exploration of ideas. They also offer opportunities to promote social goals such as empathy. During role-playing, students assume roles different than those they normally play in teacher-created situations. Enacted in front of a class, role-plays typically involve two to five students. Simulations may involve role-playing, but they typically present the whole class with situations in which they face a series of problems and decisions.

Linda Strait's skating-rink simulation well illustrates this latter method. After the preparatory small-group work, Strait presented a situation to the whole class (i.e., the need to convince her, as the skating rink operator, to allow minorities access) during which they had to both enact their prior strategies and respond on-the-spot to Strait's retorts. The activity demonstrated both cognitive and social elements as students were not only expected to use protest strategies discussed in class earlier, but also to come away with a sense of empathy for those who lived similar sorts of experiences.

Choosing Curriculum Materials

As with teaching practices, teachers can choose from a plethora of curriculum materials. Textbooks reign, but increasingly teachers and students are adding in materials such as primary source documents, computer programs (including mapmaking programs), multimedia presentations, and tradebook literature (National Center for Educational Statistics, 1999). The caveats around instruction apply equally here: Any material can be used well or poorly, and there is little to be said for restricting one's choice of materials. Computer programs are currently in vogue, but they are neither a panacea nor appropriate for every instructional activity. Teachers must make wise choices about materials based on their sense of the subject matter and the students in front of them.

The use of primary source documents represents the latest development in history curriculum materials. Employing the many possibilities of the Internet, many institutions now offer huge databases of historical documents.[11] Documents do not teach themselves, however. Yeager and Davis's (1996) study of three teachers' ideas about using documents related to the Battle of Lexington gives us a glimpse into the varied ways teachers think about and plan to use historical artifacts. Meredith sees documents as a means of developing students' historical thinking, particularly in terms of interpretation and research skills. Julie, interested in capturing students' attention with dramatic and entertaining stories, screens documents for their usefulness in advancing this objective. Finally, Jordan places emphasis on the accuracy of historical fact. In Jordan's hands, historical documents be-

---

[11]See, for example, the U.S. government web site at http://www.ed.gov/free; the National Archives site at http://www.nara.gov; and the Crossroads Project at Georgetown University at http://www.georgetown.edu/crossroads/asw.

come the means of amplifying the basic "cut-and-dried version" of history he articulates to his students. Using the same documents, the teachers Yeager and Davis profile demonstrate the range of choices teachers can make around a common curriculum material.

Coordinating Teaching Practices and Goals

Identifying individual, small-group, or whole-group instructional practices is one way of grouping instructional strategies. Another way is to consider teaching practices in light of one's instructional goals. In this section, I illustrate how some common teaching practices can facilitate different instructional goals. Some of those goals are largely practical as they direct students to particular kinds of learning. Other goals are more lofty and aim at the target of defining and promoting good citizenship.

Teaching Practices and Practical Goals

Teachers' goals cross a wide span (Rutter, 1986). Here, I focus on the day-to-day goals teachers can address through their classroom lessons.

Some teaching practices promote the goal of achieving common understanding. Any number of ideas—the causes of the Civil War, the effects of the Industrial Revolution, the antecedents to U.S. involvement in the Persian Gulf—fit the category of things teachers want all students to know. Methods that advance common understandings include readings from a common text, lectures, and recitations. Other methods allow teachers and students to explore multiple understandings. Classroom discussions, role playing, and simulations may result in some common knowledge, but it is also possible that students may come to different understandings based on their assessments of the arguments offered. Assessing students' understanding can also take different forms. Teachers who value the imaginative use of historical data might assign a diary entry whereas those who value close argument and evidence might favor the use of essays. Finally, teachers' differing goals for students' classroom participation also suggest the use of different classroom practices. Small-group projects, for example, promote a much higher value on student participation than do individual assignments.

Reconsider briefly the practices of Elizabeth Jensen and John Price (Wineburg & Wilson, 1991) profiled earlier. The same content, the American Revolution, plays out in dramatically different ways as each teacher connects his or her instructional practices with a corresponding set of practical goals. Jensen's elaborate debate process promotes in-depth study and collaboration among small groups of students and the importance of making one's ideas public in a whole-class setting. Using a lecture and recitation mode, Price emphasizes the importance of engaging all students in a common set of ideas.

Teaching Practices and Good Citizenship Goals

Although there is a fair amount of agreement that social studies ought to be about promoting good citizenship,[12] there are competing visions of what the good citizen looks like (Barr, Barth, & Shermis, 1977; Brubaker, Simon, & Williams, 1977; Grant & VanSledright, 2001). Some argue that the good citizen is alternately:

- *Knowledgeable about the past*—This view emphasizes deep knowledge and appreciation of past, especially American, accomplishments, heroes, and struggles.
- *Able to analyze current situations using social science methods*—This view emphasizes the power of social science concepts and methods as ways to organize and extend one's understanding of social situations.
- *A reflective thinker*—This view emphasizes inquiry into and assessment of cultural beliefs, actions, values, and policies with an eye toward consequences, implications, and alternatives.
- *Committed to social action*—This view emphasizes the extension of one's beliefs and values into actions.

These views are not necessarily mutually exclusive: A citizen engaged in the social action of protesting unfair housing practices is also likely to know a good deal about how those practices developed in the past. Similarly, a reflective thinker may use some of the methods of social scientists to explore a current issue. Teachers may do more or less to promote any or all of these goals through their classroom practices.

Let's consider a couple of examples. Lecture and recitation best support a knowledge of the past view. Teachers adopting these methods may tell students to become socially active, but their instruction supports the view of good citizenship that privileges what they know rather than what they think or do. By contrast, small-group projects and discussion could support either social science methods or reflective thinking goals. Assuming the small-group work goes beyond filling out a worksheet and that the discussion is more open-ended than a recitation, these methods promote the idea that there are ways (i.e., the approaches social scientists take) to analyze and understand issues and problems and that it is important to share one's thinking. The social science and reflective thinker views of citizenship presuppose some knowledge of the past. Teachers who hold to those goals, however, are not content to define good citizenship in knowledge terms alone.

In this light, we see a clear contrast between George Blair and Linda Strait. Blair's narrative lectures suggest his allegiance to a knowledge of

---

[12]The "agreement" on good citizenship as the goal of social studies is problematic, however. Not only are there many views of what good citizenship means, but there is some reason to doubt that social studies ought to claim primary responsibility for achieving this goal (Grant & VanSledright, 1996).

the past view of good citizenship. He hopes his students will develop "humanity and understanding," and presumably he would applaud their involvement in public affairs. In his classroom, however, Blair sees students as vessels to be filled with historical knowledge. Linda Strait is concerned about her students' knowledge of history, if for no other reason than their need to pass the state exam. Her lectures, notes, and the like are expressly designed to build students' knowledge base. Strait is not willing to define good citizenship as only knowledge, however. Instead, she promotes a view of good citizenship as reflective thinking. Students are to use the knowledge she and they construct to become more thoughtful actors. Thoughtful actors know the facts and are expected to share (and modify) their ideas in classroom discussions. But thoughtful actors also know and feel something of the experiences of historical actors. "I wanted knowledge about what happened," Strait said, "and I wanted feelings.... I wanted to appeal to them on an emotional level."

Teaching: The Connection Between Subject Matter and Learners

The statement "all children can learn" echoes throughout recent educational reforms. What that statement means, in real terms, is open to question as states increasingly rely on standardized test scores alone to measure students' understanding. Leaving the measurement issues aside, it is worth noting that the psychologist Jerome Bruner issued a similar statement 40 years ago. Bruner (1960) argued that all teachers must "begin with the hypothesis that any subject can be taught effectively in some intellectually honest form to any child at any stage of development" (p. 33). Safe to say, we have yet to realize Bruner's assumption as students routinely decry their social studies classes (Shaughnessy & Haladyna, 1985). Nevertheless, good teachers find ways to link the subject matter of history together with the interests and experiences of their students in ways that push far beyond the pedantic.

Think about the teachers profiled in this chapter. Think about how they craft pedagogies that reflect both honest attention to the subject matter as well as an honest respect for their students. The range of teaching methods they use—lecture, discussion, role-play, debate, brainstorming—and the range of teaching goals they work toward—knowledge of the past, reflective inquiry, use of social science methods—vary widely. What does not vary is each teacher's commitment to bringing students and ideas together in meaningful ways. The teachers who make a deep impact on their students' lives possess no extraordinary knowledge of history, they access no special cache of teaching methods, they hold no special insights into students. They do, however, push themselves to know more about history, teaching, and students and to act on that knowledge in more ambitious ways. These are uncommon teachers, but only because they act on their beliefs while many of their colleagues do not.

TEACHERS AS GATEKEEPERS
OF CLASSROOM TEACHING AND LEARNING

At their core, teachers act as classroom gatekeepers (Thornton, 1991). The simple fact is that there is far too much content and far too little classroom time for teachers to be passive. Deciding what to teach and how to teach it is often contested outside of classrooms, and there are many influences on teachers' decision making (Grant, 1996, 1998; Kirst & Walker, 1971; Romanowski, 1996). In the end, however, teachers exert considerable control over the critical decisions about which ideas get the most attention in their classrooms (Sturtevant, 1996; Thornton, 1991). As Shaver, Davis, and Helburn (1979) point out, teachers play the "primary structuring role" (p. 5) in pedagogical affairs. So although some (Apple, 1979; Giroux, 1981) cast teachers as pawns of larger power structures, that argument fails to account for the many and varied decisions teachers make.

Thornton (1991) defines *gatekeeping* as "the decisions teachers make about curriculum and instruction and the criteria they use to make those decisions" (p. 237). As gatekeepers, teachers "make day-to-day decisions concerning both the subject matter and the experiences to which students have access and the nature of that subject matter and those experiences" (p. 237). Drawing on Beard (1934), Thornton argues that teachers make these decisions from a more or less explicit frame of reference:

> Since all things known cannot be placed before children in the school room, there must and will be, inevitably, a selection, and the selection will be made with reference to some frame of knowledge and values, more or less consciously established in the mind of the selector. (p. 182)

I argue above that Linda Strait's and George Blair's teaching can be understood, in part, through their pedagogical content knowledge—the interaction of their ideas about subject matter, learners, and the like. Strait's and Blair's teaching can also be understood, however, through the concept of gatekeeping.

In their decisions, Blair and Strait clearly act as instructional gatekeepers. Teaching the same students, in the same school, and with the same state curriculum and exam in mind, these two teachers make radically different instructional decisions. Strait chooses to employ a range of teaching practices—lecture, small-group projects, essay practice, role play, and simulation. She is under no directive to do so and only rarely are her instructional decisions challenged.[13] Blair chooses to lecture and lecture alone. Class discussions, oral presentations, simulations, and the like have

---

[13]Recall that some of the modifications Strait made to her civil rights unit this year were in response to previous students' complaints. The only time her principal has questioned her teaching came after a parent complaint about a Madonna video Strait had used in class. "He questioned whether it was appropriate," she said, "but he didn't tell me not to use it again. So I did; I just didn't tell him."

no place in his classroom pedagogy. He knows that district-sponsored workshops promote activities like cooperative learning. He also knows that he, and he alone, will decide if he ever uses such practices.

That Blair and Strait act as instructional gatekeepers is no surprise. Most reformers are generally content to focus on revising the expressed curriculum and leaving instructional decisions up to teachers (Grant, 1995b; Grant, et al., 2001). Thornton (1991) observes that teachers tend to see themselves as having more control over instruction than curriculum:

> Teachers tend to characterize their planning as concerning instruction, not curriculum. To many teachers, "curriculum" appears to be synonymous with a body of knowledge identified by "experts" and encapsulated in a textbook. In other words, many do not appear to be aware of, and may not be particularly interested in, the degree of control their gatekeeping exercises over the curriculum they plan for their students. (p. 245)

But if George Blair and Linda Strait gatekeep instructionally, so too do they manage the curriculum they teach. These teachers do pay attention to state U.S. history curriculum, yet the curriculum decisions they make speak to their roles as gatekeepers.

George Blair chooses to include information about the Federal period even though the state curriculum downplays this era. Linda Strait chooses to forgo a chronological treatment of civil rights when she creates a unit that explores issues related to several oppressed groups in American society. Each teacher attends to the basic ideas of the civil rights period, but as each crafts his or her unit of study, differences in their curricular decisions surface.

The other teachers introduced in this chapter gate keep as well. Meredith, Julie, and Jordan decide, albeit quite differently, what sorts of curriculum materials students will access and how those materials will be used. Many teachers report using primary source documents, for example. How they use those documents, however, varies according to each teacher's impulse. Elizabeth Jensen and John Price illustrate the ways that teachers gate keep the kind of instruction they offer. Both teach the American Revolution in ways that elevate key concepts and events. The variation in their approaches, however, underscores the ability of each teacher to craft a teaching practice that reflects the goals she or he holds.

In these several ways—content decisions, materials decisions, and instructional decisions—teachers gate keep their classrooms. The autonomy or agency they exert is not absolute. But understanding the teachers' roles in constructing their practices is key to understanding the classroom lives of teachers and students.

CONCLUSION

This chapter covers considerable ground. Beginning with the stereotypical view of history teachers, I use several cases of teachers to examine the issues of whether teachers ought to be knowledge givers or facilitators, whether they should be content or pedagogical specialists, and what sorts of teaching practices they might employ. Underlying all these questions is the notion of teacher decision making, that is, the role teachers play in choosing the classroom paths they take. Those paths can seem quite different in the aggregate; we see cases of ambitious and far-reaching teaching as well as traditional and stereotypical teaching. The notions of teachers' pedagogical content knowledge and teachers as gatekeepers offer useful ways of understanding the decisions teachers are making. These constructs also help us understand, however, just how much agency teachers have over the classroom practices they construct.

PART II
Learning History

3

Learning History:
What Blair's and Strait's
Students Understand About History

What did the students in George Blair's and Linda Strait's classes learn? Each of the students described in this chapter completed the activities assigned, each passed the requisite quiz or test with a grade of A or B, and each passed the New York State Regents examination in U.S. History and Government. But what did they learn about history in general and the civil rights movement in particular, and did they all learn the same things? How is what they know related to their teachers' instructional practices?

As part of my study of George Blair's and Linda Strait's classrooms, I decided to interview a range of students regarding their understandings of the civil rights unit just taught, their view of history as a school subject, the sources of their ideas, and how this year's social studies course compared with previous year's courses and with their current English and mathematics courses.[1] Similarities and differences surfaced across the students' responses. As I reflected on those responses, what the students know and think about the civil rights movement seemed less interesting than what they understand about the nature of history. And what they understand about the nature of history became an interesting lens on the different instructional practices their teachers employ.

Before proceeding, two issues merit explanation. The first revolves around what counts as student understanding—that is, how do students represent what they know about the past? The second issue concerns causation, as in, what relationship exists between how teachers teach and what students learn?

---

[1] This chapter draws largely on a paper I published in *Theory and Research in Social Education* (Grant, 2001a). A more complete description of the research methodology can be found there.

Those researchers interested in student understandings of history tend to emphasize how children make sense of history (Barton, 1995; Barton & Levstik, 1996; Epstein, 1998; McKeown & Beck, 1994; Seixas, 1994, 1996; VanSledright & Brophy, 1992), how they read texts (McKinney & Jones, 1993; VanSledright & Kelly, 1995; Wineburg, 1991), where their ideas about history come from (Barton, 1995; Epstein, 1998; Seixas, 1993b; VanSledright & Brophy, 1992), and what defines the nature of their historical thinking (Holt, 1990; Leinhardt, 1994; Spoehr & Spoehr, 1994).

Others focus on the processes by which students develop historical understanding. The authors of a report by the National Center for History in the Schools (1994) argue that those processes include chronological thinking, historical comprehension, historical analysis and interpretation, historical research capabilities, and historical issues analysis and decision making. Peter Seixas (1996) offers a different view of the ways student historical understanding can be represented. He categorizes students' understandings in terms of significance, epistemology and evidence, continuity and change, progress and decline, empathy and moral judgment, and historical agency.

Although my data speak to each of the categories Seixas presents, I focus here on three elements of historical understanding that surface most prominently in the student interviews. One of those elements is *historical knowledge*, by which I mean how students perceive the outcomes of historical inquiry. The apparent distinction is around history as a set of undisputed facts versus history as a set of complex and tentative interpretations. The second element is *significance*. Here, I highlight the connections students see (or not) between the past and present, and between the past and their lives today. The third element is *empathy*, which includes the notion of understanding multiple perspectives on peoples' actions and on historical events, and the ability to take an empathic stance.

The second issue is how to analyze the relationship between the students' understanding of history and the teachers' instruction. I dismiss the possibility of a direct and causal connection, that is, what students learn depends exclusively on what teachers teach. Teaching and learning are richly complex activities (Cohen, 1988; Dyson, 1999), and the research on student learning (e.g., Barton, 1995; Epstein, 1998; Seixas, 1993; VanSledright & Brophy, 1992) emphasizes the many influences on what students know and understand. Teachers' instruction does factor in, but so too do family, media, and lived experience. Such factors influence, but do not control, the ideas and actions of classroom actors. Instead, teachers and students construct and co-construct a range of classroom realities. Although no causal relationship can be established, the data do suggest a correlation or points of coherence, if you will, between each teacher's practices and the views their students construct of history. And those points of coherence suggest that Linda Strait's and George Blair's students know different things about history, and that Strait's students hold richer and more substantive views of history than Blair's students do.

LEARNING HISTORY: STUDENTS' UNDERSTANDINGS
AND TEACHERS' PRACTICES

Researchers have studied both teachers' practices and students' historical understandings, but rarely in conjunction. During the classroom observations of the respective civil rights units, I was struck by the different
instructional choices the two teachers made. As I conducted the interviews with students, however, I was struck by the very different ways students from each class talked about history. In this chapter, then, I explore
the relationship between each teacher's classroom practice and the historical understandings of their respective students.

Before proceeding, let me introduce the students. The first four are from
George Blair's class:

- *Alice* is a medium-height, thin girl with long, dark hair, who seems quiet
  and reserved. A Westwood native, she is a second-generation Italian
  American. Alice's class average in U.S. History is in the 90s, but she said
  she has done better in past years.

- *Ann* began high school in a private school; this in her first year at Westwood High. A tall girl with a serious countenance, Ann belongs to the
  Westwood chapter of Amnesty International. Although she reports not
  liking social studies, she holds a high 90s average in Blair's class.

- *Bill* has always attended Westwood schools. A lacrosse player, he is of average height, muscular, and soft-spoken. Like Ann, he has a class average
  in the high 90s.

- *Kate* plays on the girls' varsity basketball team. Tall and thin, with a nervous giggle, Kate is a Westwood native. Her class average is in the low to
  mid 90s. Like her peers just described Date's classroom behavior consists
  of quietly taking notes.

The next three students are from Linda Strait's class:[2]

- *James* is a Westwood native with a medium build, a quiet air, and glasses.
  He says little during class discussions, but he participates frequently in
  small-group situations. Although he has a mid-90s average, James describes himself as a "plugger."

- *Melissa*, also a Westwood native, is of medium build. She describes herself as a political liberal. In class, she speaks often and articulately. She reports her class average as being in the 90s.

- *Ned*, a hockey player, is a tall, athletic-looking boy who moved to Westwood from a first-ring suburb when his mother remarried. Like Melissa,
  Ned makes frequent contributions to class discussions. He reports that
  his class average has slid into the 80s.

---

[2]A fourth student in Strait's class decided not to participate.

Before I draw the contrasts between Blair's and Strait's students, let me mention one important similarity: All seven students express a generally positive view of the United States and of their future lives. Even the student most critical of the U.S. record on civil rights, Melissa, said, "There have been a lot of success stories and ... it's [the United States is] a democracy and there's freedom and people have made it in America." Later, she added, "I still think America is a good country. I'm not going to move away because I don't like what we did in the past." Such sentiments should not surprise because they correspond with recent research (Barton & Levstik, 1998; Epstein, 1998; Seixas, 1994; VanSledright, 1997) that suggests that, although students may be critical of U.S. history, they see that that history largely in terms of progress, and they see a bright future for themselves.[3]

This similarity aside, it is the differences among the students that stand out, especially the differences around the students' views of history as a field of study and as an influence on their lives. These differences suggest that Strait's students hold views of history that are consistently more thoughtful, nuanced, and complex than those that Blair's students hold. Moreover, Strait's students seem to view history as a more vibrant and powerful influence on their lives than Blair's students do.

HISTORICAL KNOWLEDGE

Although historians have long debated the relationship between objectivity and subjectivity (e.g., Carr, 1961; Novick, 1988), educators have been more concerned about the relationship between fact and interpretation. On the one side, some educators (e.g., Hirsch, 1987), argue for the primacy of objective facts, or what Greene (1994) calls the "tradition of archivism." The assumption here is that interpretation is a meaningless exercise until one has accumulated all the relevant facts. On the other side are the proponents of meaning-centered approaches (e.g., Seixas, 1996; Wilson & Sykes, 1989). Here, the issue is not whether or not facts are important (they are!), but rather the idea that facts become meaningful only in service of interpretations.

Clearly, historical knowledge need not reduce simply to the fact–interpretation distinction. In the student interviews, however, a clear difference arises around what counts as knowing history. In Blair's students' view, historical knowledge consists entirely of facts about which there are no arguments. Strait's students, by contrast, tend to see historical knowledge as complex, tentative, and open to reinterpretation.

---

[3]Those findings tend to represent European American sentiments, however. As Epstein (1998) points out, African American students are less convinced that U.S. history is one of progress for everyone.

Blair's Students: History as the Facts

Blair's students see history in terms of immutable facts. "You know, when you're in a classroom like social studies or history, you just learn, like, basic facts," Ann said. "In history, it's just, like, plain facts, like, know this and know that, and, you know, I don't … feel anything."

History reduces to facts in these students' minds, and those facts are largely beyond dispute: History is a straightforward chronicle of past actors and events. Alice explains, "In history, it's just, like, given to you, you know? This is your history, just learn it." Kate adds: "History's already set for you." Like his classmates, Bill believes that history is but a set of facts about which there is nothing to discuss: "It's like history is already made, you know what I mean? It's facts. So I don't know if there's much you could discuss."

Blair's students do express some concern with and questions about the specifics of some historical events. For example, Ann questions the U.S. role vis-à-vis "underdeveloped countries or underprivileged" and American problems with "like Asia and China." Asked specifically about civil rights, however, Blair's students maintain that what they learned in class echoed things they had learned before. Bill observes, "I already knew about that [civil rights]…. I mean, it was interesting to me, but I already, like, looked into the Civil Rights myself through other projects, like through English and stuff, and movies and other things." Students say that Blair's coverage of civil rights was "more in depth" than previous teachers' instruction, and they appreciate Blair's stories about the era. Yet none see anything new or provocative in either the content or the stories. Like all the other history they have learned, understanding civil rights means knowing the facts.

Strait's Students: History as Complex Ideas

If Blair's students see historical knowledge as a wall of facts, Strait's students are more likely to see it as complex, tentative, and ambiguous. All talk about what they learned in Strait's unit, but they also question what they know. Moreover, Strait's students express these ideas in light of her civil rights unit whereas Blair's students talk more globally.

James's comments suggest that, although he has gained some knowledge, the knowledge gained is thorny. James has learned that "there's been discrimination against certain minority groups in the past … certain laws that have been passed, and cases in the Supreme Court." He credits Strait with much of what he now knows: "I knew discrimination, for example, existed, but I didn't know it quite to the extent that I've learned about this year." Confident of some knowledge, James also comes away from the unit uneasy about some of what he understands. For example, he now wrestles with the juxtaposition of laws and court cases that presumably protect people's rights and his sense that discrimination is a state of mind:

I don't know. I know it's difficult for people to … stop their discrimination based on laws. I mean, I know, traditionally certain groups have been discriminated against, and sometimes you just can't prevent people from having their same … state of mind about these people.

Asked why he thinks this way, James said, "It's just their values that they've been raised with, and after years and years of having similar values like that, it's just very tough to change." James's struggle is a common one: Public sanctions may change some people's actions, but do they change people's hearts and minds?

Ned and Melissa also talk about learning new things through Strait's unit and about how this new knowledge alternately promotes new ways to think about civil rights and elevates new questions. For Ned, the in-class activities introduce ideas that "I never learned till …[now]." Asked how he makes sense of the unit, Ned offers a brief but telling statement: "I think that just the past couple of weeks has really turned my mind about stuff." It is hard to tell what this means for Ned is negotiating a range of new ideas about which he has had only passing knowledge. Combined with his fledgling efforts to sort out his own responsibility, however, the notion that Strait's unit "really turned my mind about stuff" suggests the possibility that Ned is thinking in new ways. Supporting this notion is Ned's comment that even when people are armed with new knowledge, there is little predictable about their behavior. "I mean, not that it's [new knowledge] totally going to solve it [ongoing civil rights problems]," he said, "but, just give you a different perspective on what it was like. Or it could worsen it. So you never know."

Ned credits Strait with helping him understand that historical events can be viewed from more than one perspective:

> Yeah, I think she says an opinion and what, you know, what she feels and what she thinks, and I think she lets us do the same with what we think, and she takes both views into consideration, and she doesn't say, "Well, this is how it has to be, and this is how it should be." You know, she brings up a question, and she'll ask the class, and kids will say pretty much what they want to say. And she accepts what we say, and we accept what she says, and, we might have totally two different views, but you still have to take into consideration other people's … views of certain things.

From this quote, it is not clear that Ned understands that the views Strait and his peers offer fit within an enduring historical debate about how to interpret the U.S. civil rights movement.[4] By honoring students' views alongside hers, however, Strait makes space for students to see that historical knowledge includes both fact and interpretation.

Strait's unit also seems to push Melissa to a deeper sense of historical knowledge. Like her peers, Melissa claims she learned much that is new.

---

[4]For a particularly cogent discussion of that debate, see Novick (1988).

She sees a sharp contrast between the surface coverage given to cultures in her 10th-grade Global Studies class and the deeper study characteristic of Strait's U.S. History course. "I like [Strait's class] better because I learned more specifics about things," she said, "and that's the way I like it. I like specifics. I mean, generalizations are fine, but I like to know what's behind them and what makes them, you know, why can you make them generalizations." Questioning the relationship between generalizations and the evidence that supports them is a sophisticated insight. It suggests that Melissa senses the malleability of historical facts ("specifics") as one constructs interpretations ("generalizations"). As with Ned, we do not know how Melissa makes sense of these ideas, but one senses the possibility of a complex view of historical knowledge.

Understanding Students' Historical Knowledge

Examining students' views of historical knowledge offers one lens on their understanding of history and on the influence of their teachers' practices.

George Blair's students see history as a set of undisputed facts that chronicle past events. Linda Strait's students, by contrast, see both facts and interpretations as central to history. Strait's students may not know how to think deeply about the relationship between fact and interpretation, but their realization that history encompasses both seems richer than those of their peers.

Of course, Strait's students may have come to her class predisposed to seeing history in more nuanced ways than Blair's students. But even if this is true, Strait's students credit her with reinforcing that more complex view of history. Blair's students assert that his instruction reinforces the traditional conception that history is about facts. Lacking baseline data on the students' views of history before entering their respective classes, we cannot assume that either teachers' practices *caused* their students' views. We can, however, see that a correlation exists between Strait's more expansive instruction and the more complex and nuanced views of history her students hold. Similarly, Blair's narrative style correlates with his students' sense that history reduces to facts.

This last point seems problematic, however. George Blair emphasizes factual information, but he does so within an interpretive frame, a "story well told." If, as literary theorists tell us, every story is an interpretation, then one could argue that Blair's stories do highlight the importance of historical interpretation.

Why then do Blair's students fail to appreciate either the narrative he constructs about the civil rights era or the idea that history is an interpretive field? Why do they see in his lectures only the facts? One possibility is that teaching history as a narrative lulls students into thinking of history as only one story (Barton, 1997a, 1997b; Levstik, 1989, 1993b, 1995; VanSledright & Brophy, 1992). Students seem to miss the point that if history is being presented as a story, then alternative stories can be told. In short, they see the narrative or story they are told (or read in their textbooks) as the one true story rather than as an interpretation. The second reason Blair's students might fixate on facts is related to the first: He never tells them that other interpretations are possible. Blair creates and delivers the narratives that he alone constructs, and those narratives are monologues both internally and externally. Internally, Blair's narratives feature only his synthesis of the events. He allows historical actors (e.g., Dwight Eisenhower, John Foster Dulles, Melba Beals) to speak, but their words fit into the story he crafts. Dissident views, alternative perspectives of events, and the like do not surface in his lectures. And they do not surface when he delivers his lectures because students, who might offer a different view (Barton & Levstik, 1998; Epstein, 1998), are silent. So just as Blair silences the alternative views of historians and historical actors, so too does he silence his students. With no recognition of the interpretative side of history from their teacher and no opportunity to question the interpretations he offers, it makes some sense that Blair's students would hone in on a fact-based view of history.

There is much less sense of a particular narrative line in Linda Strait's teaching. By not providing a single interpretive frame, Strait may be allowing her students more latitude to construct their own interpretations, to see the possibility that historical knowledge is complex and tenuous, and to understand that others might construct different views of the same events.

SIGNIFICANCE

What is historically significant is no less an issue for historians than it is for high school students (Seixas, 1994, 1997). The growth of social history, in particular, pushes historians to confront questions about what counts as significant vis-à-vis historical actors and events (Novick, 1988). Students may be naive about the arguments in the history community, but their sense-making impulse provides entrée into discussions of historical significance (Barton & Levstik, 1998; Epstein, 1998; Seixas, 1994, 1997).

Researchers observe that students use a range of criteria to evaluate historical significance. Peter Seixas (1994) finds that, among other things, the impact on the contemporary world, understanding of personal circumstances, potential for lessons learned, and extreme events or conditions figure prominently in students' constructions of significance. Keith Barton and Linda Levstik (1998) take a broader cut. Their investigation suggests that students' views of significance can be grouped into two primary strains: the "official" view of the past as a legitimate, unifying, and progressive force, and the "vernacular" view that presents history in a more ambiguous and critical light.

Elements of both Seixas's and Barton and Levstik's findings emerge in the interviews with the Westwood students. Two particular patterns of talk—the connection of past and present, and the connection between the past and students' lives today—surface throughout the interviews, and it is on those patterns that I focus in this section.

Connecting Past and Present

Although both teachers' students see connections between the past and present, the connections George Blair's students offer seem thin and weakly developed. Moreover, none of the connections they describe relate directly to Blair's course in general, or to the civil rights unit in particular. Instead, when his students see relationships between past and present events, the sources they cite are family, media, and other coursework, particularly in English. Linda Strait's students see quantitatively more associations between past and present events. Even more striking, however, is the depth of their talk, and the clear connections they make back to Strait's instruction.

Connecting Past and Present: Blair's Students

Asked about connections between past and present events, Blair's students often seem taken aback. All are able to make those connections, but the connections seem weak at best. For example, Kate's responses suggest that she has given little thought to any relationship between past and present. She said that she sometimes wonders "what it was like in the old days." The images she comes up with, however, are lifeless. "It's like a black-and-white movie," she said, "It wasn't color, or anything. [laughs] It just looks weird, and different." Asked what this means, she seems unsure. People in the past were "not so much [different] in, like, their ideas, probably, but, how they looked, how they dressed, and all that. I don't think—I mean, we've changed a lot, but ... not too much."

By contrast, Alice sees a clearer, and more critical, connection between past and present America:

> As we learn more about our history ... the first images, it's like such a free and such a great place to be, and then, now that you really think about it, I mean, there are like terrible things about it, and different things that are bad in our society and stuff.

Asked for an example, Alice replies, "I don't know ... greed and killing and ... I mean, those would all just go on here." Beyond the fact that Alice offers one of the few critical points of view by a Blair student, what is most relevant is her attribution of this perspective: television. Blair does not sugarcoat the U.S. history he teaches. Yet Alice's sense that her views are based in what she sees in television suggest that she sees little in Blair's teaching that helps her connect past and present.

Blair's class also goes unmentioned when Bill talks about relationships between past and present. Bill has studied the Great Depression in Blair's history class, but Bill argues that his interest in the era grows out of long conversations with his grandparents, who suggest that, among other things, he "should be grateful for what I have, and stuff like that." The ribbon between past and present apparent in family discussions is reinforced in Bill's English class where he did a literature project on the Depression.

From these sources, Bill constructs a sense of how the past influences the present. Asked if people's lives during the Depression seem much different than those today, he argues that they do:

> Yeah, completely. To me it does, because ... it seemed like it was a different like, completely different swing. Like after the Depression, we still basically have the same ... like, we have all the aid coming to poverty-stricken people like welfare, and everything like that. And before that, during the Depression there were so many people that were, like, suffering and they couldn't do anything about it and there was no, like, direct relief. Like today there is. Like if you're really, if you're, like, in the dumps, you can still look to the government for aid. And back then there was, like, many people that couldn't. So it seems like a completely different time. 'Cause like, nowadays, there's always a, like, a plan B for you. And back then, like, it was just all or nothing, in a way.

Although Bill's account is in rough accord with a traditional view of the Depression, some would argue that his notion of a current "plan B" is naive. Maybe so, but for our purposes what seems interesting is that Bill attributes his conception of the relationship between the Depression and the 1990s not to his U.S. history course, but instead to family members and to his course experiences in English.

Ann is like her peers in that she draws on her English courses when she makes connections between past and present, and in that she attributes no particular understandings to Blair's course. Unlike her peers who attribute their knowledge to family, media, and other coursework, Ann cites the influence of her work with Amnesty International (more on this influence later).

Connecting Past and Present: Strait's Students

Linda Strait's students cite the influence of family, media, and other courses on their views of history. In striking contrast to Blair's students, however, all three of Strait's students ascribe many of their ideas to the civil rights unit they studied in U.S. history.

James is taken by two comments Strait made in class. First, Strait proposes that people today are only responsible for the misdeeds of their forebearers if they perpetuate them. Second, she connects the ill treatment of African Americans in the 1950s and 1960s with that of homosexuals today. Both points impress James:

> Just not to make the same mistakes as our forefathers have made. That's the point she brought up in today's class.... Basically, you know, think of everyone as equal, and like I said, not make those same mistakes in the past, the

discrimination of the past. She also brought up one of the most ... targeted groups now for discrimination are the homosexuals. And ... the type of discrimination they face is similar to the type that blacks faced back in the mid-nineteen hundreds. She's trying to stress to us not to make that same mistake.

Taken at face value, one might be tempted to characterize these views as naive: After all, there is little evidence to support the idea that "mistakes" no longer happen. When James said later in the interview, "I like to think that's [discrimination] changing," he echoes some of the naive hopefulness about the present that students routinely report (Barton & Levstik, 1998; Epstein, 1998; Seixas, 1994; VanSledright, 1997). Yet this boy is not content with simple answers. James tempers his hopefulness with the very real possibility that "it's difficult for people to ... stop their discrimination based on laws." Confirming the need to change both people's "hearts and minds" (Banks, 1994, p. 89), James points to the very real possibility that the present may not be all that different from the past, that laws may not prevent "people from having their same ... state of mind about these people [i.e., African Americans and homosexuals]."

Ned's hopefulness about the move from past to present also seems naive when, early in the interview, he says, "I don't think anything like that [discrimination against African Americans] would happen again." As he continues to talk, however, he modifies that claim in a way that demonstrates a more thoughtful understanding of how past and present intersect:

> I never thought that, I mean, the United States would ever let something like that happen, and just be so ... racist. I think that's a lot of problems. I mean, Blacks think that of Whites, we [European Americans] think that of Blacks, I mean, it's just ... I think it's happened a lot more ... as the years go on.

He then describes the impact that understanding the past has had on his sense of the present:

> You know, that certain stuff's happened, but I've never seen it. I mean when you hear something, it's different than if you actually can see it, witness it.... I wasn't there, but you saw the footage of it in the film [documentaries], and ... I believe it.... I think the kids should know, because I think that might be able to stop racism in the U.S. if they see that. I mean, not that it's totally going to solve it, but just give you a different perspective on what it was like.

Ned tempers his earlier sense that discrimination would never "happen again." He sees powerful images in the documentaries shown in class, and he is convinced that they are not only accurate reflections of the times, but that they "might be able to stop racism in the U.S. if they [students] see that." Ned is not so guileless as to think that images alone will help his peers to, at once, understand the past and change their behavior: As he notes, "It's not totally going to solve it." Nevertheless, Ned recognizes the power that comes from viewing events from multiple perspectives. So when he observes that the class lessons he has learned "just give you a different perspective on what it was like," he speaks to the possibility that appreciating a different perspective is fundamental to changing behavior (Banks, 1994). In comparing perspectives from then and now, Ned ties together knowledge of the past and possibilities for the present.

Melissa, too, expresses a hopeful view connecting past and present, although she moderates that view even more quickly and more directly than do her peers, James and Ned:

> I'd say that there are opportunities. But it's not exactly as everyone else that sees it, I mean so many other foreign countries say, "Oh, we have to go to America, it's the land of the free," but it's really not everything it's cracked up to be because there are a lot of limitations.

Asked what those limitations might be, she ties today's problems to the past:

> I think there's definitely like the racism and prejudice. You know, there's still problems with the African Americans, minorities getting jobs, women getting jobs, getting equal paying jobs, and just some people's attitudes towards different people.

In these quotes, Melissa couples past problems of racism and prejudice with current problems. She recognizes that groups who have historically had problems cracking the U.S. economy continue to experience difficulties.

Understanding Students' Sense of Past and Present

As with historical knowledge, Linda Strait's students connect their ideas more closely to her instruction and they make more nuanced sophisticated claims than do Blair's students. Without implying causation, we can nevertheless see ways that each teacher's instruction influences his or her students.

In Linda Strait's instruction, we see several instances where she makes explicit connections between the past and present. Some might argue, however, that those connections are weakened by the trap of *lineality* (National Center for History in the Schools, 1996). Lineality is the notion that present events can be improperly connected, in straight-line fashion, to the past. Expressed this way, lineality reflects the notion of presentism, which implies an overemphasis on the present as a means of interpreting the past (Rogers, 1987; Stern, 1994; VanSledright, 1998).[5]

---

[5]Thanks to Bruce VanSledright for helping me see this connection.

Critics of presentism object to the use of the present to interpret the past on the grounds that past actors can not be held accountable for societal changes they could not forecast. From that vantage, one might argue that lineality surfaces in the connection Strait makes (which James picks up on) between the experiences of African Americans in the 1950s and 1960s and those of homosexuals in the 1990s. Both groups have faced discrimination, but the different contexts of the times and the different social situations of each group undercut any direct correspondence between their experiences. From another vantage, however, Strait's connection between African American and homosexual experiences reflects an effort to use the past as a means of understanding the present. Past and present movements to protest discrimination may show some surface similarities, but studies of past movements are more likely to enable understandings of current movements than the reverse.[6]

Although some historians decry any instances of presentism, Rogers (1987) notes that strict avoidance of presentmindedness is probably impossible for teachers faced with the need to help their students construct a personal relevance to history.

George Blair avoids the trap of lineality in that he offers virtually no explicit connections between past and present. The one ostensible, but oblique, reference surfaces in his assertion that Chief Justice Earl Warren's actions "change the court forever." Blair's narrative of the civil rights movement within the context of Eisenhower's administration has the advantage of avoiding the presentism problem, but it runs up against a second trap, that of *inevitability* (National Center for History in the Schools, 1996). This trap manifests in the idea that historical events unfolded as they did in a natural, predetermined fashion, and that factors like human agency and chance do not influence the course of history. The decisions historical actors make do surface in Blair's narrative, but any sense that those decisions and their effects could have unfolded differently goes unexplored. Blair's instruction nicely ensconces students in the context of the times. Interviews with them, however, suggest that the past remains just the past.

Connecting the Past to Students' Lives

If one lens on significance is the relationship between past and present, another is the connection between the past and students' lives today. Here again, big differences surface between Strait's students and Blair's. Strait's students see many connections between past and their lives today. More specifically, they see themselves as actors in their community, and they see the impact past civil rights battles have had on how they and others view the world today. Blair's students see virtually no impact of the past on their lives. This is not to say that they have no interest in the past, but they seem to view history as irrelevant to the way they live their lives. Other fac-

---

[6]Thanks to Keith Barton for helping me see this point.

tors—school activities, coursework, family—influence them; the study of history does not.

Past Connections to Students' Lives: Blair's Students

One of Blair's students, Ann, talks about her involvement in Amnesty International. How directly Amnesty's work influences her life is unclear, but Ann does take part in letter writing and awareness-raising campaigns. "We write to other countries," she said, "saying that they shouldn't, you know, do something to this person. We try to, like, get a better outcome, or try to persuade the person, the leader, to not do that." Ann's interest in Amnesty International reflects her sense of America's historic responsibility to help others. "Well, since we're such a large, powerful country," she said, "I think we should get involved ... in some matters ... that help underdeveloped countries, or underprivileged."

Ann's work in Amnesty International marks her as distinct, for she is the only student who volunteered information about her involvement in any organized activity promoting a better world. Like most of her peers in Blair's class, however, her interest and involvement are unrelated to his class. Ann makes no mention of any connection between course material and her life now.

Neither does Kate or Alice. Kate even seems nonplussed by the idea that history might be meaningful to her. "History's already set for you," she said, "I mean we're learning about stuff in the past." By contrast, in English classes she and her classmates read, think about, and discuss the ideas and experiences represented in text, and how those ideas and experiences relate to their lives. "In English we're doing stuff in the present," she said, "talking about ourselves." Alice senses the importance of history, but that sense is nascent at best, and she flatly denies the import of Blair's instruction: "Listening to [Mr. Blair] doesn't do anything for me." Asked if she could imagine discussing ideas in history class as she has in English, she describes the limits of history as means of understanding her life:

> Alice: Actually, yeah! You could do that. But ... I don't know. Not in Mr. Blair's class, but ... yeah, it might be easier to learn that way too if you had discussions on it, on what you thought about different things. Civil rights, and your opinions, and stuff.
>
> SG: Do you think there are things to discuss? In history?
>
> Alice: Some things. Not a lot. Not as ... I mean, like, English, there's more things to discuss, it seems. I don't know, history ...
>
> SG: I'm curious about why you say that.
>
> Alice: I don't know. The way I, I knew my history, I, like, read the book, study it, memorize it, and, that's it. You know? I don't, like, go searching for more information, and stuff.

Bill provides a more complicated story. More so that his classmates, Bill is interested in historical events and he senses that there is something important for him to know. Influenced, for example, by the books he reads in English and by the stories his grandparents tell, he professes an enduring interest in the Great Depression, and in topics like organized crime. Despite these sources, Bill sees only distance between the past and his own life:

> I mean, I just can't picture like, being back then, like, how they were in the Depression. But when [his grandparents tell him about it], it really has no effect on me because I can't, like, even picture that, you know what I mean? So, I think that's why I feel so separated from it, you know?

Bill is no apathetic teenager, living for MTV and the next party, but he struggles to see any connection between the story of America's past and his life. "Nothing's really happened that affected me," he explains. "I really don't feel as though I'm part of the country." Given that much of the history Bill has been taught is about people like him—White, male, and well off—it is astounding to hear his claims of feeling disconnected from his past. Terrie Epstein (1998) and others (e.g., Barton & Levstik, 1998; VanSledright, 1995a) report that female and minority students see little of themselves in the textbooks and lessons taught in most U.S. history classrooms. Bill's assertion suggests that they may not be alone.

Past Connections to Students' Lives: Strait's Students

In contrast to Blair's students, Strait's students see important connections between historical events and their current lives, they reference the civil rights unit as examples, and they use what they learned in class to talk about their lives in contexts outside of school.

One way James expresses a lived connection with the past is through his reaction to the documentaries shown in class. After recalling several scenes, he notes, "It just makes me nauseous, some of what I see." James also cites the skating-rink simulation as cause for reflection. In that exercise, "We actually encountered somebody who discriminated against Black, minority groups." Although he took only a small speaking part during his group's presentation, James claims that this kind of activity "got us more involved, [the activity] involved students more in actually learning about it."

Ned and Melissa also connect classroom ideas and experiences with incidents in their daily lives. For Ned, part of the connection he makes is that he did not understand the severity and the extent of racial discrimination:

> The fact that, how people, well, mostly the Whites, were so against the Blacks and how people were treated. Like, they beat them, and just the way they were treated and how they thought their rights were violated.... The real

issues showed.... I never saw that till then. I never learned that till then. And a lot of kids in class were like that, too. They didn't know that. I got that just from talking to the kids.

Part of what grounds Ned's understandings of the past are the comments of classmates who were also taken aback by the documentary images. Although many students seem intent on forgetting their last lesson as soon as possible, Ned and his friends talk about the activities they experience in class.

This is no small point. Nor is Ned's insight into the different world he and his friends inhabit compared with those students in the nearby urban center. Westwood is a second-ring suburb. Ned moved to Westwood from a first-ring community 4 years ago. He understands, however, that a change of a few miles can mean a world of difference:

I grew up in Kastor, and I moved here, so there was a lot of Blacks and Hispanics, and I grew up around that, so it didn't bother me at all. And then when I moved here, kids are like sort of iffy about ... if you go in the city. They'd be like, "Oh, like that's some ... like a different world" or something.

Ned is reluctant to disparage his new peers. At same time, however, Strait's civil rights unit reminds him of the "different world" in which he now lives. "I think both places are good," Ned explains, "but, I think, I wish kids that are here would go live where I was. And then I think they'd ... see the same thing I would. Maybe they wouldn't, but, it's totally two different things.... If people could only see it."

One other indication of the connection Ned makes between his experiences in Strait's history class and his life is the firm but complicated notion of where his responsibility as a human being lies. Asked what learning about the civil rights movement means for him, Ned hesitates:

I think that we are responsible that ... to make sure something like that doesn't happen again, but ... again, it could. Anything's possible, but, I don't think ... I don't know what I'd do if that ever happened ... or put in that situation, so I wouldn't know.

Here, Ned struggles. He perceives a collective responsibility, "to make sure something like that doesn't happen again," that he may not have felt before. Things get messy, however, when he considers his own part. Rather than put on a false bravado, he admits discomfort and uncertainty. What would he do if confronted with an ugly situation? It is no easy question for any of us to answer; recall that Strait describes her own struggles with the question during the roundtable discussion. Ned may have no answer, but that he entertains the question is noteworthy.

As with James and Ned, Melissa is moved and even angered by classroom experiences during Strait's civil rights unit:

It kind of disappoints me that this country, in our Constitution is, you know, equal for everyone and they tried to be different from the other countries by not limiting anyone. And they were, you know, hypocritical, went back on their word and did destroy these people's lives just because of their race and color.

Thinking about her own social relationships, Melissa translates the feelings arising from Strait's class directly into her own experiences:

I have a lot of friends who are minorities and I see how they're treated. And how, you know, it's really uncomfortable for me when I go to their, when I like go to their family gatherings and they've got all Koreans there and I'm the only White person there. And I feel uncomfortable. I told my one friend that, and she said, "Well how do you think I feel everyday?" And I, you know, it just blew my mind. And then we started something about the civil rights movement and everything and I realized that our country is a little more backward than I thought.

The civil rights movement means more to Melissa than a set of past events. Her experiences in Strait's class give her leverage on understanding not only her own experiences and how she feels about them, but also how others feel and experience the world.

Melissa knew something about social inequities before taking Strait's class. Since the civil rights unit, however, she sees even more clearly that her race and social class provide privilege. She explains, "Me, being where I'm living now and, and the race I am, and you know, just this status that I, that my parents have given to me, it's, I feel comfortable in America. I think that I'm probably a privileged American."

Like Ned, Melissa is not sure where her responsibility lies. In class, she is a strong and vocal proponent of equity and justice. These themes surface in her interview as well, but her assurance is undercut when she talks about trying to negotiate the complex dynamics of race:

We [in Westwood] don't really have to deal with race issues that much. And I don't like to think that I'm racist. I really try, you know, but coming from Westwood I don't know how to deal with people.... And it's kind of embarrassing to me, but I don't have like good public relations like that. I don't know how to act.... And I kind of feel uncomfortable because I don't know how to deal with everything. I mean, I feel really secluded that I live in Westwood.

Melissa's discomfort dealing with people unlike herself is a remarkable admission, one that few European Americans make (McIntosh, 1992). Also interesting is the way Melissa uses the insights gained in class to help her think about her own position in her community. Her frank admissions about feeling "secluded" in the largely White world of Westwood and feeling "uncomfortable because I don't know how to deal with everything" suggest a sharp insight into the complex interaction between her life and the greater community. Melissa gives some credit for this insight to her parents, but she seems equally indebted to Strait. "It kind of helped me this year, just being able to deal with her," she explained, "and the way that she [Strait] thinks and the way she presents things." Strait's civil rights unit has not given Melissa any easy answers. In fact, one could argue that Melissa is more disconcerted, more uncomfortable for having taken Strait's class. Yet, as psychologists (e.g., Nisbett & Ross, 1980) remind us, cognitive challenge is key to conceptual change.

Understanding the Connections Students Make Between the Past and Their Lives

As the work by Seixas (1994) and others suggests, students may come at the notion of historical significance from several angles. Making connections between past and present events is one, but no less important is seeing a relationship between one's own life and the past. And as is apparent in the preceding descriptions, each teacher's instruction shapes some part of students' views.

This is no simple matter, however, for two complex issues surface across these student interviews. One is the notion of what students connect to. George Blair's students report that family stories, coursework in English, and school activities help them think about their lives. None cite as influential the narrative history Blair presents. That the females in Blair's class might feel this way is no particular surprise, for although women do appear in his narrative, the focus on political, economic, and international events, and on the roles that the largely male actors have played, is unlikely to appeal to the females in the class (Brophy & VanSledright, 1997; Fournier & Wineburg, 1997). More surprising is Bill's apparent ennui. Blair's version of U.S. history is replete with White, male characters, and yet Bill senses only distance between their lives and his own.

Bubbling below the surface in earlier sections, it now seems that George Blair's influence on his students can be explained as much by what he does not do as what he does. We sense that Blair's students do not see history as an interpretative field, in part, because he makes no effort to help them see it as such. And we suspect that his students make few connections between past and present, in part, because he neither makes these connections explicit nor does he encourage his students to do so. In this section, the emerging pattern takes hold. Blair hopes his students will develop "humanity and understanding," but they seem to be on their own.

The distance Blair's students see between the past and present contrasts sharply with the perceptions Linda Strait's hold. Although the civil rights movement is mere backdrop for Blair's students, for James, Ned, and Melissa it becomes a useful lens on their lives.

This last point is interesting because it appears that the unit Strait teaches provides students with an opportunity to juxtapose their own experiences, their "vernacular" history, with the "official" history of school curriculum and textbooks (Barton & Levstik, 1998). Nonmajority students may be more likely to see how their and their families' histories vary from that generally taught in classrooms (Epstein, 1998; Seixas, 1994), yet each of Strait's European American students also sees discrepancies, if not between their lives and traditional views of America, then between different images of America.

They can do so, in part, because Strait pushes them to do so. Traditional accounts of historic events surface in Strait's classroom, but so too do accounts that challenge mainstream interpretations. Strait's interpretation of the civil rights movement is not hard to find, and she may well wish that students would come away with the same understanding of movement that she has. By pushing students to consider multiple views of events, including their own and those of their classmates, however, she opens up the potential for students to realize something of importance for their lives today. Not all students do, but the words James, Ned, and Melissa speak are indications that they can.

EMPATHY

The third element of historical understanding I explore in this chapter is empathy. A popular construct among theorists across the political spectrum, *empathy* is an amorphous term. Noting the "constellation of empathies," Susan Verducci (2000) describes four categories of definitions: affective empathies (which include aesthetics, sympathy, and compassion), cognitive empathies (which refer to Freudian therapeutic and moral philosophical empathies), a complexion of feeling and thinking empathies (which she defines largely in terms of contemporary therapeutic empathies), and epistemological empathies (which include focus on theories of knowledge).[7]

Writing in the context of history teaching and learning, Stuart Foster (1999) keys in on the qualities of empathy that cross between Verducci's (2000) cognitive and epistemological categories. Discounting affective notions of empathy, Foster notes that, contrary to popular sentiment, empathy is not a synonym for either sympathy or imagination,[8] nor is it the ability to see through the eyes of another. He argues that "historical empathy" encompasses six qualities: understanding and explaining why actors behaved as they did, appreciating the context of historical events, analysis and evaluation of historical evidence, appreciating the consequences of past actions, recognizing that the past differs from the present, and understanding the complexity of human action. Foster's view is helpful, but

---

[7]Thanks to Steve Thornton, who suggested this citation.

[8]For a contrary perspective on the relationship between empathy and imagination, see Lee (1984).

seems less like a coherent view of empathy than a description of historical thinking generally (cf. National Center for History in the Schools, 1994).

Peter Lee (1984) takes a narrower view. Focusing primarily on what Verducci (2000) terms affective empathy, Lee defines empathy alternately as a *power* (the ability to discern others' thoughts and feelings), as an *achievement* (the realization of understanding what others have believed, valued, or felt), as a *process* (the means by which we understand the actions of others), and as a *propensity* (a disposition to look for other perspectives on events). This last characteristic, Lee argues, is "an essential part of learning to think historically" (p. 90).

The notion of empathy as a disposition to imagine other perspectives surfaces most clearly in the student interviews for this study as both sets of students demonstrate an understanding of multiple perspectives. The key difference is that although Blair's students do not demonstrate this ability in the context of the civil rights portion of their history class, Strait's students do.

Empathy in Blair's Students

Ann, one of Blair's students, suggests an understanding of different perspectives when she explains that her friends of "other races":

> might see ... America differently 'cause ... we're on kinda like different levels, maybe? You know ... like I'm an American. She maybe came from a different country, but she's still a U.S. citizen, you know? But, you know she still has that, like, bind with her country. And I'm an American, so ... we're just on different levels.

Although Ann does not believe that the differences she perceives "affect, like, anything," she implies that she and a nonnative friend may see the world differently.

The notion of multiple perspectives also surfaces when Ann talks about her English classes. In a course on African American literature, she found Richard Wright's *Black Boy* "gave me insight on, like, their side." Ann's insights into African Americans' experiences expand when she reads Zora Neale Hurston's *Their Eyes Are Watching God*. Moreover, in the classroom activities that follow, Ann comes to see that her European American classmates also hold a variety of views:

> We had lots [of class discussion]. Like, we would read the chapter, and then we would write logs about them, like, how we saw something, or what we felt by it, and then we would get in the group and just talk about it. And like, you would hear other people's views, and you would say, "Oh, I didn't see it that way." We would learn a lot more. It was helpful.

Ann sharply contrasts the insights she develops in English with what she perceives of as a lack of opportunity for insights in history:

You know, when you're in a classroom like social studies or history, you just learn, like, basic facts. Like, yeah, they [African Americans] were discriminated against, yeah, they were not allowed here. But then with English, in the books, you learn, like, how they felt. Like, what they wanted to do, like how it hurt them, how it affected their lives and family. So, you could really feel for them. But in history, it's just, like, plain facts, like, know this and know that.

The empathic understandings Kate, Alice, and Bill report echo Ann's, especially the sense that these are more obvious in English classes than in history. For example, Bill claims to have read extensively about civil rights and other historical topics in his English classes. What strikes him is the fact that the characters he reads about breathe the same air he does. For example, in reference to *The Jungle*, Bill talks at length about the corruption of politics and society. As he continues, however, he focuses on the plight of the novel's main character, Jurgis Rudkus:

Like, you were actually like able to sympathize with these people.... It [*The Jungle*] focused on one guy and how he was, he would just lose his job one day, and he'd be working for a while, and then an accident would happen in the factory that was caused by, like, bad machinery, and he would be affected by it. But there was, like, no justice in it, you know what I mean? So he would lose his job again, and you were able to actually sympathize and see what it was like for these people, and, like, they were objects and not, like, human beings to these people, like the higher levels of employers. They were more objects. They didn't care about the human beings, they care about money.

Like Ann, Bill senses that different actors hold different views. Although one might argue that his contrast of workers and owners is simplistic, Bill distinguishes between the actors' competing perspectives. Also like Ann, Bill attributes that understanding to his English class. George Blair covered the plight of European immigrants in cities like Chicago, but Bill's sense of that coverage pales against the experience of reading *The Jungle* in English class.

Empathy in Linda Strait's Students

Linda Strait's students also report instances where they see multiple perspectives and feel empathic toward characters they encountered in their English classes. Unlike their peers, Strait's students also see multiple perspectives throughout the civil rights unit they studied. And even more importantly, Strait's students seem to draw inferences to their own lives.

Although empathy is considered a key element of historical understanding, James suggests this is no easy thing. The skating-rink activity, he said, gave him a "good idea" of what life was like for minority citizens in the 1950s. Even so, James knows that this one exercise ill equips him to know how people felt at the time. "It's hard to imagine what black people actually encountered," he said, "and how degrading it must be ... I couldn't imagine living [like that]." After a pause, James adds, "I don't know about you, but I'd be suicidal." Although this comment might be dismissed as hyperbole, James's quiet and cautious demeanor suggests that his claim represents a fledgling attempt to put himself in the shoes of another. His effort may be thin, but it suggests a step toward empathic thinking.

Ned uses scenes from the civil rights documentaries to push his empathic thinking. Not only does he sense the possibility of different perspectives on these scenes, but he also tries to imagine White and Black perspectives over time:

> I think that if Black people saw it—'cause I was thinking about this during the movie—if black people saw this, that mostly all the Whites were beating on them, that they'd think that we were totally ... I mean, if I were Black and I saw that I'd be, I'd hold a grudge against the Whites. I mean, I'm not saying I wouldn't like them, but ... they did that to us. It'd be different if, you know, the Blacks did that to the Whites.... If I were White then I would ... see it differently too.

Here, we see a student struggling with some complex ideas. Ned supposes that African Americans might respond differently to the video images than do his largely European American classmates. He also hints at a sense of what the White antagonists felt at the time. Ned does not tell us if and/or how he resolves this tension. But by imagining his reactions from different perspectives, he suggests an insight into empathic thinking.

So does Melissa. She credits several pieces of Strait's instruction—the videos, handouts, and skating-rink simulation—with sensitizing her to "both sides" in the struggle over civil rights. "She [Strait] didn't blame anyone per se," Melissa said, "She just showed us who did what, and she's pretty fair to everyone." Melissa also credits Strait with helping her see herself in the context of a wider society:

> I feel comfortable in America. I think that I'm probably ... a privileged American. And if ... I was another race or something I probably would see America totally differently. I think it's just how you are placed in life and somewhat what you make of it. But when you're born, you know, most people are born into something and there's some things you can do about it and some of it is just beyond control.

Melissa points both to the notion of multiple perspectives and to the import of those perspectives for how she views her life. Born under different circumstances, Melissa senses the possibility that she might "see America totally differently." Also interesting, however, is Melissa's puzzling through the complex dynamics of birth and initiative. Many observers cast the disparities in American society as a case of either–or: One's position is determined either by birth, or by one's own achievement. Melissa seems to see a middle ground where constraints like race, class, and gender matter, but matter in no exclusive or predetermined ways. Melissa's perspective is intellectually complex, and by avoiding a simplistic dichotomy, she holds a potentially powerful position from which to empathize with others.

Understanding Students' Empathy

Although variously defined, empathy promotes sensitivity to historical actors and their actions and to the notion that those actors and actions can be viewed through multiple perspectives. Because it is a living person who feels (or not) empathy, this is a condition that demands a connection between our lives and the lives of others. George Blair's students demonstrate a capacity for empathy, but they do so outside the context of his class. The lived experiences of Linda Strait's students figure into their empathic accounts, but so too do the ideas and experiences they encounter in her class.

George Blair's students see multiple perspectives, but they do not often center themselves within those perspectives, nor do they see anything in their history course that promotes alternative points of view. This is less surprising, however, if we credit Flavel's (1974) distinction between the capacity to see multiple perspectives and the recognition of the need to do so. Blair's students seem not to see multiple perspectives in history (as opposed to in English) because they do not need to (McIntosh, 1992). Representing the common conclusion Blair's students project, Ann said, "History is just given to you. This is your history, just learn it."

Ann's perception is ironic, for although one might suppose that Blair's narrative style could lead to empathic responses with featured characters like Dwight Eisenhower, this does not seem to happen; in fact, only Bill ever mentioned Eisenhower. Strait's instruction, by contrast, is much less narrative and her students get nothing close to Blair's narrative focus on Eisenhower or any other historical actor. What they do get, however, is access to a series of different perspectives. They also get opportunities to try out a range of perspectives in public forums. It is not always clear what sense students make of these perspectives, but the comments of the students profiled here suggests that they sense the importance of understanding multiple perspectives, and that this is more than an academic exercise.

CONCLUSIONS

Although there is more to what these students have learned about history than I have just presented, articulating their views of historical knowledge, significance, and empathy offers insights into their understandings of history and into the relationship between their understandings and the instruction they experienced. I accept the argument that prior knowledge and experience influence students' views more than was once understood (Barton, 1995; Epstein, 1998; Seixas, 1993a, 1994). Nevertheless, the role of teachers' practices in shaping, supporting, and extending students' conceptions of history seems important to examine. There is little empirical work in this area and we do not understand this relationship well, but studies suggest that there is a connection (Evans, 1988; Leinhardt, 1994; VanSledright, 1995b, 1996b).

If students are to see any value in the study of history, then how to engage their interest becomes a key question. Dewey (1902/1969) warns teachers not to rely on tricks and sugar coating. Neither George Blair nor Linda Strait falls in to that trap, but what about the kinds of instruction their students encounter? Stories excite some, but stories or narrative history may not be enough (Barton, 1997a, 1997b; Levstik, 1989, 1993b, 1995; VanSledright & Brophy, 1992). Blair's students experience a seemingly coherent and engaging narrative centered on the beginnings of the civil rights movement. Yet neither that narrative nor the ones that Blair presents in other units seem to inspire students' engagement with or their understanding of history. Instead, Blair's students seem to equate what they learn about history to "school knowledge" (McNeil, 1988), information that helps them pass tests but means little to them otherwise. Moreover, the historical understandings that Blair's students do hold come largely from sources outside his classroom—their personal experiences, the media, their other coursework.

Some might argue that Blair's students have simply worked their history class learnings together with their other learnings into a seamless web. And others might suggest that there is no reason to despair because Blair's students manifest a measure of historical understanding. Both these possibilities should be considered, but two considerations undercut them. One is the thinness of the historical understanding that Blair's students present. This is most obvious in their collective sense that history is simply a set of facts to learned for school purposes, and in their seeming inability to see connections between the past, the present, and their lives today. Blair's students notice some connections between the past and present, and they seem generally cognizant of multiple perspectives and empathic thinking. In neither instance is their thinking particularly insightful, however. Moreover, when asked to attribute their ideas, they invariably cite sources other than Blair's history course.

But if they are developing a sense of history, do we need to worry about its source? I think so, for although experiences with the media, literature, and family and friends are important, it is the thoughtful study of the past that provides a context in which to develop historical thinking skills and understanding (National Center for History in the Schools, 1994; Seixas, 1996). There is also the problem of enduring perceptions of history. Put simply, if Blair's students' shallow sense of history continues unchallenged, their suspicion that history holds little value is likely to endure.

Linda Strait's students seem on firmer ground here. Although they may or may not be more skilled at constructing arguments or evaluating evidence, they consistently project a more thoughtful and substantive view of history than do their peers in Blair's class.

But let's be clear here: The fact that Strait spends more concentrated time on civil rights than Blair does obviously figures into this differential. On reflection, however, this observation is not as simple as it seems.

First, we must recognize that Strait and Blair are making conscious choices about what content they emphasize and how they structure their teaching practices. Blair chooses to teach civil rights in the context of larger narratives that he spreads out following his textbook's table of contents, and he chooses to give the information to students as lectures. Strait's content and instructional choices are dramatically different. Part of what makes their differences so interesting is that their decisions emerge within the same social context of students, school norms, state curricula, and Regents testing. These factors figure into a complex mix of influences that help shape each teacher' classroom practice. With these influences in mind, the point remains that each teacher has the autonomy to make real decisions about content and pedagogy.

And that leads to a second point: The kinds of decisions Blair and Strait make are qualitatively different. Strait's unit is decidedly broader, less storylike, and more experiential than Blair's. Her students read, write, listen, view, and interact in a range of instructional settings that seem far more intellectually open-ended than Blair's narratives. Strait's students may not always rise to the occasion, but the comments of the students profiled here support the idea that history is by its nature complex, tenuous, and interpretive. Strait's students do not always know what to make of this ambiguity, but unlike Blair's students, they use history as a way to make sense of their lives. Given the thin uses most students assign to history (Seixas, 1994; VanSledright, 1997), this is no small achievement.

4

Learning History: The Nature of Student Understanding in History Classrooms

The "endemic uncertainties" of education include the ill-defined nature of teaching and the unpredictable nature of learning (Lortie, 1975). Simply put, teachers worry that they "are not sure they can make all their students learn" (p. 132). As Linda Strait, George Blair, and their peers enter school each day, they do so with great hopes, but with no guarantee that their efforts will result in powerful student learning.

In chapter 3, I describe how seven students in George Blair's and Linda Strait's classrooms make sense of the instruction they experienced, and I argue that Strait's students walk away with a considerably richer and more nuanced view of history than do their peers. Students are not blank slates, patiently awaiting the deft strokes of a master's pen. Each of the students in these classes understands history in general, and the civil rights era in particular, in part through their prior knowledge, beliefs, and experiences. These influences are not absolute; the classroom activities of their teachers also figure into their understandings. Learning, then, is neither purely individual nor is it purely social; it is less about the direct transmission of knowledge than it is about the active translation of classroom activities into meaningful understandings (or not).

This view of learning, generally labeled *constructivism* (Bruner, 1986, 1990; Piaget, 2001), contrasts sharply with the long-held theory of *behaviorism* (Skinner, 1974). As a learning theory, behaviorism represents the view that all human behavior can be explained as a series of stimulus-response actions. Involuntary responses, such as blinking when a light strikes one's eyes, are fundamentally the same as learned responses, such as answering "George Washington" when asked who was the first U.S. president. Rewards and punishments further learning in that responses that are rewarded tend to persist more than those that are not. In schools, we see behaviorist theory at work when historical knowledge is divided into distinct pieces, when teachers teach those pieces through direct instruction, when students rehearse the pieces through discrete activities, when teachers test frequently to ensure that the pieces are memorized, and when students are praised or punished according to how well they recall the pieces.

Much current thinking challenges the behavioral view. Constructivist theory assumes that people play an active role in their lives: We construct what we know and do rather than merely react to external stimuli. Constructivists do not ignore the importance of environmental stimuli: They blink when light shines in their eyes, too! Instead, they differ from behaviorists in distinguishing between reflexes and learning, in defining what a stimulus is, and in understanding how people respond. Simply put, constructivists assert that learning is a far more complex activity than is a physical reflex, that a wide range of factors—both external and internal—influences our behavior, and that the same factor may influence different people in different ways. Taking constructivism to school means that knowledge is viewed as complex and multifaceted, that something may be lost when ideas are reduced to elementary pieces, that teaching is about creating opportunities for students to think about and work through big ideas, and that learning is more about understanding than simply memorizing those ideas.

Although the contest between behaviorism and constructivism continues to play out in school classrooms, observers of those classrooms find strong evidence for the constructivist vantage when examining students' understandings of history (see, for example, Barton & Levstik, 1998; Epstein, 1998; Keedy, Fleming, Wheat, & Gentry, 1998). Constructivism is no panacea (Philips, 1995), but it seems a useful lens on student learning.

Every teacher wants to think that he or she is the chief influence on what students learn. Teachers' actions do matter, an argument I make near the end of this chapter. But students like those in Linda Strait's and George Blair's classes come to school with all kinds of ideas and the sources of those ideas are many. From this background, the questions I explore in this chapter focus broadly on what and how students learn history. More specifically, I look at: (a) the influences on students' learning; (b) the historical understandings students hold; and (c) the dispositions teachers embrace and the actions they take that most positively affect student learning.

THE INFLUENCES ON STUDENT LEARNING

Before examining *what* students know, let's look at the factors that influence how they learn and understand history. Constructivists argue that learning occurs when students use their prior knowledge, beliefs, and experiences as ways of making sense of or interpreting the influences around them. Two related conditions fall out of this view. One is that two students may make very different sense of the same influence. The second condition is that each student's sensemaking can be affected by a wide range of influences. Those influences can include family, friends, media, and lessons learned in nonhistory classes. History teachers, too, can influence a student's understanding, but their influence is neither assumed nor exclusive.

The Role of Prior Knowledge in Learning

Although controversy reigns over the notion that ideas learned in one context "transfer" directly into a new context (cf. Anderson, Reder, & Simon, 1996; Brown, 1994), there is little question that what we learn in the present is influenced by what we have learned in the past. That past learning, typically called our *prior knowledge*, consists of our beliefs, experiences, and understandings. Constructivists argue that our prior knowledge influences what we attend to in our environment and how we make sense of that information.

The role prior knowledge plays in new learning is complicated, however, by two conditions. One condition is the idea that, in order to learn anything new, we must already have some preliminary knowledge about it. Hallden (1994) notes that, "the learner must have a general idea about the subject matter of the instruction that can provide a framework for interpreting the information presented" (p. 34). In short, we graft new understandings onto old as what we already know helps us understand that which we don't. This is all well and good, but this condition suggests a second: Our prior knowledge can interfere with our new learning (Nisbett & Ross, 1980; Resnick, 1987). We generally hold tightly to that which we know—so tightly, in fact, that we may resist new learning, even when it is more accurate and/or useful.

Consider how each of these prior knowledge conditions works in this example: Ask yourself the question, "Who discovered America?" Chances are the word "Columbus" popped into your head. Knowing that Christopher Columbus was an explorer, that he landed in the Americas, and that some would attribute their discovery to him helps us understand something about exploration and colonization. At the same time, however, "knowing" that Columbus "discovered" America can inhibit our learning about other discoverers, and even what the notion of discovery might mean.[1]

To put the point on this discussion of prior knowledge, recall how James wrestles with the thorny relationship between laws and court cases that

---

[1]Historians propose numerous individuals and groups as better "answers" to the question of who discovered the Americas. Although there is general consensus that Native Americans were the first inhabitants in the Americas (see, for example, Morgan, 1993), the arguments become intense as various authors pitch the importance of the Vikings (Wahlgren, 1986), Irish (Fell, 1976), and Africans (Van Sertima, 1976).

presumably protect people's rights and his sense that discrimination is a deep-seated and powerful state of mind:

> I don't know. I know it's difficult for people to ... stop their discrimination based on laws. I mean, I know, traditionally certain groups have been discriminated against, and sometimes you just can't prevent people from having their same ... state of mind about these people.

James explains, "It's just their values that they've been raised with, and after years and years of having similar values like that, it's just very tough to change."

This is a powerful example of prior knowledge, for it works on two levels. First, James demonstrates an appreciation for how strongly people's experiences can shape their "state of mind." Then he hints at how his own past experiences help him understand the "state of mind" of those who would discriminate. Researchers are just beginning to understand this phenomenon of prior knowledge. It seems like a powerful influence on learning, but how it works and when it works have yet to be determined.

The Many Influences on Students' Learning

In chapter 3, Ann describes how the books she read in her English classes, Richard Wright's *Black Boy* and Zora Neale Hurston's *Their Eyes Are Watching God*, influence her thinking about the experiences of African Americans:

> We had lots [of class discussion]. Like, we would read the chapter, and then we would write logs about them, like, how we saw something, or what we felt by it, and then we would get in the group and just talk about it. And like, you would hear other people's views, and you would say, "Oh, I didn't see it that way." We would learn a lot more. It was helpful.

What students learn in English classes is one of several influences on the knowledge they construct and then bring, as prior knowledge, to their study of history. Family, friends, and the media also figure prominently (Epstein, 1998; Keedy et al., 1995; Nuthall & Alton-Lee, 1995; Seixas, 1993b). So powerful are these many influences that "by the time children have celebrated a decade of Thanksgivings and Martin Luther King days, they are already seasoned students of American culture and history" (Wineburg, Mosburg, & Porat, 2000, p. 55). Sam Wineburg and his colleagues demonstrate that what students (and their parents) know from these sources can be problematic. Nevertheless, the importance of such influences can not be denied.

Although their storehouse of lived experience may be limited, those experiences can be a powerful influence on students' understandings (Barton & Levstik, 1998; Epstein, 1998). Recall Ned's analysis of his life before moving to Westwood:

I grew up in Kastor, and I moved here, so there was a lot of Blacks and Hispanics, and I grew up around that, so it didn't bother me at all. And then
when I moved here, kids are like sort of iffy about ... if you go in the city.
They'd be like, "Oh, like that's some ... like a different world" or something.

Ned adds, "I think both places are good, but, I think, I wish kids that are
here would go live where I was. And then I think they'd ... see the same
thing I would. Maybe they wouldn't, but, it's totally two different things.... If
people could only see it." Like James as described earlier, Ned illustrates
how his experiences influence his understanding of civil rights and his
sense of how others might interpret similar experiences.

A second potential influence on students' understandings of history is
family. The stories families tell one another, whether explicitly designed as
history "lessons" or not, figure into the prior knowledge students bring to
class. Patty, an eighth grader studying colonial America, clearly benefits
from her parents' involvement in and support for her learning. Not only do
they take her to museums and historical sites, but they began encouraging
her understanding of history in grade five: "Actually our fifth grade teacher
was not that great, but my parents reinforced me on that [understanding
the colonial period].... They wouldn't, like, let me go to sleep until I understood what I was reading" (VanSledright, 1995a, p. 328). African American
students report that family members "filled in the facts" about the history
of non-White Americans (Epstein, 1998, p. 408). Sheree, a high school student, appreciates the comparison between the racial uprisings around the
Rodney King beating and those in Detroit and St. Louis in the 1960s because her father discussed them with her: "You just never learned anything about them [in school] ... my father talked about people getting
killed and everything. They were just like Los Angeles, but I never learned
anything about them" (p. 410). She adds, "School tries to fix it up and make
it look pretty; home tells it to you like it really is" (p. 410).

The media constitutes a third influence on students' learning. The documentaries Linda Strait's students see are one form; Walt Disney movies,
newspaper and television reports, and music are others. For example,
Wineburg et al., (2000) cite the heavy influence of certain scenes in the
movie *Forrest Gump* on students' and their parents' understandings of
how Vietnam veterans were treated on their return to the United States.

Teachers' Influence on Students' Learning

With so many factors shaping students' knowledge, can teachers influence
what students know? Of course they can! Teachers' lectures, assignments,
and tests send many messages about what is important to learn. Teachers
must understand, however, that their influence on what students know is
neither exclusive nor guaranteed. Rogers and Stevenson (1988) note:
"Teachers teach and children learn, but what they learn, if we probe deeply
enough, often bears little resemblance to the 'taught' curriculum" (p. 74).

Alice, a student in George Blair's class, makes this latter point clear: Although she appreciates her English teacher's efforts to help her and her classmates understand themselves and others, "Listening to [Mr. Blair] doesn't do anything for me." By contrast, James acknowledges the importance of his teacher, Linda Strait: "I knew discrimination, for example, existed, but I didn't know it quite to the extent that I've learned about this year." Another of Strait's students, Ned, adds, "I think that just the past couple of weeks has really turned my mind about stuff."

The research literature is replete with examples of teachers who powerfully influence their students' understandings of history (Evans, 1988, 1990; Keedy et al., 1998; Rossi, 1995; Rossi & Pace, 1998; Wineburg & Wilson, 1991). These observers assert that teachers can make a powerful, if not exclusive, impression on what their students know. Students are meaning-makers, and as such they use their knowledge, beliefs, and experiences to interpret what they learn in school.

And sometimes what students learn in school conflicts with their prior knowledge. Wineburg et al., (2000) point to the possibility that "lessons learned at home contravene those learned at school" and that "what we hear at school conflicts with what we hear at church or synagogue—if not in the pews then certainly in the bathrooms" (p. 55). Students, like all members of a culture, must "navigate the shoals of the competing narratives that vie for our allegiance" (p. 55). One example of this phenomena is apparent in Sheree's claim that "School tries to fix it up and make it look pretty; home tells it to you like it really is" (Epstein, 1998, p. 410). Another is Isabella, a middle school student, who explains that her understanding of civil rights comes from different sources, and that those sources conflict with what she learns in school:

> You don't really learn about [civil rights] in school. You know I've read books about it. My parents have books and I've gone to the library and I've seen movies and stuff and I mean at this school and at my other school I didn't learn too much about it 'cause like you celebrate Martin Luther King but you don't hear about it ... you just hear that he helped. (Barton & Levstik, 1998, p. 493)

With so many influences, both potential and real, students' prior knowledge can be scattered and thinly developed (Evans, 1990; Keedy et al., 1998; VanSledright, 1995a; Wilson & Sykes, 1989). But as Sheree's and Isabella's experiences suggest, important disjunctures between school knowledge and prior knowledge can erupt.

None of us are fully conscious of all the influences on our thoughts and actions. But in many ways, students, both individually and collectively, decide what they will learn, for the influences of teachers, family, media, and the like are just that: influences. Influences are not determinants; they may shape, but they need not coerce. For example, Karen, a high school student, describes how she navigates multiple influences, while reserving final judgment:

I've always been taught to have an open mind. To get the real facts you compare several viewpoints and average them together and look beyond surface value.... Mrs. G [her history teacher] lays it out. I accept it within an academic context, but I won't just agree with it because she says it is so. (Keedy et al., 1998, p. 628)

Her parents matter, her teacher matters, but in the end, Karen understands that their influences can only contribute to what she understands and to the decisions she must make.

The prior knowledge students bring to class is not always historically accurate, relevant, developed, or useful. It is, however, an important consideration if teachers are to understand their students' learning. We are all able to learn, in large part, because we have already learned. But what we have learned, our prior knowledge, shapes our new learning in many and various ways. Much about students' prior knowledge remains a mystery. We really do not know how much prior knowledge is necessary to understand new ideas, what kinds of prior knowledge are most useful, or how prior knowledge interacts with new learnings. But we do know that to ignore the relationship between what our students know and what we want to teach them is to misunderstand a fundamental element of learning.

STUDENTS' UNDERSTANDINGS OF HISTORY

Although many assert that students know little if anything about history, the issue of what students know and how they think is worth untangling. Popular opinion holds that television, video games, and the like drive all thoughts of history from kids' heads. Three national assessments of historical knowledge seem to support this view. What such data mean, however, is not at all clear. Students like those in Linda Strait's and George Blair's classrooms *may* not know very much history, they *may* know less than their parents, they *may* be "at risk" because of this. At this point, though, the research to confirm these suspicions does not exist.

The research literature does suggest a profitable distinction between (a) what students know and (b) what counts as historical understanding. The first question asks what students remember about the facts, concepts, and generalizations they have been taught, whereas the second asks how students represent their understandings of history.

What Do Students Know?

What *do* students know? It seems like a simple question. Teachers teach, students learn, and tests confirm what they know, or so common perception would have it. And yet, the complex, contextualized, and messy worlds of teaching, learning, and testing yield little in the way of hard conclusions. Part of the problem is figuring out what we want to hold students responsible for knowing; another part is figuring out how to assess them accurately.

Understanding What Students Know

The news isn't pretty. Reports detailing student performance on national assessments of historical knowledge (Beatty, Reese, Persky, & Carr, 1996; National Center for Education Statistics, 2002; Ravitch & Finn, 1987) suggest students know very little. Diane Ravitch and Chester Finn term "shameful" the performance of a national sample of 11th graders on the 1986 National Assessment of Educational Progress (NAEP). This group of students, they conclude, is "ignorant of important things it should know, and that it and generations to follow are at risk of being gravely handicapped by that ignorance upon entry into adulthood, citizenship, and parenthood" (p. 201). A different group of students and a different NAEP test in 1994 yielded distressingly similar results: "Simply put, students are not performing as well ... as the [National Assessment of Educational Progress] Governing Board and the many panelists and reviewers think these students should perform" (Beatty et al., 1996, p. 31). The preliminary results from the 2001 NAEP history exam, released as this book is going into press, show no significant changes from the 1994 test: Scores of students in Grades 4 and 8 rose slightly, but the Grade 12 results are virtually unchanged.

On each test, students knew some things quite well. Most 11th graders could identify the contributions of Thomas Edison, George Washington, and Adolph Hitler, they could locate the former Soviet Union and Italy on a map, and they could recognize the importance of the Underground Railroad and the assembly line (Ravitch & Finn, 1987). Twelfth graders could interpret William Jennings Bryan's "Cross of Gold" speech, compare Franklin Roosevelt's 1933 and 1937 inauguration speeches, and explain differences between White and Native American attitudes toward land ownership (Beatty et al., 1996).

Most other test items proved more challenging. Few 11th graders could correctly connect the Puritans with the founding of Boston, Betty Friedan and Gloria Steinem with the women's movement of the 1970s, or Abraham Lincoln with the decades of his presidency (Ravitch & Finn, 1987). Similarly, 12th graders struggled to interpret documents around FDR's New Deal, identify the *Brown v. Board of Education* decision, and recognize rights protected by the 14th amendment (Beatty et al., 1996).

A limited number of qualitative studies confirm these quantitative results. For example, in a pair of studies, Bruce VanSledright (1995a, 1996b) finds that students' knowledge of historical events is spotty, even after direct instruction. Before their classroom unit on colonial America, 6 eighth-grade students demonstrate that their knowledge of explorers, early colonists, and early governmental structures is relatively weak, that their sense of what a colony is is pretty keen, and that, although they often express highly opinionated views, they occasionally demonstrate the ability to understand multiple perspectives (VanSledright, 1996b). Postunit analysis reveals a good deal of the same, and in a few students, even more confusion. But that analysis also shows that despite a unit heavy on "information overload," students do pick up on central elements of the European colonial experience and on the different experiences Native Americans.

And yet, when 79% of 11th graders fail to recognize the role of Reconstruction and when 59% of 12th graders cannot identify the purpose of the Monroe Doctrine, it is easy for those who hold history dear to shake their heads and ask, "How can they not know these simple ideas?" "How can they forget that which they just learned?"

The fact of the matter is that we really do not know why students know (or don't know) what they do. There are lots of reasons why we don't know this, but a huge part of the problem is that, as educators and as a society, we have yet to decide *what* we want students to know. Rhetorically, the old argument about whether students should know basic facts or what those facts mean (as in concepts and generalizations) is over: They need to know both. Ravitch and Finn (1987) put the matter bluntly:

> A knowledge of disconnected facts that are joined, related, or explained by no concepts is obviously without significance; we learn particular facts in order to grasp ideas and develop generalizations. At best, concepts explain the facts of a given situation, while facts provide examples with which to illustrate or test concepts. (p. 16)

The authors conclude, "In order for history to make sense, concepts and facts must be blended. It is not necessary to choose between them" (p. 17). Kathryn and Luther Spoehr (1994) agree, making that argument that facts are to generalizations as the alphabet is to reading:

> Facts (and letters) are essential building blocks; without them you cannot do history (or read). But, just as reading necessitates looking at how the letters and words stand in relation to one another ... , thinking historically requires going beyond chronology or chronicle and looking at the relations that the facts bear to one another. (p. 71)

Okay, so students need to know facts, concepts, and generalizations. But which ones? The New York State curriculum for 11th grade U.S. history is 33 single-spaced pages long. Is every item on that list of such importance that students will be "gravely handicapped" if they cannot recall them? And if not all, which of those facts, concepts, and generalizations do students *have* to know in order to function as good citizens?

Assessing What Students Know

The problem of *what* students need to know is compounded by *how* we assess their knowledge. I discuss the problems of testing in chapter 6. Here, I want to point to several issues that tests, especially national tests, pose for answering the question, "What do students know?"

One problem is that the older and newer NAEP exams are different. Not only were the tests given to different age groups, but the 1987 exam assessed only basic factual knowledge, whereas the 1994 exam (and the 2001 test) was purposely constructed to be a "challenging" test (Beatty et al., 1996). Rather than assess straightforward who, what, when, and where information, the authors of the 1994 and 2001 exams created questions that pushed students into higher levels of thinking, asked students about the nature of history as well as about historical events, and demanded that students answer questions where they had to write out their answers as well as select the right multiple-choice answer. Although we can now begin comparing the 1994 and 2001 results, pushing our analysis of student knowledge back to 1987 is problematic.

The incommensurate nature of the NAEP exams points to a second problem: Until now, we have no baseline from which to compare the tests' results. Ravitch and Finn (1987) and Beatty and her colleagues (1996) can assert that students' performance is substandard, but both sets of authors lacked the data with which to compare those performances. With the 2001 test replicating the 1994 exam, we can now use the 1994 results as baseline data such that we now can make and support claims about student performance over time.

A third problem is even nastier: Even with similar tests and good baseline test data, there is still the issue of how well tests measure what students know. Graham Nuthall and Adrienne Alton-Lee (1995) study how students respond to standardized, test-like questions. After analyzing how and why students choose the answers they do, Nuthall and Alton-Lee conclude that "students with the same scores on the achievement test were unlikely to know, or have learned, the same content" (p. 192). In short, gross errors in understanding what students know can develop when we only count right and wrong answers to a test question.

Evidence for this last point comes in Sam Wineburg's (1991) study of how high school students and college history professors interpret various kinds of text. The substantive differences in students' and professors' interpretations aside, Wineburg points to the fallibility of tests as a measure of knowing. Wineburg begins his study by giving students and professors the same short quiz asking them to identify elements of the American Revolution period—What was Fort Ticonderoga? What were the Townshend Acts?—that sort of thing. Although the students do not read the texts Wineburg gives them as wisely as the historians, they do almost as well as the historians on the quiz. In fact, two students outperform one of the eight historians, while another historian answers correctly about the same number of questions as do most of the students. Wineburg makes no wild claims about such findings and neither will I, but this report underscores the problematic nature of deeply understanding what students know based on test questions alone.

Don't misunderstand: I outline these problems not to minimize the issue of what students know or to argue that we should be sanguine about what little students seem to know about history. It is discouraging to think that students are unaware of seemingly basic information, especially if it has been recently taught to them. But in the face of all that we do not understand about what students know, we ought to avoid making hasty and hard judgments.

What Counts as Students' Historical Understanding?

Understanding what students know, although a tempting research area, turns out to be less interesting to most researchers than the question of what counts as students' historical understanding. This issue is not completely unrelated to the question of what students know, but it assumes that what they remember and can recall is only part of the story. Also key, especially if our goal is to have students know more than basic facts, is exploring how they understand the history they learn at home, in the media, and at school.

Two issues surface when we examine the notion of students' historical understanding. The first is what their understandings look like. Here, we ask *what* students are thinking about when they demonstrate an understanding of history. The second issue focuses on *how* students think historically. Here, we explore whether or not their thinking develops in stages, and the special role narrative plays in students' understanding of history.

What Student Understanding Looks Like

Peter Seixas (1996) offers perhaps the most comprehensive vision of student historical understanding. In this section, I briefly review his six elements and then look more closely at the research on one of those elements—significance.

Seixas (1996) identifies six elements of historical understanding—significance, epistemology and evidence, continuity and change, progress and decline, empathy and moral judgment, and historical agency—and comments on how these elements relate to student learning. He defines *significance* as "the richness and complexity of its [a historical event's] connections to other events and processes, and ultimately to ourselves" (p. 768). Students, Seixas notes, typically lack the breadth of knowledge historians have so their choices about significance are "severely constrained" (p. 769) and they may decontextualize the past as they search for meaning in the present. Seixas asserts that *epistemology and evidence* involve "separating warranted belief from that which is not" (p. 769). In other words, he asks, what traces of the past are worth examining and believing, and on what grounds and with what reservations should people do so? Here, Seixas cites Denis Shemilt (1987), who argues that although students often accept historical accounts as written, they can question the reliability and authenticity of sources, see the usefulness of evidence as a basis for inference, and understand the need to question all accounts. *Continuity and change*, Seixas notes, are relational concepts that provide context for one another. "In order to identify historical change," he argues, "we have to set a phenomenon against an unchanging, or continuous, backdrop" (p. 771). In short, understanding change entails understanding continuity. Students, however, often seize on one pole or the other, fixing either on a world in constant motion or on one that is essentially static. As with continuity and change, students typically see the fourth element of historical understanding, *progress and decline*, as a dichotomy, although they are far more likely to see progress across historical events rather than decline (Barton & Levstik, 1998; Wertsch, 1994). A much more complicated set of elements are *empathy and moral judgment.* Judgments involve "understanding historical actors as agents who faced decisions, sometimes individually, sometimes collectively, which had ethical consequences" (p. 776). Empathy involves an "understanding of the differences between our moral universe, or ideological surround, and theirs (historical actors')" (p. 776). Each construct requires that students entertain the possibilities of historical actors performing in ways both common and distinct from our own. Finally, the notion of *historical agency* asks about the consequences of historical actors' deeds. Historians debate the roles that individuals and groups play in constructing their lives. This debate is useful, but it raises real issues for students as they negotiate a seemingly endless list of people, the places they inhabit, and the records of their actions.

The research literature gives more attention to some of Seixas's categories than others. We know far more about significance, epistemology and evidence, and progress and decline than we do about elements like historical agency.[2] Space prevents me from delving into all of these areas, so to get a sense of the research, I focus on significance.

Understanding Students' Views of Historical Significance

Seixas (1997) notes that "students do not swallow whole what this year's teachers and textbooks tell them is historically significant. Rather, they filter and sift and remember and forget, adding to, modifying, and reconstructing their frameworks of understanding through their own often unarticulated values, ideas, and dispositions" (p. 22). This observation tells us two things about significance. One is that students come to the study of history with some sense of which people, places, and events are

---

[2]On epistemology and evidence, see Doppen (2000) and Foster and Yeager (1999); on continuity and change and progress and decline, see Barton and Levstik (1998) and Wertsch (1994); on empathy and moral judgment, see Foster (1999) and Lee (1984); and on historical agency, see Penyak and Duray (1999).

significant. That sense may be thinly developed, but it is a disposition students bring with them. The other point Seixas raises is that what students define as significant may vary from that which their teachers offer. Just as students construct the knowledge they hold, so too do they construct ideas about historical significance.

Knowing that students hold ideas about historical significance and that those ideas may be colored by a wide range of influences, let's look at two dimensions of students' understandings of significance. One dimension focuses on how students' conceptualize significance; the other highlights what they determine to be significant.

Seixas (1997) argues that students' conceptualize significance along a rough objectivist-subjectivist scale. The *basic objectivist* can identify significant events, but when asked why they are important, the student falls back on authorities (e.g., teacher, textbook, historians). For example, Marco asserts that the writing of the Bible is the most significant historical event because "I was taught to respect the Bible and I even learned from the Bible. It is the only communication to God" (p. 24). A second type of significance is defined as *basic subjectivist* in that this student sees historical significance only in terms of his or her own experience and interests. As Seixas notes, "The student might see the history of hockey as significant because he likes sports. The history of religion is not significant because she is not interested in it" (p. 25). The *advanced objectivist* student typically determines significance by focusing on the perceived impact of an event. Cindy explains that "movable type has entirely revolutionized the speed, range, efficiency with which we are able to communicate. It has changed the world" (p. 25). An *advanced subjectivist* also emphasizes an event's "impact," but restricts the scope of meaning to a specific culture. Born in Macau, Helen cites as significant those events that focus on "her people, her country of origin, the impact of recent world events on them" (p. 25). Seixas's final category is *narrativist*. These students create interpretive frameworks whereby they define significance in terms of how events relate to one another. These linkages may be temporal, spatial, or related to trends (e.g., population growth) or moral judgments (e.g., "crushing the world's aboriginal people"). Nancy cites European exploration of the Americas as significant because "it spread our western culture throughout the world. It crushed and ravaged the natives all over the world. Set a world standard for civilization—what was civilized and what wasn't" (p. 26). In this response, Nancy links past and present in ways that imply a continuum of human experience. The past is not just the past, but instead provides key insights into the contemporary world.

Seixas's categories help us think about how students conceptualize the significance of historical events. Keith Barton and Linda Levstik (1998) help us think about the kinds of events students identify as significant.

Like many adults, middle school students hold "alternative and even conflicting images of the past" (Barton & Levstik, 1998, p. 479), and those images translate into constructions about the significance of events. Many of the students Barton and Levstik interviewed select as significant those events that legitimize the present, that is, events that reflect the creation of the United States as a social and political entity, the creation of perceived American freedoms and opportunities, and the benefits of technology. For example, Brenda identifies the first Thanksgiving as significant because it illustrates "the start of the United States, when we all became possible, because we all came from over there, and a bunch of immigrants came over here, and that's basically how we started our nation" (p. 483). Most students list the American Revolution as significant with such justifications as it "kinda started our country," and that without it, "we would have no country" (p. 481). These students articulate a basic premise of historical significance: the connection of past to present. They do so, however, within a framework that emphasizes the progress of American ideas, or what Barton and Levstik call, the "legitimation for the present" (p. 482).

Although for many students historical significance revolves around legitimizing the present, a countertheme can also be detected. Drawing on Bodnar's (1994) work, Barton and Levstik (1998) argue that students construct alternative or "vernacular" accounts of significant events. These accounts often arise from lived experience and draw on values and experiences ignored by the mainstream. Students identify issues of continuing racism and sexism, the Great Depression, and Vietnam as events that run counter to the theme of progress.[3] Students who cite the significance of the Great Depression offer that it "just changed the country so much. They realized that they weren't the god of all countries" and "[life's] not going to be perfect all the time" (p. 496). Vietnam also proves problematic. Although students see most American wars as beneficial to the country, they struggle to understand U.S. efforts in Vietnam. No clear or consistent viewpoint surfaces, but comments like "if they [the North Vietnamese] were going to go communist, let them … we should stay out of their business" (p. 497) suggest that students hold no rosy view of all U.S. actions.

Barton and Levstik (1998) and Seixas (1997) wisely temper their analyses, claiming that their findings neither generalize to all students nor do they exhaust all the possible ways students may conceptualize historical significance. Their research does offer, however, a way to understand how students think about historical events. Such understandings, Seixas argues, "can then become a starting point for history instruction" (p. 22).

The Development of Students' Historical Thinking

With some sense of *what* students' historical understanding looks like, we turn now to *how* their understanding develops. Traditionally, two related

---

[3]Interestingly enough, these middle schoolers believe the U.S. civil rights movement is successfully over, so although it is still significant, it is seen as a legitimizing rather than vernacular event.

questions have guided the study of children's thinking. One question asks whether or not children pass through discernible stages of development; the second asks when children are ready for sophisticated thinking. According to some researchers, children's thinking matures in clearly recognizable stages, and higher levels of thinking are attainable only by older students. Others discount these views, arguing that even very young children are capable of robust thinking and that, rather than progress through age-defined stages, each child's thinking develops along an idiosyncratic trajectory. Although the questions remain, current thinking generally supports the second conception. The narrative view of thinking assumes that children acquire early on the ability to understand and present narrative accounts that include people, places, and events. The accuracy and sophistication of these accounts can vary widely, but the role of narrative in understanding children's thinking seems prominent.

The Stage Theory of Children's Historical Thinking

Jean Piaget (1962), the famous Swiss psychologist, argued that all children pass through discrete, identifiable, and general stages of thinking. Very young children (birth to 2 years) are deemed *sensorimotor* thinkers. At this age, children explore and begin to understand their environment largely through sensation and movement. The second stage, *preoperational*, characterizes children from ages 2 to 7. More sophisticated than their younger peers, preoperational children are developing a facility with language that allows them to begin using symbols to represent real-world objects. *Concrete operations*, Piaget's third stage, is exemplified by children from first grade through early adolescence. Characteristic of children at this age is the ability to manipulate objects and representations of objects, although they tend to operate more successfully in present than in future contexts. Finally, children in the *formal operations* stage (age 11 or 12 on) can appreciate hypothetical situations where they consider possible variables and posit potential relationships. Children at this stage, for the first time, can understand multiple perspectives on an issue.

Piaget's ideas spawned the belief in "developmentally appropriate" education, which presupposes that children's thinking develops sequentially from concrete to abstract, from simple to complex, and from known to unknown (Lyle, 2000). So fixed and age-dependent are these developmental shifts that Piaget deemed meaningless teachers' actions to advance children's thinking: "Teaching children concepts that they have not attained in the spontaneous development ... is completely useless" (Hall, 1970, p. 30).[4]

---

[4]This quote comes from Lyle (2000).

Kieran Egan (1989) applies stage theory to children's historical thinking.[5] Although he criticizes some of Piaget's assumptions, Egan supports the idea of developmental stages. His four "layers" of historical thinking are: (a) developing and extending one's identity as a continuation of the past (mythical understanding); (b) building empathic understanding of past actors (romantic understanding); (c) searching for patterns upon which to build grand theories (philosophic understanding); and (d) focusing on particulars as a way to understand what happened for its own sake (ironic understanding). Egan claims that the first two layers "are not left behind or beneath" (p. 291) the second two. The latter two layers, however, "are accessible only through the earlier layers." (p. 292). Further reflecting Piagetian logic, Egan argues that the first layer is appropriate for students up to age 8 while the second is apropos of students ages 8 to 15. The philosophic and ironic layers characterize adult thinking.

A Critique of Stage Theory

Stage theory has engendered considerable criticism (Lyle, 2000). Researchers interested in how children learn to think historically have exploded all three of the major stage theory premises: that children's thinking is age dependent, that all children pass through definable stages, and that teachers can only support the natural development of children's thinking. Some researchers (e.g., Bruner, 1986, 1990; Vygotsky, 1962, 1978) challenge these premises generally, whereas others (e.g., Booth, 1980; Dickinson, Lee, & Rogers, 1984; Levstik, 1986; Seixas, 1994, 1997; Shemilt, 1980) focus on children's thinking about history.

Alaric Dickinson and Peter Lee (1984) summarize the case against the stage view:

> The age-stage relation is only statistical, and, more important, the stages themselves are necessarily simplified models. Even where a child's thinking may in general be allocated to a given stage, his performance on any particular task may fluctuate widely according to the nature of the task, the variety of his experience, and the surrounding circumstances. For many teaching purposes cognitive states are therefore likely to be at best misleading and unhelpful, and at worst rigid and stultifying, leading to a kind of "stage prejudice." (p. 118)

Three points are worth developing. First, the notion of "stages" is problematic, as Dickinson and Lee call them "simplified models" that are

---

[5]Egan does not credit Piaget with the idea of thinking stages, nor is his notion of stages or "layers" of historical thinking based on empirical study. The argument that Piaget's stages are directly relevant to children's historical thinking is best made by Hallam (1969, 1970) and Peel (1967).

"only statistical." What they mean is that when stage theorists "see" clear-cut categories of students' thinking, they are identifying general tendencies rather than the full range of behavior. Seeking general tendencies in children's thinking can be useful, but it can also hide important variations (Seixas, 1994, 1997; Shemilt, 1980). Those variations become especially important when realizing Dickinson and Lee's second point: A child's thinking can "fluctuate widely according to the nature of the task, the variety of his experience, and the surrounding circumstances." Here, they question the stage theorists' premise that thinking is age dependent, that thinking matures according to a child's physical development. Rather than viewing thinking as biologically based, Dickinson and Lee argue for the importance of context and experience. Children think in more or less sophisticated ways depending on the kind of assignment they are given, their prior knowledge, and other elements that have little to nothing to do with their chronological age (Levstik, 1986; Shemilt, 1980, 2000). Finally, Dickinson and Lee reject the stage theorists' premise that teachers do not influence children's historical thinking. To accept stage theory, one must accept the idea that teachers may offer only learning activities that support the level of thinking deemed appropriate to the students' age group. Offering more challenging tasks is, in Piaget's words, "completely useless." Such an assertion is bound to rub teachers wrong. And it should, as many researchers also discount this premise. Lev Vygotsky (1962, 1978) counters stage theory with the notion of a "zone of proximal development." That "zone" is the boundary between what children can do on their own and what they can do with assistance from a teacher or a more capable other. Vygotsky's view, like that of other researchers (Booth, 1980; Bruner, 1996; Shemilt, 1980), presumes that skillful teachers assess each of their students' current capabilities and provide assignments that both build on and push beyond those levels. One of the more complete accounts of children's cognitive growth when experiencing ambitious teaching is Denis Shemilt's description of the Schools Council History 13–16 Project (Shemilt, 1980). Rather than being confined to an age-dependent category, the students Shemilt studied were "more accustomed to giving and seeking explanations, see more problems and puzzles in History, proliferate ideas more readily, frequently—if implicitly—arrange these ideas into the germ of what deserves to be called a 'theory of History,' and were generally more bold and vigorous in their thinking" (pp. 13–14).

The notion of a defined progression makes the stage theory of student thinking attractive. Yet, the issues critics raise cut deeply. If the available evidence suggests that children can think beyond the age-dependent stages and that good teachers can push students' understanding, then we need to consider other ways to explain how children think their way into history.

The Narrative View of Children's Historical Thinking

Okay, so if students don't think in definable stages, how do they think about history? Although the argument continues, there is some consensus that narrative plays a large role in children's historical thinking.[6]

Jerome Bruner (1986, 1990, 1996) believes human thinking manifests in one of two ways, paradigmatic or narrative. Paradigmatic thinking emphasizes analytic modes of inquiry typically associated with mathematics and the sciences. Narrative thinking emphasizes the creation of organized and coherent accounts of people, places, and events. Such thinking, Bruner asserts, is innate in the sense that it emerges naturally as children construct and verbalize their understandings of the world.[7] Narrative thinking is sometimes equated with story-telling. Stories can be part of a narrative, but narrative thinking is more broadly conceived of as a process of creating coherence that may or may not reflect the elements of story.

Researchers interested in how children learn history find much to support Bruner's theory about narrative thinking. Although some (e.g., Levstik, 1986, 1995; Seixas, 1994; Shemilt, 2000; Wertsch, 1994) worry that children and textbook authors get stuck constructing naive and simplistic narratives, many accept the notion that children's first understandings of history develop in narrative form (e.g., Beck, McKeown, Sinatra, & Loxterman, 1991; Cronon, 1992; Paxton, 1997).

The argument that young children can construct coherent historical narratives is well established (e.g., Barton, 1997a; Levstik, 1986; Levstik & Pappas, 1987; VanSledright & Brophy, 1992). For example, Bruce VanSledright and Jere Brophy (1992) observe that upper elementary-age students "possess interest in historical detail, are concerned about motives in human interactions, demonstrate preliminary understanding of cause and effect relationships, and are able to construct and appreciate historical drama" (p. 851). That said, young children's narratives can be ungainly. Consider how Helen, a fourth grader, accounts for the origins of the United States:

> The United States was really poor and it didn't have that much, but the British had fabulous stuff and they weren't poor. They had clothes and stuff like that. Then America was just this poor country. There were people there but they weren't the richest part of the world. The British agreed to never fight the Americans again and America agreed to that. They never fought again but the British, I'm not sure about this part, but I think the British went against their promise and the British left and they had to do something like sign a paper or something to get it together, a promise and then the British left and

---

[6]Susan Lyle (2000) offers a particularly useful overview of the development of narrative thinking as an alternative to stage theory.

[7]Intererestingly enough, although Egan's work can be seen as supportive of stage theory, he is also a major proponent of narrative understanding (see, for example, Egan, 1988).

they never got to sign or do whatever they had to do to make the promise but then a few years later, I think they fought. But this time America was rich and had a lot of soldiers and the Americans won over the British and that's how we got our country. (p. 848)

In Helen's narrative, chronology, drama, cause and effect all surface, but so too do conflations, contradictions, and confusions. VanSledright and Brophy point out that although Helen's imagination helps her create a vivid story with plenty of plot twists and turns, it also helps her slide over relevant details, perspectives, and evidence.

Older students' narrative accounts can also be problematic. First, they get the people, places, and events mixed up (VanSledright, 1995a, 1996b). Constructing a narrative is not the same thing as constructing a narrative faithful to the known facts. Asked how the Jamestown colony was organized and governed, Randy offers an account that includes the English king, the Virginia governor, and a royal charter. As the details begin to escape him, however, he sighs, "it's, like, all jumbled up in my head" (VanSledright, 1995a, p. 317). Randy is not alone. Because "information overload always lurks in the shadows" (VanSledright, 1996b, p. 137), many students find it difficult to keep both the storyline and the facts consistent.

A second problem with narrative thinking is the tendency to construct accounts that offer only a single perspective. When Wertsch (1994) asked students to write an essay describing the "origins of your country," he finds they produce "monological" or "univocal" narratives. Some students offer a form of critique, but they have trouble including more than a single perspective. For example, after finishing a fairly traditional account of European settlement, a student appends a description detailing his discomfort with his narrative:

So as far as the "beginnings," it is necessary to distinguish *whose* beginnings. My upbringing and historical knowledge has been grounded in the nation's "Founding Fathers" and the ideals of democracy. I am not 100% sure I agree with all the original premises, but according to the perspective I've been born into, it is these values which have influenced me. But to be objective is to say that the beginnings of this land we live on are not those of the White man, but of the Indians. (p. 335)

This student is not alone in adding a "vernacular" element (Barton & Levstik, 1998) to his essay. Like virtually all of his peers, however, the bulk of his essay presents a "single set of events and a single set of agents and allowing other events and characters into the picture in a subordinate role at best" (Wertsch, 1994, p. 336).[8]

---

[8]James Voss and Jennifer Wiley (2000) offer an interesting addition to Wertsch's findings. When they analyzed the essays college-age students wrote using primary source documents, they found that students who used multiple sources to write argumentative or analytic essays tended to demonstrate higher cognitive processing than students who wrote more storylike narrative essays.

If students fail to include multiple perspectives in their narratives, so too do they falter in knowing what to do with the sources available to them. Interviewing high school students, Sam Wineburg (1991) discovers that they are generally blind to subtexts and that they typically read multiple documents for right answers rather than to compare one account with another. Frans Doppen (2000) reports that when given multiple accounts of the atomic bomb decision, students tend to divide them into only two sides (us vs. them). And Stuart Foster and Elizabeth Yeager (1999) find that students tend to believe that the "truth" of any event lies in eyewitness accounts and that students sometimes have trouble assessing the credibility of a source.

One last problem students encounter involves the scope of the narratives they create. Shemilt (2000), like many of the researchers noted thus far (e.g., Foster & Yeager, 1999; Wineburg, 1991), finds that students can answer testlike questions and construct narratives around single historical events. Students can, Shemilt argues, "make rational sense of the past and perhaps even to bring historical perspective to bear upon the analysis of contemporary events and options" (p. 85). Where they struggle, however, is in "the knowledge or even the sense of the past necessary to exploit this understanding" (p. 85). In short, students can think historically about "fragments of the episodes of the past, but not to the past as a whole" (p. 85). Shemilt's conclusion brings to mind Seixas's (1997) categories of historical significance. The bulk of the students he interviewed focus their accounts of significance on the impact of or lessons learned from a single event. Rare is the student who offers a "narrativist" account, one in which the student "successfully united personal interests and concerns with broad historical trends and developments" (p. 27).

Given this list of problems, one might assume that the narrative theory of children's historical thinking is as unruly as stage theory. Perhaps, but the evidence that children, beginning at young ages, use narratives to construct historical accounts cannot be ignored. This remains thorny ground, in part, because *what* students tell us they understand depends in no small part on *how* they are asked to respond (Foster & Yeager, 1999; Nuthall & Alton-Lee, 1995; Voss & Wiley, 2000) and *how* they have been taught (Evans, 1990; Keedy et al., 1995; Young & Leinhardt, 1998). This last point offers hope, however, for although the origins of children's historical thinking may remain clouded, there is some indication that teachers can have a salutary effect on students' understanding.

WHAT TEACHERS KNOW AND DO
TO ENABLE STUDENT LEARNING

History teachers like Linda Strait and George Blair face a rough road. A broad curriculum and insufficient time conspire with students who come to class with widely varying prior knowledge and with uneven abilities to construct coherent narratives. On top of all this, a teacher's instruction may be only one of several influences on what students know. It's enough to make one consider another profession.

But it is also not the whole picture. Although the problems teachers face are real, research suggests that teachers can have a real and substantive effect on what students know and think about history. That research is far from conclusive, as there are many areas yet unexplored. Rally points exist, however, and around these teachers can examine and reconstruct their classroom practices.

One of those rally points concerns the dispositions ambitious teachers hold, whereas a second revolves around the classroom actions they take. Key to both is a sense of agency: Good teachers believe they can spark positive results and they take specific actions to do so. Students can learn some history on their own and from the various family, media, and social influences around them. They can learn more and more powerful history with thoughtful teachers beside them.

The Dispositions and Actions of Ambitious Teachers

When I interview prospective teachers for the University at Buffalo teacher preparation program, I hear story after story about teachers who "made a difference." These stories serve as powerful indicators of the dispositions ambitious teachers hold. Those dispositions include both general attitudes toward students (e.g., "She respected me as a person") and more specific ideas about teaching and learning history (e.g., "He really believed that we could learn things from history"). The students' stories also outline the compelling classroom actions taken by their favored teachers. Those actions cohere with the teachers' dispositions: Teachers who believe their students can think their way deeply into historical issues are the ones who provide lots of instructional opportunities to do so.

Talented history teachers know that no magic formula exists. But the recent research literature describing powerful teaching and learning provides clues about the dispositions such teachers hold and the actions they take.

Students and the Purpose of History

One set of useful dispositions and actions responds to the ways students think about the purpose of history. Elementary students struggle with this question (Barton, 1995); older students do, too. Asked directly, many respond with a version of Santayana's (1968) dictum that those who ignore the lessons of the past are doomed to repeat them (Seixas, 1994; VanSledright, 1997). Ron Evans (1988) argues that students can talk about the purpose of history, but when pushed, their ideas soon become "vague, incomplete, and poorly formed" (p. 217). Martin Sleeper (1973) takes a slightly more optimistic view. He asserts that whether it is obvious to them or not, history helps students in "acquiring a sense of identity" (p. 260). A distinction he makes, however, is key: The students who best connect the study of history with their own sense of self are those who talk about the history they learn outside of school. School history, by contrast, often seems to these students to be distant and separate from the concerns of their lived experiences.

Accomplished teachers understand that although some students come to them with a rich appreciation of history, most do not. They also know that admonitions ("You need to know this for the test"), exhortations ("You'll like this part. Really!"), and negotiations ("If we just get through this stuff, then we can do something fun") persuade no one. Good teachers deal with the question of why we study history both explicitly through discussion and implicitly through the messages their instruction approaches send (Doppen, 2000; Wineburg & Wilson, 1991). For example, John Keedy and his colleagues (1998) find that, in the hands of a capable teacher, "most of our students demonstrated an understanding that history was not just a collection of dates and events … to be memorized. History consisted of subjective meanings about why events happened and their consequences to our citizenry" (p. 632). Evidence of this finding emerges in the words of Linda Strait's students as they consciously strive to connect that past to the present and to their own lives.

Students as Constructivist Learners

A second set of dispositions and actions revolves around the notion of students as constructivist learners. Behaviorist theory works pretty well to describe why humans do some of the things they do, but it does not work well to explain how students learn history. As active constructors, what students come to know and believe about history reflects their prior knowledge and the range of influences they encounter that support, challenge, and extend that knowledge. Effective teachers know that they can be one of the more powerful influences on their students, but they also know that other influences matter, and that as various influences mix, a sort of "fact stew" can result (VanSledright, 1995a). As Wineburg and Wilson (1991) note, "teachers who are unaware that students filter, twist, construct, and reconstruct the information they hear are naive about the processes of learning" (p. 273).

To teach well, teachers need to know well the range of ideas their students bring to class. Among the actions teachers can take are providing occasions when students can "expose their often partially submerged frameworks for orienting themselves in historical time" and using their "own understandings of their (students') understandings [as] a starting point for history instruction" (Seixas, 1997, p. 22). Key to both ideas is putting students in places where their lived experiences intersect with historical events. For example, consider how Bill's understanding of the Great Depression in George Blair's class might have expanded had he been encouraged to share his stories about his grandparents' experiences. Another way is to help students find a particular question or issue that nettles them. A boy dissatisfied with standard explanations of how Thomas Jefferson could own slaves at the same time that he wrote "All men are created equal" is unlikely to sleep through his history class.

Taking the time to uncover these pressure points is low on many teachers' lists, especially because many believe either that students approach all of history apathetically or that they lack the ability to think beyond the facts (McKee, 1988). Such views are ultimately disabling, however, for they fail to give students either a reasonable impetus for studying history or the credit for being able to do so in engaging ways. As VanSledright (1995a) observes, "the point is to put the students back into the picture, linking their immersion into the past to a personalized quest or odyssey, making their questions and curiosities as important as the putative historical facts" (p. 338). Taking VanSledright's advice means acting on the belief that students can and will construct important historical meanings when they are engaged in important studies.

The Variation in Students' Knowledge

If what students know reflects a wide array of influences, then it makes some sense to realize that as students construct meaning, those meanings will vary. Both quantitative and qualitative assessments demonstrate that students' recall of historical detail is relatively weak, and that what any two students might know can differ dramatically even if they experience the same instruction (VanSledright, 1995a) and are asked the same questions on a test (Nuthall & Alton-Lee, 1995). Good teachers understand that instruction and assessment—how they teach and how they understand what students learn—are intimately connected (Rogers & Stevenson, 1988; Wiggins, 1995).

These dispositions are enacted when teachers teach and assess widely. Teachers like George Blair can be effective with lectures and objective tests. The research literature, however, offers more successful examples of teachers like Linda Strait, who employ multiple teaching and assessment approaches (e.g., Evans, 1990; Rossi, 1995; Rossi & Pace, 1998; Wineburg & Wilson, 1991). Julia Smith and Richard Niemi (2001) cite evidence for this assertion through their analysis of the 1994 NAEP history test. Comparing students' responses to the questionnaire with their performance on the exam, Smith and Niemi conclude that although several factors correlate with higher test scores, the strongest relate to the nature of classroom instruction. In particular, higher test scores correlate with student reports of instruction that includes complex writing tasks, in-depth reading (meaning from sources outside the textbook), extensive student discussion, and learning tools such as outside speakers, film, and computers.[9] Smith and Niemi conclude that, "in history as well as elsewhere, active involvement promotes student achievement" (p. 34).[10]

Qualitative research supports these quantitative results (Evans, 1990; Newmann, Secada, & Wehlage, 1995). In findings that parallel what students said about George Blair's and Linda Strait's practices, Ron Evans (1990) reports that students are more responsive to teachers who employ a more ambitious pedagogy. Susan, an engaging storyteller like George Blair, gets high marks from students for offering clear and appealing lectures. Interviews with students, however, suggest that her lecturing is "enjoyable to students, but may be having little impact on student beliefs other than giving them an image of history as story with the concomitant focus on knowing for the sake of knowing" (p. 109). By contrast, Rusty's more diverse classroom practice seems to encourage deeper student understanding of history. Key to student comments about becoming more critical, analytical, and aware is Rusty's "questioning, process-centered orientation to history and pedagogy" (p. 113). As one student said, "It has been like a total opening of the government and it is like analyzing the government this year and it is really new and I really appreciate it" (p. 112).

Diversity in assessment is just as important as diversity in instruction. One of the cornerstones of the move toward "authentic" assessment (see, for example, Avery, 1999; Mathison, 1997; Newmann et al., 1995) is the benefit realized when multiple assessments are used to understand what students know. Single assessments can provide useful information, but that information grows in value when combined with additional results (Rogers & Stevenson, 1988).

Challenging Students

One last set of research findings related to student learning offers a paradox for teachers. On the one hand, some students admit their preference for teachers with minimal expectations (Keedy et al., 1998; Rossi, 1995) and engage in complex negotiations with their teachers to avoid hard work (Sedlak, Wheeler, Pullin, & Cusick, 1986). On the other hand, students report that they find history most valuable when it most challenges them (Doppen, 2000; Ehman, 1980; Newmann, 1990; Stevenson, 1990). This apparent contradiction dissolves on further inspection. Given dull work, students naturally want it to be easy. However, when students find the subject matter interesting and they have an opportunity to actively participate in learning, they typically rise to meet higher expectations

---

[9]Preliminary results from the 2002 NAEP test in U.S. History confirm this finding (National Center of Education Statistics, 2002).

[10]Julia Smith and Richard Niemi (2001) claim that instructional factors are even more important than such traditionally important factors of family income and education. Particia Avery (1999) concurs: "Demographic variables have very little impact on authentic student performance.... It is the authenticity of instruction, however, that is the best predictor of authentic student performance" (p. 371)

(Stevenson, 1990). Students can become frustrated by problematic situations and by abstractions, but when their attempts to overcome these obstacles are supported and encouraged, these frustrations can turn into triumphs. A high school student reports, "It was satisfying to know what I finally believe. When I decide based on considering evidence and different points of view, you know you've made a good decision because you've seen both views.... The reward is when, after you reach a conclusion, you can articulate your position, knowing you've examined all sides of the issue" (p. 336). The success this student and others report reflects the intrinsic rewards inherent in ambitious learning rather than in extrinsic rewards such as grades and test scores.

Grades and test scores do matter in schools, and for some students these rewards are key motivators. Wise teachers know, however, that history will matter to their students largely because of intrinsic factors. They also know that apathy declines with engagement; students become more engaged as the cognitive challenge grows (Onosko, 1991; Stevenson, 1990; Wineburg & Wilson, 1991).

There are many ways to ratchet up the cognitive challenge in history classrooms. Students report that activities involving inference (e.g., writing papers that call for a synthesis of events) and evaluation (e.g., expressing and defending a stance on a controversial issue) are more challenging than those that call for literal comprehension (e.g., the recall of right answers) (Stevenson, 1990). They also report being more engaged when teachers offer them opportunities to explore genuine historical questions (Foster & Yeager, 1999; Wineburg & Wilson, 1991). One way to do this is through the use of primary sources. For example, Frans Doppen (2000) describes how high school students in a world history course navigate their way through a series of documents related to Harry Truman's decision to drop atomic bombs on Japan. He finds that students' ability to recall specific information increases substantially from the pretest to the posttest, as does their reasoning about the decision. More difficult to measure, but no less important, are the end-of-unit comments Doppen summarizes:

> Many found the unit different because "they had never been able to decide for [themselves]" and it gave them "the chance to see a different side of the world and what they think about the United States." One student wrote that the class had learned not "just the unopinionated textbook side" but got to "use other sources and realize others' views." Others responded that it was "most interesting because of the depth," that they had do "most of the work [themselves]," and that it helped them to "learn quicker and develop communication skills." (p. 8)

Primary sources, by themselves, guarantee no increase in student engagement (Foster & Yeager, 1999), but when used by skillful teachers, they can help students engage historical ideas in ways traditional instruction and materials can not (Doppen, 2000).

Wineburg (1991) notes that "expert teaching entails not the *selection* of methods but the *transformation* of knowledge" (p. 517). "Selecting" instructional methods is not unimportant, but good teachers choose the methods they employ in the service of transforming knowledge (Shulman, 1987). And as these last paragraphs point out, the transformation of knowledge has to happen in students' ideas and experiences if it is to matter. Students who hear lectures hear the transformations their teachers have created. A lecture does not necessarily suppress students' ability to construct their own learning. However, their ability to construct richer learnings is enabled when they participate in more active, more demanding, and more varied instructional experiences.

The Dilemmas of Teaching and Learning

There are no guarantees. Ambitious teachers face uncertainties just as their more pedestrian colleagues do. A teacher like Linda Strait reaches many students and in deep ways, but not all. The dilemmas of classroom practice (Lampert, 1985) can unsettle even the most confident of teachers.

John Rossi (1995) describes the dilemmas of an ambitious high school teacher. Rossi's account of Kenneth Lansbury's classroom portrays him as an engaging instructor who provides multiple opportunities for students to engage with issues around freedom of speech. As a group, students do participate and they do raise and debate important ideas. But while some elements of Lansbury's teaching soar, others flop.

Rossi (1995) tries to understand both by examining three dilemmas. The *director's* dilemma has two parts, best captured when Lansbury notes, "I usually try to run from where the students are to where I would like them to be" (p. 106). On the one hand, Lansbury wants to work from student ideas and interests, and he wants them to wrestle with complexities. At the same time, he wants to provide direction and information that will nudge them toward the meanings he holds dear. In these ways, Lansbury operates like "the director of a Broadway play who has his own interpretation and conception of the script, but desires to grant his actors some autonomy" (p. 106). The *participation* dilemma develops when Lansbury's desire to create a structured and scored discussion format discourages students from participating. The rationale for a formal discussion seems sound: A thoughtful classroom investigation is more likely to develop if there are firm ground rules and an emphasis on evidence, debate, and rebuttal. As Rossi notes, however, Lansbury "paid a price" for this effort: Several students do not talk. Their reluctance stems partly from discomfort with the structure and partly from typical teenage fears of peer reactions. Lansbury's attempts to address these issues go for naught. "I have found that ... I have quite a few quiet students who have not been able to participate in the discussion," he said, "and I have not been able to get them involved" (p. 108). The third issue Rossi discusses is the *information* dilemma. Put simply, Lansbury's expectation that students will complete readings outside of class is not always realized. Unprepared, the students can not begin working directly on the issues at hand.

Most teachers face some version of these dilemmas, and ambitious teachers like Kenneth Lansbury, Linda Strait, and others portrayed in these chapters are no different. Rather than see Lansbury as a failure, then, Rossi describes him as a "dilemma manager," a teacher who acts as "an active negotiator balancing a variety of beliefs and interests that interact in the classroom" (p. 109). Ambitious teachers constitute a special case, however, as the dilemmas they face may be exacerbated because students must shoulder increased responsibility for their own learning. But if the stakes are higher, so too are the rewards. Listen to how a representative student in Lansbury's class talks about his emerging understanding of race and affirmative action:

> The race issue ... I simply thought it was you're either a racist or you're not a racist. Or blacks should advance or blacks should not advance. But now I realize that there's all these intertwined things, like poverty is a factor and discrimination in jobs which I didn't realize before. (p. 113)

Like James, Ned, and Melissa in Linda Strait's class, this student comes away from his studies with a far more complex and textured set of ideas than is seen in the average history classroom. Students do need to answer questions on tests, but they also need to be able to express the richness of ideas outside the rigid confines of multiple choice questions. Ambitious teachers do not always get it right, but comments like the one just quoted suggest they are getting closer.

CONCLUSION

Oh, that it was behaviorist world! Imagine how much easier the lot of teachers and students would be if stimulus and response, rewards and punishments operated cleanly and effectively. The world of ideas complicates this view, as does the evidence that even young children will see the world and its influences differently. We are far from a complete understanding of how students learn history, but indications are that they come to school with some naive but powerful ideas and that they build on those ideas with and without teachers' help. Teachers face strong competition for their students' hearts and minds, and they may not prevail. But if they approach their classes with big ideas, opportunities to participate, and a willingness to hear what students are trying to say, they improve their chances.

PART III

Testing History

5

Testing History: The Influence of State-Level Testing on Blair's and Strait's Practices[1]

A third-year high school social studies teacher sat in my office one day. Visibly upset, she said that her students had performed poorly on the Global Studies Regents examination and that the school board was delaying for a year its decision on her tenure in order to see how the next group of students performed. I had not seen this woman teach (she came to me as a student in a master's-level social studies course), but she seemed thoughtful, concerned about her students, and committed to ambitious teaching. And scared. She explained that she used practice test questions throughout the year and that she spent the last 6 weeks of the year reviewing for the test. "What am I supposed to do?" she asked. Clueless, I asked, "What do you want to do?" "I don't know," she said, "but I'm not going to do all that stuff again." If, as we are so often told, tests drive teaching, then where is the test driving this teacher?

Truth, myth, or some of both, the perception reigns that "tests drive ___" (fill in the blank with the object of your choice—instruction, curriculum, change). Controversy around the role of state-level testing in schools has percolated for more than thirty years, and it shows no signs of abating. Some argue that the influence of state-level assessments is overblown (Cohen & Barnes, 1993; Firestone, Mayrowetz, & Fairman, 1998). Others argue that the influence is weak, but still vibrant (Corbett & Wilson, 1991; Koretz, 1995; Smith, 1991). And still others argue that tests have a real and definite impact (or should have) on classroom teaching and learning

---

[1]Sections of this chapter were adapted from an article I published in *Teachers College Record* (Grant, 2001b).

(Feltovich, Spiro, & Coulson, 1993; Frederickson, 1984; Heubert & Hauser, 1999; Popham, 1998; Shanker, 1995; Smith & O'Day, 1991).[2]

The talk about testing seems endless. Cohen and Barnes (1993) point out, however, that most of that talk is based on interviews and self-report; little reflects observations of teachers' instructional practice. It would be silly to discount interview and self-report data, but the lack of observational data begs the questions of if and how tests influence teaching and learning. In this chapter, I return to the classrooms of George Blair and Linda Strait to explore the influence of state-level testing. My analysis suggests that although the state test figures into their teaching practices, it does so by interacting with a range of other factors, especially the teachers' views of subject matter and learners. From these findings, I argue that state tests function as an uncertain lever and that although reformers continue pinning their hopes on new tests, faith in tests as a means of driving instructional change may be hard to sustain.

REGENTS TESTING IN NEW YORK STATE

The Regents test is an established tradition in New York state.[3] Offered for over 100 years, tests are administered in all academic subjects and are tied to state curricula. For example, the 11th graders in George Blair's and Linda Strait's classrooms took the U.S. History and Government test after completing a course of the same name.

Several features of the Regents program mark it as distinctive among state testing efforts. First, the Regents exams are more than assessments of basic skills. Regents tests have traditionally been viewed as academically challenging and as strong measures of student performance.[4] The social studies tests, in particular, are content driven, with a combination of multiple-choice and essay questions that reflect the state-recommended courses of study. The Regents test in U.S. History and Government, for example, consists of two parts. The first is a set of 48 multiple-choice questions worth 55 points. These questions ask students, for example, to define terms (e.g., nativism), recall portions of the U.S. Constitution (e.g., congressional powers), and interpret political cartoons and graphs. The second part involves writing three essays. In the first section, students respond to one of two essay prompts. In the second section, they must write on two of five prompts. The three essays are worth a total of 45 points. The content

[2]See Cimbricz (2002) for a review of the research on the influence of state testing on teachers' practices.

[3]The Regents testing program is being revised in light of new curriculum standards developed in the late 1990s. For a review of the changes in the standards and the tests, see Grant (2000).

[4]Interestingly enough, however, an ERIC search failed to produce a single empirical study that examined the relationship between students' test performance and any other social value (e.g., performance in college). There is also a sense among teachers that the latest exams are less challenging than the old ones (Grant, et al., 2002).

of the essay questions varies, but a typical question asks students to explain a concept (e.g., nationalism) and to describe how that concept played out in a number of historical settings. (See chapter 6 for a description of the new Regents exams.) A second feature of the state tests is the high stakes attached: Students must pass all the exams in order to receive a Regents diploma.[5] Students may opt to take the easier Regents Competency Test (RCT) and receive a school diploma.[6] A Regents diploma, however, carries greater status.[7] One last feature of the Regents assessment program is that they are graded by the classroom teachers who administer them. State officials do pull exams randomly and check the scoring, and if questions arise, they schedule meetings to talk with teachers.

Regents tests are no less high stakes for teachers than they are for students. Since the mid 1990s, state policymakers have introduced a number of curriculum reforms (e.g., new state standards for social studies), yet it is concern about the state tests that surfaces most regularly in teachers' talk (Grant, 1997b, 2000; Grant et al., 2001). This makes sense for two reasons. First, the curriculum documents produced thus far offer teachers little assistance in making concrete instructional decisions (Grant, 1997b). Second, the messages teachers receive often promote the view that tests are intended to drive change (Grant, 1997b; Grant et al., 2001, 2002). For example, during sessions explaining the new state social studies standards, a representative from the NYS State Education Department (SED) said that new tests will "help grow change in the system" (Grant, 1997b, p. 271). During another session, a different SED representative said, "New assessments will represent a change in instruction…. Kids won't perform well until [teachers'] instruction reflects this" (p. 271). And at yet a third meeting, SED Commissioner Richard Mills added, "Instruction won't change until the tests change" (p. 271). The message that tests matter echoed throughout local school and district meetings. A suburban district social studies supervisor, for example, told teachers that "change in content will come if we change the tests," whereas an urban district supervisor observed, "If we change the assessments, we'll change instruction" (p. 271). One might question the focus of test influence—instruction, curriculum, or the "system" in general—but it is hard to miss the larger point: tests matter.

---

[5]The Regents-level exam load consists of one test in English, one in languages other than English, and two each in math, social studies, and science.

[6]The RCT program was initiated in the late 1970s as a minimum competency test for non-college-bound students. The first tests in social studies (Global Studies and U.S. History and Government) were administered in the late 1980s. The RCT follows the same multiple choice and essay format of the Regents exam with the exception that the RCT has 50 multiple choice questions and students write on two of four essay prompts.

[7]Statewide, approximately 60% of students take the Regents examinations, which are administered in January, June, and August. Tests are scored by the teacher of each class; scores are then forwarded to the State Education Department. In addition to deciding whether or not a student receives a Regents diploma, test scores also figure into each student's course grade. During the year in which this study was done, 73% of Westwood students received a Regents diploma, compared with 63% in the district, 53% in similar schools, and 40% in all NYS schools.

TEACHERS AND TESTS

George Blair and Linda Strait agree: Regents test scores greatly matter to their school and the local community. Most Westwood High students take the Regents test (as opposed to the RCT),[8] and they and their parents put great emphasis on passing. The new Westwood principal (a California native) has not said much about test scores. The previous principal, however, committed considerable energy to tracking students' scores, and he was quick to remind teachers that low scores were not acceptable.

Blair and Strait take radically different approaches to teaching U.S. history. Not surprisingly, then, these two teachers also take different stances toward the state Regents exam. In what many would see as an odd twist, George Blair gives little explicit classroom attention to the test, whereas Linda Strait spends parts of two class periods in explicit test preparation.

George Blair: Teaching and Tests

Mention of the Regents test rarely comes up in George Blair's classroom. In fact, the only explicit reference in my notes surfaces as an offhand remark. During his explanation of the Cold War, Blair describes Harry Truman's dismissal of General Douglas MacArthur and the appointment of General Omar Bradley as commander of the United Nations forces in South Korea. After mentioning Bradley's name, Blair adds, "That name is of no significance, however. It's never on the Regents." This reference aside, the state test goes unmentioned. Blair makes no apparent connections between the test and the various people, places, and events covered in unit, and he makes no in-class assignments that explicitly reflect the test content or format.

That said, one might argue that Blair's teaching implicitly mirrors the state test. After all, the content he covers reflects attention to the kind of big-ticket items routinely assessed on standardized tests. In that context, Blair's dismissal of Omar Bradley as a test concern makes sense; in effect, Blair is telling his charges that although Bradley's name and contribution are unlikely to appear on the test, there is a good chance the other people and actions he mentions will. Blair's classroom instruction may also be seen as aligned with the state test. His narrative approach to lessons seems well suited to cover the material tested. Although this approach allows Blair to weave together the relevant names, dates, and places, it also allows him to craft one or more storylines as a means of helping students remember the information. Finally, Blair's approach to assessment also

---

[8]Of the 230 students enrolled in U.S. History during the year this study was done, 205 took the Regents test. Of that number, 80% passed the test (with a cutoff score of 65) and 42% achieved "mastery" (a score of 85 or better). With these percentages, Westwood students fare well compared to students in similar schools (65% passing; 25% mastery) and those in all NYS schools (49% passing; 16% mastery).

suggests some attention to the Regents exam. The state test features both multiple-choice and essay questions, but gives more weight to the multiple-choice section, 55 points to 45 points. Not all of Blair's tests include an essay question, but they do feature objective-style questions, and of those, multiple-choice questions dominate. In these several ways, then, one might conclude that George Blair's instructional practice, if not explicitly attentive to the Regents test, is at least implicitly so.

Linda Strait: Teaching and Tests

If Linda Strait's instruction looks sharply different from her colleague's, so too does her approach to the Regents examination. Where George Blair's narrative teaching practice seems implicitly representative of the state test, Strait's teaching seems less focused on test-related concerns than on providing a rich array of instructional activities and experiences. At the same time, where Blair gives little explicit attention to the test, Strait devotes parts of two class periods to direct practice on test items.

The Regents test plays no obvious role in the first 6 days of Strait's civil rights unit during which she uses various instructional approaches and resources to provide a vivid set of classroom experiences. All this changes at the end of day 7. With 10 minutes left in the class period, Strait distributes copies of two essay questions taken from recent Regents exams:

Essay #1: During various time periods in U.S. history, groups of people have been excluded from full participation in American society.

Groups

Native American Indians (1790–1890)

Latinos (1900–1970)

Japanese Americans (1900–1970)

Women (1940–1990)

African Americans (1945–1970)

a. Select *three* of the groups listed. For *each* one selected, discuss a specific example of how the group was excluded from full participation in American society during the time period indicated.

b. For *one* of the groups you selected in answer to a, discuss a specific action taken by the Federal Govt. *or* an organization *during* or *after* the time period indicated to help this group achieve full participation in American society.

Essay #2: Since 1865, agents of change have acted to advance the cause of civil rights and civil liberties in the United States.

Agents of Change

Government

A nongovernmental group

An individual

For *each* of the agents of change listed:

a. Explain one action taken by that agent of change to help advance civil rights or civil liberties in the U.S.

b. Describe the historical circumstances that led to that action.

Strait directs students to work with a partner on one or the other essay and "to outline the question ... as you would do on the Regents." She adds, "I think you'll have enough information with the videos and notes to handle either of these essays." About half the students turn to the task; the others chatter about a range of off-task topics. A few minutes later, Strait trains the students' attention on the second essay. She asks for examples of "nongovernmental groups" that had acted as agents of change. Students volunteer a range of answers: the KKK, the NAACP, the Nation of Islam. Strait acknowledges these responses while she circulates around the room prodding students to work on their individual questions. To one pair, she explains how the test is structured (i.e., the multiple-choice and essay sections). Looking at the work of another pair, she exclaims, "See how much you know!" Then she talks with them about how little the test questions change from year to year.

The next day Strait spends approximately 30 minutes reviewing class efforts on the practice essays. She begins by asking if students had any difficulty outlining the essay questions. There is a good deal of chatter, and she gets no particular response beyond one girl who says, "no." Strait responds, "I didn't think so." She continues to the class, "In June, you should make a little outline.... I don't take BS on essays.... I might have done so before, but I don't now."

With that introduction, Strait reviews the information students might use in each section of each essay, and talks explicitly about test-taking strategies. She explains, "You always have to know what the problem is and one solution.... If you can identify a piece of legislation, talk about it.... But if you don't know, don't use it because I have to take off a point for incorrect information."

What follows are snippets of the talk around each section of the essay questions. The first question asks students to choose three of five groups and to (a) discuss a specific example of how the group was excluded from American society and (b) discuss a specific action taken by a government agency or nongovernmental agency to help the group achieve full participation. Unless indicated, the responses for each section below are the students':

- Native American Indians (1790–1890)—(a) Trail of Tears, Manifest Destiny, culture taken away; (b) (no student response; Strait volunteers the Dawes Act).
- Japanese Americans (1900–1970)—(a) put in camps, thought to be spies; (b) federal government offer of $20,000 tax free (Strait disqualifies this answer because it does not fit the time frame stated in the question; no other

student responses follow; Strait mentions the Civil Rights Act of 1964 with the reminder that it did not apply to African Americans alone, and she adds, "You can always use that piece of legislation for any of the groups").

- Women (1940–1990)—(a) women's suffrage (Strait disqualifies this response as it does not fit within the specified time period; she cautions, "You have to stay in the time period.... You don't have to memorize dates, but you have to be aware of time periods"), hiring, pay (Strait accepts these responses, adding, "Think of other groups as having the similar struggles with Blacks.... I don't think anyone could pick Blacks and not write anything about this time period").

Strait then turns to the second essay, which asks for one action by government, a nongovernmental group, and an individual who helped advance civil rights, and the historical circumstances that led to the action. Strait labels this question "very easy." A boy calls out, "No way!" Strait laughs and explains, "You could talk about *Brown* or any of the civil rights legislation ... there are no time [period] constraints." The boy asks, "Just something positive?" Strait nods, lists some nongovernmental groups— NAACP, CORE—and explains, "Then you just have to describe the historical circumstances. That's a cinch for 15 points." Students are quiet during this time, but few seem attentive or engaged; I see only a couple actively listening or taking notes.

Several points seem interesting about these vignettes. First, Strait talks explicitly, and at some length, about the Regents test structure (i.e., the types of questions and points allotted) and about the test content (i.e., distinctions between events and implications). Second, she talks explicitly about test-taking strategies (e.g., using the Civil Rights Act of 1964 as an all-purpose answer and remembering to consider question parameters such as explicit time frames). Finally, she gives students an opportunity to practice outlining their responses and comparing those responses with her assessment of the tasks. In contrast to Blair's apparent disregard for the Regents, Strait devotes the equivalent of almost a full class period—40 minutes over 2 days—to test preparation and practice.

Comparing the two teachers, then, we see variation in both the explicit and implicit attention each gives to the Regents test. Blair gives little explicit attention to the test, yet one can argue that his content selection, teaching, and assessment mirror the state test. By contrast, Strait's instructional practices seem less directly reflective of the test, yet she purposely leads her students to think about and practice test-taking strategies.

THE NYS REGENTS TEST AS AN INFLUENCE
ON TEACHERS' PRACTICE

What are we to make of such varied approaches to teaching and testing? If tests drive curriculum, then why do George Blair's and Linda Strait's content decisions vary so much? If tests drive instruction, then why do these teachers construct their teaching practices in such different ways? If tests drive teachers to focus on student test performance, then why do these two teachers give such different attention to the state exam? Finally, what might all this mean for testing as a lever of instructional change?

Tests do matter. George Blair and Linda Strait acknowledge the influence of tests on their instructional thinking, and observations of their teaching suggest, although thinly, that the teachers do take the tests into account. The differences in how Strait and Blair construct their civil rights units and how each measures the success of his or her efforts owes something to how each teacher reads the Regents test. Just as influential, however, seems to be the different sense the teachers construct of the content chosen and of the particular students in their respective classes. So although the influence of the state Regents test is apparent, that influence interacts with other factors, particularly the teachers' views of subject matter and learners. If this argument holds, then the assumption that testing drives teaching, learning, and the like seems suspect.

TESTING AND TEACHERS' PRACTICES

The Regents test is not irrelevant in George Blair's and Linda Strait's teaching. Both its visibility and influence differ, however, as each teacher's reading of the test interacts with his or her view of the subject matter and learners.

The Influence of Testing on George Blair's Practice

I argue earlier that although George Blair's instruction offers little direct indication of being influenced by the state Regents test, a case can be made for a strong implicit influence. Understanding the relationship between Blair's teaching and the test, however, proves to be complicated, for factors such as Blair's sense of the subject matter and his view of learners figure into his teaching at least as strongly as does the state test. The Regents exam matters, but it holds no privileged position.

Blair supports the Regents testing program. Asked about current school reforms in New York, he volunteers, "What scares me the most about that whole idea that's coming down from the State ... [is] ... the attitude of Regents exams being thrown out."[9] The test serves two principal functions in Blair's view. One is to provide teachers with a content "standard" and "a direction to get to the end of the course." The second function is one of accountability. "The measure is the exam at the end of the year," Blair asserts, and that measure is an accounting of his students and himself. Poor

---

[9]Although this idea was floated briefly at the end of former Education Commissioner Thomas Sobol's tenure, it has been firmly rejected by current Commissioner Richard Mills.

test scores mean something, he claims, "and if [the scores] don't measure up, the course doesn't measure up. I don't; the kids don't measure up." Test scores also provide a means of accountability for his colleagues. Blair taught middle school social studies for 13 years without a high-stakes test.[10] The result, he believes, was chaos: "Without any accountability for teachers ... I saw teachers teach whatever they wanted to teach, how they wanted to teach." Blair is quick to say that he has no "problem" with this other than when teachers fail to "cover" the material. "You can cover the material, cover it anyway you want to, that's fine," he said, "but *cover* the material."

At first glance, this talk about the Regents test seems odd given Blair's inattention to the exam in his daily practice. But perhaps not. Blair routinely stages a 2-week review session just before the test administration in early June. He discounts, however, the importance of this activity. "I don't spend a lot of time reading Regents questions or putting them together for the kids or anything like that," he said. So although Blair believes the test is important, he asserts that explicit preparation for the test counts for little. He is not alone in that view. There is little research on how test preparation affects students' performance, but as Haney, Madaus, and Lyons (1993) conclude, there may be some reason to believe that "overemphasis on test preparation in schools has a negative impact on teaching and learning" (p. 179).

Although Blair may not give much direct classroom attention to the Regents test, he is sensitive to the exam. Scoring his students' test papers provides an opportunity to see what kinds of questions and content are represented. "When you do the grading," he said, "you know generally what they hit and what they don't hit.... It's experience, that's all it is." Blair translates that experience into a range of instructional decisions, some quite obvious. Recall his observation that Omar Bradley's name "never shows up on the Regents." During an interview, he made a similar comment about military actions during the Civil War:

> I never deal with militarism in the Civil War, never, because it's never on the Regents, so I don't deal with it.... I spend about 25 minutes at the end of class, of one class, on a couple of battles, the western battles, the eastern battles, the naval blockade, the naval engagement, the Monitor and the Merrimac. It's all done in 25 minutes total. It's finished and it's because it's not on the Regents. And I tell them there's a chapter in the book on the military action, read it between now and the Regents. But there's seven essays, and if they get a military history question, I'm sure I've given them enough information that they could skip that and get some other question anyway.

These examples suggest a link between the state test and Blair's content decisions. Combined with the observations that Blair's instruction reflects

---

[10]Until recently, eighth grade students in New York took the Program Evaluation Test (PET), a multiple-choice examination focusing on U.S. history. As a program test, the PET had no direct consequences for students. Eighth graders now take a state test that mirrors the 11th grade exam. (See chapter 6 for a description of the new state tests.)

a strong, if implicit, connection to the Regents exam, the influence of the state test seems strong.

The Influence of Subject Matter and Students

Other evidence, however, complicates this picture. For although Blair gives the test its due, he does not follow the presumed dictates of the test in a slavish fashion. In fact, it appears that factors such as Blair's views of the subject matter and of his students figure as prominently in his teaching decisions as the test does.

One example of the influence of subject matter on Blair's teaching centers on the Federal period in U.S. history. That era, the period after the establishment of the U.S. Constitution, is downplayed in the state curriculum and on the Regents test. Blair finds this unconscionable:

> I find it very difficult to cut things out of American history. I'm sorry, I just find it very difficult. The new course that came out in '89 ... they removed the Federal period of American history. How the hell do you leave out the Federal period of American history? How the hell do you do this? Where's Louisiana, where's Jackson?[11]

Continuing, Blair makes the case that such curricular decisions by the state inherently disrupt the study of U.S. history, and he refuses to go along:

> There's something inside of me that says you can't do that. So I teach a survey course and I break my ass getting through it 'cause I have to do an eight-week Constitution unit and that takes eight weeks out of the course. Like somehow we get there. Would I change that? No. I'm not going to change that.

So strongly does Blair feel about presenting a coherent view of U.S. history that when asked if and how his content decisions might change if there was no Regents exam, Blair emphatically defends the notion of covering the "whole course." There "might be" some changes, he said, but "first of all I would cover the course. I think that's clear.... I think there's an obligation to teach the course and to teach it well, the best I can, the whole course. Colonialism to Clinton."

One might argue that Blair's defense of content coverage mirrors the state test emphasis on key people, places, and events. Nevertheless, Blair's general commitment to teaching "the whole course" and his specific commitment to teaching the Federal period implies a resolute view of the content to be taught that prevails even if it conflicts with state curricula and testing prescriptions. Arguably, Blair's classroom life would be

---

[11]Although the state syllabus gives substantial attention to the Constitutional period, the chronology of U.S. history in 11th grade is supposed to begin with Reconstruction.

eased and his students' test scores increased if, for example, he let go of content like the untested Federal period. He refuses to do so, largely, it seems, because of his conception of and responsibility for the subject matter he teaches.

If Blair's view of the subject matter mitigates the influence of the Regents exam on his teaching, so too does his view of his students. Two beliefs define Blair's sense of students. One is that they need a survey course in U.S. history. Blair's students come to his class with 1 year of U.S. history study in fifth grade and 2 years in Grades 7 and 8. Yet Blair dismisses any "carryover" from those experiences:

> Seventh and eighth they get this two-year program. They're twelve years old. I mean they don't know up from down anyway. When they come here they don't have the faintest idea.... You want a kid to remember a couple of things from seventh and eighth grade to eleventh grade? You've got to be kidding me. They went through three years of puberty. Do you know what they're thinking about? They're not thinking about the Wilmot Proviso. And to say there's carryover, that's absolutely asinine.

Blair's conviction that students arrive with a fragmented knowledge of history coincides with another belief—that his students have little ability to think or reason. Blair holds no truck with teaching methods that promote critical or higher level thinking. He dismisses simulations and other experiential activities as "games," doubting that they have any real or lasting effect. He explains, "I'd say I don't think the kid can make the generalization from this game to an historical event or general ideas of life or the flow of society or the flow of history, or the flow of psychology, the flow of people, the flow of culture." Similarly, Blair discounts the importance of small group work, student presentations, and nontraditional assessments. "Does learning go on?" he asks. "Is the maturity level there for these students to truly understand what they're doing?" Blair assigns a research paper, but reports, "I don't expect much."

George Blair believes he faces a simple reality: He must cover the entire history of the United States, "colonialism to Clinton," in an entirely too short school year, with groups of students whose intellects are undeveloped at best. Given those assumptions, Blair's narrative approach to instruction makes some sense. Creating a master story around the key figures and events of U.S. history helps him cover the subject matter he deems necessary and provides his students with a way of remembering the material. In fact, taking a narrative stance makes considerable instructional sense whether or not there is a state test. For although some observers criticize an exclusive focus on narrative (Barton, 1997b; Levstik, 1993b, 1995; VanSledright & Brophy, 1992), the emphasis on history as story appears both in the empirical evidence (Brophy, 1992; Evans, 1990; VanSledright & Brophy, 1995) and in educational reforms (California Board of Education, 1988; New York State Education Department, 1996a). Narrating stories of the past may or may not help Blair's students perform better on the state test. But, as with his content decisions, one suspects he would not abandon this instructional vehicle should the Regents exam disappear.

One last point involves test results as a measure of success. Test scores matter to Westwood school administrators and parents. They also matter to George Blair, who holds his students' test performance as an indication of both his and their achievement. Again, however, the picture is complicated, as other measures of success compete with test scores. One of those measures is Blair's commitment to covering the course material. Another is his sense that students need both "humanity and understanding." Blair worries, for example, about the state of race relations in America and his perception of a growing intolerance in his students and the larger public. The "problem [of race relations] seems to be getting worse, not better," he said, "and it scares the hell out of me." Although he once thought that the situation was improving, he is no longer sure. "The rift seems to be even greater," he said, "I mean, we're really in some serious trouble here. Very, very serious trouble." Interestingly enough, Blair is not sure what effect his stories about civil rights leaders and events have. "You just put the question in their mind and then walk away from it and let them deal with it," he said, "I think a lot of them forget it. But at least they've been exposed to those kinds of ideas." Some observers may worry that Blair's monopoly of the classroom conversation does little to encourage student engagement with issues such as race relations. Nevertheless, sensing that Blair holds his students' "humanity" on par with their "understanding" suggests that test scores are but one of his several measures of success.

The Influence of Testing on Linda Strait's Practice

Although there is much that is different in the classroom practices of Linda Strait and George Blair, in neither classroom does the state Regents test seem to drive teaching and learning. Although Strait gives explicit attention to the test, the influence of the test on her practice interacts with other factors such as her views of the subject matter and learners.

Perhaps because she is relatively new to teaching, Strait seems more concerned with and worried about tests and test scores than Blair does. And unlike her colleague, Strait sees little value in the Regents exam. She chafes at the content constraints she feels the state test imposes, and she is daunted by the breadth of content covered. "For the Regents exam, knowing what the exams are like, I see so much content there," she said, "The curriculum [of the test] is just too broad. There's just too much there." The breadth of content means Strait must constantly negotiate the tension between her sense of what is important and the test makers'. She explains, "Sometimes I spend a lot of time with something I think that's interesting.... I just think it's part of what they need to know as viable human beings in this society." Strait pauses, and then adds, "But the Regents doesn't test anything on it." At times this tension does not seem to matter; Strait simply goes ahead with what she thinks is appropriate. At other times she defers to the test. "It's sometimes difficult," she said, "because there's a lot of things I want to do and [given the test] I just skip over [them]." At still other times, Strait is able to accommodate both impulses—hers and the test makers'. The skating-rink simulation is a good example. This activity balances ideas and experiences that help students empathize with historical actors and prepare for a potential Regents test question (e.g., the portion of the practice essays that asks students to talk about the actions groups might have taken to protest discrimination). As her teaching experience grows, Strait is increasingly able to create these balances. She begrudges the planning time this takes, but she knows that test scores matter in this upscale, suburban environment, and so she continually walks a line between her goals and the test makers'.

If Strait's content decisions are influenced by the Regents test, so too are her instructional decisions. Were there no test, Strait still might have her students writing practice essays. Nevertheless, she clearly communicates the influence of the test in the content of the questions and in her strategic review of the students' responses. Strait's students may develop as skilled and thoughtful essayists, but with her guidance they will also know how to respond to an essay prompt on the up-coming state test.

The Influence of Subject Matter and Students

And yet, if the state test influences Linda Strait's content and instructional decisions, that influence is far from pure or direct. An argument can be made that the test drives Strait's practice no more so than her attention to the subject matter and to her students.

Strait comes to the civil rights unit with two overall goals in mind. The first is to help students understand that "[racism] is really still happening today." "I think it's pushed in the back of the memory of people that they don't seem to see that this is still a really awful problem," she said. "I see it and I have always seen it as the biggest problem in America today ... how the races get along." Although she believes students are more tolerant today, that toleration seems limited to religious differences; racial differences are another matter. "It seems like, on the surface, superficially, that they might be more tolerant in terms of religion," she said, "You [get] more heated, close-minded debates about the race issue as opposed to the religion issue."

Strait's second goal is broader in that it reflects the view that history is more than politics and economics, and more than a record of the victorious:

What I try to convey is that America is multifaceted. That there—it's not *just* White America anymore. I don't know if it ever was *just* that, but that's how it was always taught in the history books. So, I'm trying to let them see that there's another side, and it's ever increasing, that other side of the diversity in America, and we have got to see it, recognize it, and start working together.

As Strait explains, "I'm not necessarily trying to tell everyone that you've got to love everybody, but you have to accept them and you can't, you shouldn't just hate them because of the differences."

These goals suggest that Strait's instruction is sensitive to more than the state Regents test. Two examples underscore the power of Strait's view of the subject matter as an influence on her teaching practice. The first is the amount of time she devotes to the civil rights movement. If she considered only the dictates of the Regents test, planning an 8-day unit would make little sense, for the civil rights movement simply does not figure prominently on the exam. True, there is occasionally an essay question around civil rights (such as those Strait introduced in class), but there is no guarantee of one. Moreover, there are generally no more than a couple of multiple-choice questions devoted to civil rights. Given that Blair covers a good chunk of the civil rights movement in about 20 minutes, Strait's very different unit reflects her sense of what subject matter is important.

This sense of the subject matter also seems behind Strait's emphasis on social history. Regents test questions tend to focus on political and economic events. Strait does not discount this material, as, for example, her lecture notes cover the major civil rights legislation. Nevertheless, much of her unit focuses on social history or the "lives of ordinary people in all their richness" (Appleby et al., 1994, p. 84). The two videotapes, the roundtable discussion and the skating-rink simulation, and the class readings of "40 Lives for Freedom" and "Hate Crimes—Summer, 1991" all emphasize the roles and experiences of people unlikely to ever appear on a standardized state test. Make no mistake: Strait's students have access to the people, places, and events that make up conventional accounts of the U.S. civil rights movement. Yet Strait contextualizes this content within a larger picture that attempts to connect the lives and experiences of civil rights pioneers with those of her students. The Regents test may influence some of her instructional decisions, but that influence seems relatively small when one considers the influence of the subject matter she deems important.

If Strait's view of the subject matter influences her classroom decisions, so too does her view of students. The principal evidence for this point comes from the range of activities Strait designs as part of her instructional unit. If the state test is the primary influence, it is hard to imagine why Strait would spend so much time providing opportunities for students to read, watch, discuss, and write about past actors and events, and to explore their own ideas and experiences. Strait constructs a range of activities and assessments, in large part, because she believes all students can learn. She knows, however, that not all students learn the same way and that different learning experiences will engage different students. "I am of the belief that all students can learn," she said, "just in different ways, and different styles."

The range of instructional activity evident in Strait's civil rights unit owes something to her sense that students need to be ready to take the state Regents test. Scores on that test do matter, after all, and Strait would never suggest that they are an unimportant measure of success. But just as important, at least for the civil rights unit, are the developing sensitivities and sensibilities of her students.

Much rides on Strait's students' performance on the Regents test. She wants them to do well and, to that end, she pushes her students academically. At the same time, Strait wants students to feel something of what, for example, discrimination feels like. "I would like students to be more empathetic with other people," she said, "Try and just imagine if you were in their shoes. Even if they can never be your best friend, you know, try and understand others." The range of instructional activity evident in Strait's civil rights unit owes much to her sense that students need to master a considerable amount of subject matter knowledge and to experience something of the passion of the times. Knowledge without empathy, she asserts, is meaningless.

CONCLUSION

Tests matter, especially those that have real consequences. How tests matter, however, is an open question. Presumably tests like the New York Regents direct a considerable portion of teacher's practices. But do they? And if they do, to what extent and in what direction? Although I take these questions up more fully in chapter 6, they have implications here.

The analysis above suggests that state-level testing has a real but thin influence on George Blair's and Linda Strait's teaching. Their concerns about covering test-related material and about their students' scores surface in both implicit and explicit ways. At the same time, their concerns push in no particular direction. If we take their word that the state test is important, and there is no reason not to, then we must wonder how powerful an influence the test is if these teachers can construct such radically different practices.

I argue that subject matter and students matter as much to Blair's and Strait's teaching as does the state test. Other factors probably matter as well. After all, considerations of personal biography (e.g., individual knowledge, beliefs, and experiences), local organizational structures (e.g., school norms and expectations, time, and resources), and the state and district policy climate (e.g., the state social studies curriculum developed in the late 1980s and the more recent state social studies standards and revised state test) may also figure into the content and instructional decisions teachers like Strait and Blair make (Grant, 1996, 1998). Thus, my emphasis on the views each teacher holds of subject matter and students is meant to be illustrative rather than definitive; I take up more fully the various influences on teachers' pedagogies in chapter 7. In any case, the point is the same: Although state tests influence Blair's and Strait's practices, they are not the only influence and, in fact, may not even be the principal influence. In short, I see little direct, deep, and consistent influence of tests on these teachers' classroom teaching. The pervading sense that tests drive content, instruction, and the like seems alternately overstated, ill-informed, or misplaced. If tests are an influence on practice, then they may be an uncertain influence at best.

6

Testing History: The Nature of State-Level Testing in History Classrooms[1]

Of George Blair's approximately 50 students in two classes, 10 failed the Regents test in U.S. history during the year of this study; of Linda Strait's approximately 100 students in four classes, 16 failed. What does this set of facts tell us about teaching, learning, and testing?

I wonder. Is Linda Strait a "better" teacher than George Blair because her passing rate was 84% while his was 80%? Are her students "smarter" than his? Or are any such comparisons a wash? In chapter 3, I argue that Strait's students have an edge over their peers in their understanding of history. Does the closeness of the state test results negate that seeming advantage? These and other questions perplex me, but none more so than this: Should the results of a single test determine whether or not students pass a course and graduate?

Tests have long been a part of the American education landscape and, if anything, their presence is increasing: Central to George W. Bush's "No Child Left Behind" legislation is more testing. Policymakers' faith in testing continues despite a curious lack of consistent evidence that tests induce positive change. As the first decade of the recent wave of educational reform crested, Stake and Rugg (1991) note "In sixty years of vast international research on school testing, the policy of emphasizing test performance in order to improve education has never been validated" (p. xx). In the 10 years since this accusation, the scene is hardly any clearer (Camilli, Cizek, & Lugg, 2001; Clarke, Madaus, Horn, & Ramos, 2000; Dorn, 1998). G. W. Bush campaigned on the "Texas miracle" of increasing test

[1]Sections of this chapter were adapted from an article my colleagues and I published in *Journal of Curriculum and Supervision* (Grant et al., 2002).

scores, but many questions about the validity of those results remain (Haney, 2000; Klein, Hamilton, McCaffrey, & Stecher, 2000; McNeil, 2000). Still, the press continues for more tests and more consequences of those tests despite the absence of occasions for "independently evaluating a testing program before or after implementation, or for monitoring test use and impact" (Clarke et al., 2000, p. 177).

Critics of testing cite a litany of problems with state-level testing programs. Their critiques, as well as the arguments of testing advocates, play a part in this chapter. Instead of stopping there, however, I choose to explore three questions on which a measure of research exists. One question asks about the purposes of tests. Here, I sort through some of the chaos around testing terminology by linking different forms of assessment with the functions they are intended to serve and the values those functions suggest. The second question asks whether testing drives teaching and learning. This notion has considerable currency in teachers' rooms and in state departments of education. I argue, however, that the research literature offers little direct support for such claims. The final question asks whether increasing the stakes on students and teachers increases educational standards. The premise that more tests and higher stakes will yield better academic outcomes makes common sense. The research evidence, however, undercuts this optimism. Tests do matter to teachers, students, parents, and policymakers, but whether they matter in effective and beneficial ways is far from clear.

Three caveats bear mentioning at this point. One is that only a small measure of the testing literature is research-based. The majority of the words written about tests consists of advocacy, historical, and/or theoretical (and often rather whiny) pieces rather than empirical studies. Kurfman's (1991) admonition that "there has been far more argumentation about test effects than there has been actual research" (p. 310) still stands true. Of the empirical literature on testing, the bulk focuses on reading and mathematics rather than on history.[2] So despite a huge potential literature, little relates directly to impact of testing on teachers' practices and on students' historical knowledge and understanding.

The second caveat concerns incommensurate data. Part of the issue here is one of moving targets. The testing literature reflects several trends—from low stakes to high stakes, from minimal competency to higher order thinking, and from generic to standards-based testing parameters. Assessing complex learning is difficult enough; doing so under differing conditions and across differing contexts presents myriad problems (Linn, 2000). This general issue of incommensurate data becomes magnified in the special case of testing historical knowledge and understanding. As I noted in chapter 4, only recently has national data concerning students' history test performance begun to employ similar testing condi-

---

[2]A brief report of a national survey of 200 social studies teachers (Burroughs, 2002) is the exception.

tions. Comparing state-level tests with these national data or with one another only magnifies the problem of drawing coherent conclusions based on incommensurate measures. Moreover, because the kinds of questions asked heavily influence the kinds of responses that ensue (Nuthall & Alton-Lee, 1995), even if we did have multiple test results on the same group of teachers and students, drawing any firm inferences would be dicey (Amrein & Berliner, 2002; Linn, 2000).

The final caveat is that, given limited space, I focus here on state-level tests rather than on classroom assessments or national exams. I do so because the realm of classroom assessments is well covered by folks like Grant Wiggins (1998) and his colleague, Jay McTighe (Wiggins & McTighe, 1998), and because there are so few relevant national exams. State-level testing, by contrast, is growing dramatically and, as such, is an area that garners the attention of teachers, administrators, parents, and the public. I draw heavily on the New York state Regents testing program throughout this chapter, but I allude to testing programs in other states as they are relevant.

THE PURPOSES OF TESTING

One of the biggest issues around testing concerns purposes. The seemingly simple proposition—that the purpose of a test is to measure learning—turns out to be hugely complicated. One part of that complexity comes from the many formats tests can take—a basic skills, multiple-choice test, for example, is a far different thing from a more robust, essay exam. Another part of the problem is language: "Evaluation," for example, seems like a far different thing from "assessment." And a third part of the problem is that different kinds of tests and assessments (I sort this division out later) can serve very different needs.

So let's begin with some basic distinctions in language and purposes. *Evaluation* refers to a summary activity that functions as a form of judgment on what students know and can do. *Assessment* can include evaluation, but typically goes beyond the notion of summary judgment to emphasize understanding (Grant & VanSledright, 2001). This distinction matters because it highlights differences in purposes and values. First, where evaluation occurs at the end of a unit of study, assessment is an ongoing part of teaching and learning. The value of assessment, Rogers and Stevenson (1988) claim is "the insight it gives us about the quality of the teaching–learning act in a given classroom and the opportunity it provides to revise and re-teach intelligently" (p. 75). Second, where evaluation typically relies on a single instrument, assessment encourages the use of multiple measures, or what Wiggins (1993) calls a "comprehensive, multifaceted analysis of performance" (p. 13). Because what we know depends in part on the questions we are asked, it makes sense that more opportunities to show what we know and can do produce richer understandings. Finally, where evaluation generally focuses on cognitive or academic outcomes, assessment can include affective and social goals. The standards movement in the United States has a cognitive flavor; policymakers and the public want higher standards to ensure that students know more. Teachers, and most parents, know that academic outcomes are important, but they also believe that affective (students' attitudes, values, and dispositions) and social (how students work and learn, both individually and in groups) outcomes are also key.

The distinction between evaluation and assessment is useful because it helps frame additional distinctions and definitions. A *test* is "an 'instrument,' a measuring device" (Wiggins, 1993, p. 13) or "a means for measuring something that is predetermined" (Mathison, 1997, p. 214). The purposes tests serve include measuring student abilities and achievements, grouping students for instruction, identifying students for special programs, informing students and others about their progress, and evaluating teacher and program effectiveness (Haladyna, Nolen, & Haas, 1991; Messick, 1988). In serving these purposes, tests promote several values, perhaps the most important of which is efficiency (Clarke et al., 2000; Madaus & Kellaghan, 1992a) or "the ability to test more people at less cost and in less time" (Mathison, 1997, p. 215). Public perceptions of tests also include the values of precision and fairness, accountability and judgment, and individuality and competitiveness (Mathison, 1997). Tests have an aura of science, accuracy, and objectivity; they imply that what is important can be measured, and that no-nonsense decision making can be based on those measurements. Koretz (1988) adds one more attribute of testing—accountability. He argues that although tests can be about measuring learning, increasingly they are about making teachers and students answerable: "Tests are increasingly used, not only to show how well students do, but also to judge the competence of the educational enterprise and to hold the participants—students, teachers, principals, superintendents—accountable" (p. 8).

Often tests are viewed only as evaluations, as a means of summary judgment. They can also be used, however, as a form of assessment. Where this gets tricky is when tests and the scores they generate become the only measure that counts, and when tests measure only school-related abilities. The multiple-choice test is a good example. Loved by test makers for its precision and economy, the multiple-choice test rankles many critics because it tends to emphasize discrete information rather than more complex understandings (see, for example, McNeil, 2000; Smith, 1991). Such tests are "typically *inauthentic*, designed as they are to shake out a grade rather than allowing students to exhibit mastery of knowledge in a manner that suits their styles and interests and does justice to the complexity of knowledge" (Wiggins, 1989, p. 58; emphasis in original). A multiple-choice test *can* serve as part of a larger assessment plan, but only as one of several measures that teachers and others use to understand what students know and can do. Inherent in this view is the idea that although tests can be a form or instrument of assessment, assessing is a far bigger construct than testing. Assessing is primarily about understanding, about trying to figure out what students know or how well teachers teach; testing is about quantifying, about measuring the phenomena under study.

Long-held concerns about multiple-choice testing have induced educators to seek more and better forms of assessment. The outcome of that effort goes by many names—authentic assessment, authentic achievement, performance assessment—but typically pushes students to demonstrate their understandings in real and genuine ways. *Authentic assessments*, Wiggins asserts, "would be much more a simulation or representation or replication of the kinds of challenges that face professionals or citizens when they need to do something with their knowledge" (Nickell, 1992, p. 92). Newmann et al., (1995) propose that *authentic achievement* results when students construct knowledge through disciplined inquiry that has value beyond the school setting. *Performance assessment* differs from these ideas only in the sense that it emphasizes an active demonstration of what students know and can do. Although the distinctions among these ideas can be useful, it is the similarities in purpose that occupies us now. So whether an essay should be classified as an authentic, but not a performance, assessment is less important in the long run than realizing that the notion of assessment represents purposes and values that are some distance from those under the label of evaluation.

Although the definitions and distinctions just given describe classroom assessments, increasingly they have become important for state-level tests, especially in history. In the last few years, there has been a movement to push state-level tests toward greater authenticity, with the idea being to design more genuine tasks and to increase the academic challenge.

Traditionally, state and national history tests have used multiple-choice formats. Questions ask students to identify major historical actors, to locate places on maps, and to compare one event with another. Pervasiveness is no substitute for satisfaction, however. Critics of tests, and of multiple-choice tests in particular, complain that interpretive subjects like history are ill-suited for objective-style tests that put a premium on forced-choice responses. More appropriate, they argue, are more authentic activities such as interpreting political cartoons, drawing comparisons, and writing essays, which call for the analysis and synthesis of data. Sensitive to these critiques and suggestions, test makers at both national and state levels have responded with new forms of test items. High school students in New York, for example, still answer multiple-choice questions, but since 1999 they also respond to a document-based question (DBQ). Similar to the DBQs on the Advanced Placement exam, the New York DBQ presents students with 6-8 primary and secondary source documents (e.g., quotations, political cartoons, graphs) related to a single topic. Following each document are one or more questions that probe for the main idea of the representation. After completing these "constructed response" questions, students respond to an essay prompt drawing on the information from the documents and on their prior knowledge. On the first new U.S. history exam, the DBQ documents reflected various U.S. foreign policy actions and programs—such as neutrality, imperialism, containment, and interna-tionalism. The essay prompt asked students to describe two of those poli-cies and to discuss and evaluate an illustrative action or program for each. Although there are problems with such tasks (Grant, Gradwell, & Cimbricz, 2002), inclusion of DBQs is clearly intended to strengthen the au-thenticity of state-level tests.

If greater authenticity is on policymakers' minds, so too is greater ac-countability. Here, the idea is to use tests as levers for ratcheting up the stakes on students and their teachers. More authentic than their predeces-sors, state testing programs like the New York Regents, the Massachusetts Comprehensive Assessment program, the Kentucky Instructional Results Information System, and the California Assessment Program still function primarily as evaluations because of the high-stakes associated them: Stu-dents must pass a single exam in order to pass U.S. history and to graduate from high school. If students are feeling more pressure, so too are their teachers. New York teachers are told, for example, "New York State is en-gaged in a serious effort to raise standards for students.... Classroom teachers ... must bring reality to the *teaching and learning* process in order to assure that *all* of their students will perform at higher levels" (New York State Education Department, 1996b, p. 5; emphasis in original). Key to the "strategy for raising standards" is "setting clear, high expectations/stan-dards for *all* students and developing an effective means of assessing stu-dent progress in meeting the standards" (p. 5; emphasis in original). In New York and other states, then, tests are expected to leverage the im-provement of classroom instruction (Cimbricz, 2002; Grant, Gradwell, Lauricella, et al., 2002; Heubert & Hauser, 1999).

That new state-level tests aim at greater authenticity at the same time they promote greater student and teacher accountability illustrates the idea that tests have always been expected to serve multiple purposes. Like any multipurpose tool, however, tests serve some needs better than others (Camilli et al., 2001). State-level tests are well designed to provide a snap-shot of student achievement, information that could be useful to teachers and others as part of a wider assessment plan. More and more, however, these tests are being viewed as final evaluations, a purpose that even some testing advocates worry about (Camilli et al., 2001; Haladyna et al., 1991; Linn, 2000; Messick, 1988).

THE EFFECTS OF TESTING
ON TEACHERS AND STUDENTS

As the amount of state-level testing increases, understanding what effects these tests have becomes critical. Because tests have purposes is no guarantee that those purposes are achieved. In this section, I explore the question of whether or not testing drives teaching and learning. Tests like the Regents exam are intended to promote ambitious teaching and higher levels of student achievement. But what does this intent look like in schools and classrooms? The empirical literature is far from clear here, but we can draw some tentative conclusions about how tests affect students and teachers.

Testing and Students

It is hard to imagine American schooling without tests. Students take kindergarten readiness tests, they take classroom tests in every subject from English to physical education, they take standardized IQ and aptitude tests, general achievement tests, college entrance tests, and school, district, and state-level graduation tests. These tests have many purposes, but presumably most or all of those purposes have the best interests of students in mind. Some of those interests involve placement in appropriate classes, grades, and programs; others involve ranking students and making decisions about the colleges they can attend; and still others involve judgments about what students know and can do. It is this last set of purposes that I am most interested in, for it is the area that most concerns students, teachers, parents, and the public. More specifically, I am interested in exploring what tests can tell us about students' academic achievement.

If we want to know what kids know, give them a test. The logic of this proposition seems so obvious as to be beyond question. Yet there can be big problems associated with the kinds of questions asked, the number of opportunities students have to convey what they know, and the circumstances under which they are tested. It also turns out that interpreting the scores that tests produce is problematic in two ways.

One problem highlights the fairly stable pattern test scores exhibit over time. It tends to be true that when students are tested, their scores rise (Grissmer & Flanagan, 1998). Linn (2000) cites long-term studies, however, that invariably show that early gains soon level off. Moreover, the race and class differences that appear in most standardized testing situations remain: Affluent and White kids fare better than poorer and Hispanic and African American kids. This tendency leads some (e.g., Kornhaber, Orfield, & Kurlaender, 2001; Mathison, 1997) to conclude that tests confirm rather than confront prevailing school patterns.

The second problem with test scores lies in what they measure. Psychometricians, experts in the field of testing, are proficient at developing test items, cut scores, and the like. They are less able to guarantee that their tests assess knowledge worth knowing. Lee Cronbach (1963) puts the psychometrican's dilemma this way:

> Whenever it is critically important to master certain content, the knowledge that it will be tested produces a desirable concentration of effort. On the other hand, learning the answer to a set of questions is by no means the same as acquiring understanding of whatever topic that question represents. (p. 681)

In addition to the specific criticisms of multiple-choice items, many observers worry that state-level tests best measure trivial information. James Popham (1999), a long-time advocate of "measurement-driven instruction," now questions the real potential for tests to assess significant learning. As tests are increasingly used as accountability measures, Popham concludes that "the most serious consequence" of state-level tests are that they "contribute only modestly, if at all, to the central mission of education—namely teaching children the things they need to know" (p. 14). Camilli et al., (2001) put the matter more bluntly: "There is, lamentably, little evidence currently available that suggests a causal link between assessment information and increased student learning" (p. 466).

These problems of stable patterns and of the mismatch between tests and learning become magnified when state-level tests are used as evaluations. Most experts (Camilli et al., 2001; Haladyna, Nolen, & Haas, 1991; Linn, 2000) believe state-level tests can be an effective component of an larger assessment plan: A Regents test score in New York offers a useful snapshot of what students know and can do. But just as a snapshot cannot replace a panoramic view, neither can a state-level test provide anything like a rich assessment of a student's capabilities. And so, when state tests are used as one-shot measures of learning and, more importantly, as one-shot judgments of who graduates, the connection between tests and meaningful student achievement weakens.

Tests and Teachers

If a weak link exists between tests and student learning, what about the notion of testing driving teaching? A flurry of popular books (e.g., Kohn, 2000; Rothman, 1995; Sacks, 1999) sharply criticize state-level testing both as poor measures of student achievement and as foul influences on teachers' classroom practices. Researchers (e.g., Corbett & Wilson, 1991; Noble & Smith, 1994; Smith, 1991), too, have pointed to pernicious effects of tests on teachers. Others (e.g., Firestone et al., 1998; Salmon-Cox, 1981; Zancanella, 1992), however, are less sure that a direct relationship exists between standardized testing and teachers' classroom practices. Thus the research around teachers and tests shows no clear pattern of influence (Cimbricz, 2002). Tests seem to matter, but how and to what extent, is unclear.

Advocates of tests as a vehicle for driving educational change tend to cite general good effects rather than specifics. Some (Feltovich et al., 1993; Finn, 1995; Ravitch, 1995; Shanker, 1995) make the all-purpose argument that good tests inevitably drive good instruction. With neither any more specificity nor any empirical evidence, Popham, Cruse, Rankin, Sandifer, and Williams (1985) suggest that what is being tested is important and that good results equal good education. Advocates of systemic reform (Fuhrman, 1993a; Smith & O'Day, 1991) believe that testing must be part of an overall strategy aimed at school change. Still other observers (English, 1980; Glatthorn, 1987; Heubert & Hauser, 1999) assert that because standardized tests are a reality in most school districts, they should be used as a fundamental part of curriculum planning. Chester Finn (1995) makes the general case for testing this way: Forecasting a dismal end to the national education goals the first President Bush and the nation's governors endorsed in 1990, Finn asserts, "A sizable part of the reason will be the refusal to construct any sort of meaningful examination or assessment system tied to those [national] goals" (p. 121).[3]

Although some critics of testing (Kohn, 2000; Ohanian, 1999) rely more on principle than research, many back up their claims with empirical evidence. George Madaus (1988) argues that teachers teach to the test, that they adjust their instruction to follow the form of the questions asked (e.g., multiple-choice, essay), and that tests transfer control over the curriculum to whoever controls the test. LeMahieu (1984), Koretz (1995), and Romberg, Zarinnia, and Williams (1989) are a bit more tentative, but they too conclude that teachers tailor their curricula to the content covered on a test. More recent empirical work supports some of these claims. H. Dickson Corbett and Bruce Wilson (1991), for example, argue that testing, especially minimum-competency testing, has a harmful effect on teachers in that it causes them to narrow their sense of educational purposes and to focus on activities designed to raise test scores whether or not they think those activities are good for students (see also Miller, 1995; Noble & Smith, 1994; Smith, 1991). They conclude that squeezing teachers in this fashion encourages them to rebel against reform measures, both good and bad: "Statewide testing programs do control activity at the local level, but the subsequent activity is not reform" (Corbett & Wilson, 1991, p. 1). Mary Lee Smith (1991) makes the more specific claim that testing "significantly reduces the capacity of teachers to adapt to local circumstances and needs of pupils or to exercise any discretion over what to teach and how to teach it" (p. 10). She worries that tests "result in a narrowing of possible curriculum and a reduction of teachers' ability to adapt, create, and diverge" (p. 10). She concludes that multiple-choice testing leads to "multiple-choice teaching" (p. 10).

Still other researchers are less sure that any direct relationship exists between state-level testing and teachers' classroom practices. Earlier studies by Freeman et al., (1980), Salmon-Cox (1981), Kellaghan, Madaus, and Airasian (1982), and Mehrens and Phillips (1986) found little direct impact of standardized testing on teachers' daily instruction. More recently, Rita O'Sullivan (1991) asserts that testing is "part of teaching but not really as immediate instructional reality ... testing is the pale rider on the various

---

[3]Sandra Cimbricz (2002) reviewed all the research literature related to the effects of testing on teachers' thinking and practice. She first determined that the bulk of the literature consists of advocacy, theoretical, and historical pieces rather than research. She also determined that not a single piece of empirical work supported claims of testing as a positive influence on teachers' thinking and practice.

educational trails" (p. 144). Her survey results show little explicit influence of tests on teachers' practices: Teachers do more reviewing and teaching of test-taking strategies, but few say that tests have any dramatic effect on their content selection, instructional practices, or classroom assessments. Bill Firestone, David Mayrowetz, and Jean Fairman (1998) also see weaker than expected testing influences on teachers' practices in both low- and high-stakes settings. Teachers do make changes in their practices, especially in terms of the content they teach, but major changes in pedagogy do not surface. James Pellegrino (1992) makes the point bluntly: "[Standardized] test information is of little practical assistance to teachers and other individuals involved directly in the instructional process" (p. 277).

Tests do matter to teachers, but how they matter is uncertain. Consider the example of Paula, a third-year global history teacher.[4] Although she believes in promoting an active, engaging, and substantive pedagogy reflecting the tenets of "teaching for understanding" (Cohen, McLaughlin, & Talbert, 1993; Prawat, 1989), these views clash with the evaluation and accountability directions she perceives the state curriculum and test promote. "The message that I got," she said, "and this was not explicit, was that the objective was to get these kids to pass this test and that the state education people were using the test to change teaching."

The state's efforts, Paula believes, lie squarely at odds with her own sense of powerful teaching and learning:

> I think the curriculum should have gone in a very different direction, and maybe even if they wanted to change it from the more social science approach I would have liked to have seen it go to some kind of thematic approach where history, great themes of history, and teachers would be free to pick out examples of those themes and teach those themes, not necessarily in chronological order.... That seems to me more how history really is written, how historians write, and it seems more meaningful to me certainly and, I think, to kids as well.

With such convictions, one might conclude that Paula can substitute her own more ambitious inclinations for the state's. Paula complicates that impression. "Generally I think it's forced me to teach history in a way that I'm philosophically at odds with," she said, "and in a way that I don't think kids are going to remember or care about, and I feel obligated to do that because of this test at the end." Disposed toward more powerful instruction, Paula nevertheless feels "forced" to teach history in traditional ways:

> I just feel this sense of breathlessly running through a curriculum, never having an opportunity to relax enough to do that, to bring the materials (primary source documents) in and work with kids, take the time to work with kids

---

[4]This case draws on recent work I have done with several current and past students (Grant et al., 2002). These data reflect the teacher's views about the new global history exam the semester before it was administered.

through those materials. Because clearly it would take lots of time, and if I've got to get through World War II in two weeks, you know, I just don't know how to, how I could do that at this point.

In addition to racing through the curriculum, Paula feels a need to teach test-taking skills, especially for lower ability students. "I feel a pressure to drill certain kids on methods of passing a test," she said.

With the information just given, one now might see Paula as captive to the state policies: Paula's more ambitious intentions seem impotent next to the more conventional approaches she perceives advocated by the state. Paula's response could be read as an overreaction to the policy-makers' intent. After all, the rhetoric of the state policies seems to support the kind of pedagogy Paula espouses. What underlies her doubts about this rhetoric?

Paula's relative inexperience figures prominently. A newly tenured teacher, Paula still considers herself a novice, both curious and uncertain about her teaching. Believing that students need provocative and substantial experiences to become thoughtful learners, she does not know if such instructional activities will, by themselves, help students on the state test. She finds herself in an awkward position: trusting what she believes the state is telling her to do—that is, emphasizing content coverage and test-taking skills—until she knows otherwise. "I don't even know what [the test's] going to look like," she said, "so I'm going to take their word that this is going to work, I'm getting [the students] through the exam and, you know, do what I am supposed to, what they [the state] think I'm supposed to be doing."

Another dimension of Paula's seeming embrace of traditional practices is that it only explains part of her practice. For Paula has created, in effect, two teaching approaches: One is explicitly state curriculum and test di-rected, while the other is explicitly self-directed. Paula's use of primary source documents is a case in point: "I use [documents] the way I thought I would use them. I think, well, I use them the way I would like to use them sometimes, and I use them the way I think the state would like me to use them sometimes." Paula describes how she uses documents to execute these different teaching objectives:

> The way I use documents is for kids to make interpretations of them, of the documents, based on their knowledge of the topic. And that means that there may be a very wide variety of answers to whatever the question is. When I use them how I think the state wants to use them, there is probably not a wide variety of answers to the question. There's probably a pretty spe-cific answer to the question that goes with the document that I'm present-ing to them....

> I'm not sure I've ever used the same document two different ways.... I used a political cartoon which showed a Red Army soldier helping a peasant plow a field. And the caption underneath it was, "How can I ever repay you?" And it wasn't clear who was saying it to whom. As I looked at it, I realized it could have gone either way. So that was the question I asked: "If the peasant was

asking the soldier, what was the response? If the soldier was asking the peasant, what would the response be?" But I think if I were to use that same document for a DBQ essay, I would make it clear who was speaking to whom, and ask maybe a more direct, explicit question, like what kinds of, I'm not even quite sure what I would ask. But it would be a different kind of question, and it would not be as ambiguous to what was going on in the cartoon. I would not allow for that kind of ambiguity in the document.

I think when I'm doing it [using documents] for the way I'd like to do it, I have an idea of the response I'm looking for, but if [the students] come up with something that is different from what I was expecting but it makes sense and they can back up with some reasoning, then that's acceptable. But if I were using it for the state test-taking skill thing, then there would be one response, and if they didn't get that, then it would be wrong.

The tension this teacher feels resonates. On the one hand, documents such as the Red Army cartoon help push her students to think about the historical context of the situation, to draw from their prior knowledge, and to build both an argument and the evidence for that argument. Such actions are what some call powerful instruction (e.g., Wineburg & Wilson, 1991) and promote what the authors of the National Standards for American History call "real historical understanding" (National Center for History in Schools, 1994, p. 17). And yet, Paula feels compelled to use other documents that support more limited understandings, understandings from which students presumably will draw the right "state test-taking skill thing." Instead of crafting an instructional plan that coherently promotes ambitious teaching and learning, then, Paula constructs a wobbly mix of the rich and the dull, the engaging and the pedantic. The latter of these pairs reflects her sense that she cannot afford not to; the former reflects her hope to offer something more than a superficial treatment of the subject matter. But here is the kicker: Paula's ambitious teaching comes *in spite of* rather than because of the new state test. Tests are driving a portion of Paula's teaching, but not the part that seems most beneficial to students. Rothman (1995) points to the apparent irony in this kind of situation: "The emphasis on raising test scores has thrown into doubt the meaning of the higher test scores. If test scores go up because schools have focuses extensively on preparing students for the test at the expense of other material, what does the increase signify?" (p. 62).

Paula's case suggests that one reason tests may not have a dramatic influence on teachers' practices is that they can conflict with deeply held beliefs. Teachers can hardly ignore tests, especially of the high-stakes variety, but tests are like many influences on teachers: They are more potential than direct (Grant, 1996; Romanowski, 1996; Sturtevant, 1996).

Another reason for the diminished influence of tests is that they typically do not provide the kind of information teachers value (Kellaghan et al., 1982). Testing advocates argue that test scores provide insights into students' strengths and weaknesses; information that can then be used to modify instruction (Popham et al., 1985). Problems with getting test scores back in a timely fashion, with drawing direct parallels between test and instructional tasks, and with issues of "test score pollution" (Haladyna et al., 1991) undercut this argument. Over 10 years ago, Kurfman (1991) noted that "there is little research evidence on one potentially positive instructional effect of testing: the diagnostic use of test results by teachers to modify their teaching practices to provide remediation for students who need it" (p. 317). More recently, Camilli et al., (2001) add, "performance standards embedded in high-stakes achievement tests have little, if any, formative value for individual students" (p. 466).

Whatever the reasons, the proposition that tests drive teaching and learning must be qualified. For although researchers detect some influence of tests on the content teachers choose to teach (Firestone et al., 2000; Firestone et al., 1998; Grant, Derme-Insinna, Gradwell, Lauricella, Pullano, & Tzetzo, 2002; Grant, Gradwell, Lauricella et al., 2002; Smith, 1991), far less evidence shows profound influences on teachers' instructional practices. Kellaghan, Madaus, and Airasian (1982) observe, "while the cooperation of teachers in administering the test program was good, their commitment to using test results, even on their own admission, was not great" (p. 128). Tests, then, influence how teachers construct their practices, but that influence is less direct, powerful, and predictable than most observers believe.

HIGH-STAKES TESTS AND HIGHER
EDUCATIONAL STANDARDS

The last big question for this chapter asks if raising stakes propels higher standards. In the cases of George Blair and Linda Strait, and in the review of the research just given, I argue that testing is an uncertain lever at best. In the time since I collected the data on Blair and Strait, however, New York policymakers have upped the ante under the assumption that raising the stakes will raise educational standards (Grant, Gradwell, Lauricella et al., 2002). Again we confront a commonsense assumption: Increasing the pressure on students and teachers should make both more accountable, and ultimately improve education for all. And again, common sense fails the test of reality, for the research literature challenges the relationship between high stakes and high standards. High-stakes tests induce some changes in teachers' practices, but as Corbett and Wilson (1991) observe, change is not the same thing as reform.

The Cases for and Against High-Stakes Testing

The former president of the American Federation of Teachers, Al Shanker (1995), makes the case for high-stakes testing this way:

> School reformers who are working to solve the problem of students' low achievement levels have come up with all sorts of new and creative things,

but as long as students are given no reason to work, it is hard to see how any reform, however ingenious or creative, will achieve what is needed. The absence of stakes makes the whole system trivial. (p. 147)

Shanker, like many advocates of testing, argues that real educational reform demands high curriculum standards and high stakes tests. This advocacy rests on two premises: that tests are a reasonable way to decide if schools are working, and that increasing the stakes represented by test scores will impel the desired kinds of changes. Those changes are generally described as more ambitious teaching and learning for all students. "High stakes," then, refers to the twin notions of "examinations are associated with important consequences for examinees" and "examinations whose scores are seen as reflections of instructional quality" (Popham, 1987, p. 680). Amrein and Berliner (2002), Madaus (1988), and Koretz (1988) expand the definition of high stakes to include the publication of test scores. The conditions Popham describes highlight the efforts of students and teachers in the classroom; the condition that Amrein, Berliner, Madaus, and Koretz describe puts those efforts on public display.[5]

New York state policymakers, like their colleagues in Massachusetts, Virginia, and elsewhere, have embraced the premises and conditions of high-stakes testing as a means to educational reform. The Regents tests have been revised, but so too has the context in which the Regents test is administered and the implications of taking the test. First, the importance of state testing has been pushed into lower grades. Elementary and middle school teachers used to give program evaluation tests in social studies. These tests and the scores they produced were to be used by teachers and administrators to make content and instructional decisions; no individual student scores were generated. The exams were almost exclusively multiple-choice in format and the scores were reported only to local school and district offices. Today, fifth- and eighth-grade students take tests that mirror those given at the high school level, including DBQs, and the school scores are reported in local newspapers. Moreover, low scores are now used to mark individual students for remedial work and more testing. A second sign of the increased stakes attached to the NYS testing program comes at the high school level. Students have always had to pass a 10th- grade global studies and an 11th-grade U.S. history exam in order to graduate. Students could, however, choose either to take the less-demanding Regents Competency Test (RCT) and receive a local diploma or to take the more challenging Regents test and receive a higher status Regents diploma. Calls for higher standards for all students ended in the decision to phase out the RCT and to require that all students take and pass the newly designed and presumably more rigorous Regents tests. Newspapers anxiously await the release of Regents scores and publish them by school and

---

[5]See Amrein and Berliner (2002) for a thorough analysis of high-stakes testing practices and effects.

district. The last indication that the stakes are higher now is that although no explicit state-level sanctions have been created for individual teachers whose students do not perform well, schools whose test performance lags for 3 years can be taken over by the state education department.

Policymakers in New York and across the United States pin their hopes on the power of new tests to drive educational reform. Those hopes seem to be falling on hard ground, however. Analyst after analyst points to the same conclusion: Tests, even high-stakes tests, fail as levers of policy change (Clarke et al., 2000; Darling-Hammond & Falk, 1997; Firestone & Mayrowetz, 2000; Grant et al., 2001; Popham, 1999). Robert Linn (2000) laments the chasm between the promise and problems of high-stakes tests:

> In most cases the instruments and technology have not been up to the demands that been placed on them by high-stakes accountability. Assessment systems that are useful monitors lose much of their dependability and credibility for that purpose when high-stakes are attached to them. (p. 14)

Gregory Camilli and his colleagues (2001) conclude that the research evidence confirms the "diminishing returns of high-stakes assessment as an educational reform strategy" (p. 466)

The seeming exception to the consensus view on high-stakes testing is the state of Texas. The Texas Assessment of Academic Skills (TAAS) began in 1990 as a criterion-referenced test (like the New York Regents exam) designed to measure students' higher order thinking skills and problem-solving abilities. Results from the TAAS tests of reading and mathematics were dubbed the "Texas miracle" because they showed enormous gains in student achievement and demonstrated a reduction in average score differences among racial and ethnic groups. This latter point seemed especially important because African American and Hispanic American students have not done well on standardized tests in the past. Then-governor Bush and state education department policymakers were ecstatic: Texas teachers and students seemed to be fulfilling the promise of high-stakes testing.

That initial enthusiasm muted some of the criticism that the new exams promoted an unhealthy focus on test scores alone, which in turn promoted excessive teaching to the test and even cheating scandals. That criticism took a new turn, however, when researchers began comparing students' TAAS scores with their performance on the NAEP, which is generally considered the "gold standard" of standardized testing (Klein et al., 2000). As that research came in (Haney, 2000; Klein et al., 2000), the bloom began to fade on the Texas rose. In short, the huge gains registered on the TAAS failed to register on the NAEP exams. Moreover, the gap between White students and students of color in Texas increased on the NAEP. Klein and his colleagues (2000) believe two implications result from this analysis: The Texas miracle is suspect, as is faith in high-stakes tests as a means of reform:

Our findings from this research raise serious questions about the validity of the gains in the TAAS scores. More generally, our results illustrate the danger of relying on statewide test scores as the sole measure of student achievement when these scores are used to make high-stakes decisions about teachers and schools as well as students. (p. 2)

The discrepancy between TAAS and NAEP scores is not unusual.[6] Linn (2000) reports that there is a questionable relationship at best between state-level tests and the NAEP. Barton and Coley (1998) go even further. Their analysis shows an inverse relationship between students' performance on the NAEP and those states that have high-stakes graduation exams: the higher the stakes, the lower the NAEP scores.

Bizarre as all this sounds, it points to a key realization: High-stakes tests *may* result in higher test scores, but strong doubts surface around what those scores mean and whether those scores represent real academic achievement. Evidence for this conclusion arises in work graduate students and I have done around the new New York global history test (Grant et al., 2001; Grant, Derme-Insinna, Gradwell et al., 2002; Grant, Gradwell, Lauricella et al., 2002). State policymakers promote new exams as a means of elevating education standards. Teachers' reactions to and students' performance on the new global test undercut that premise. The teachers we studied contend that the new exams are far less challenging and that the scoring process is far more generous than under the old system. Student test scores bear this out: Passing rates at all the schools in our study are either the same as or above the rates for the old exams. The state passing rates, too, reflect a large increase: Where 60.9% of tenth graders passed the last global studies exam, almost 10% more students (68.5%) passed the new, presumably more difficult global history exam. This increase is even more astounding given the conditions of the test: Virtually all 10th graders took the new exam as schools moved to drop the RCT option. So not only did test scores rise dramatically, but they did so when many students who once would have taken the easier RCT now took the reportedly more challenging Regents test. An experienced teacher put the matter bluntly: "It's dumbing down the content so they [the state] get higher numbers.... You can do anything you want with numbers, it doesn't show that [the students] are gaining." Teachers scoff at policymaker claims that the new, high-stakes test inspires higher educational standards:

No, I don't think [the test] reflects higher standards. But they're [the state] going to be getting different numbers that they'll be happy with to say that everything is working. But the kids don't know as much or aren't doing as well as they could be doing.

We [the teacher's colleagues]) sat there and chuckled and said, "Oh yes! We are raising standards, aren't we?" A billy goat can pass them, but that's okay.

---

[6]An analysis published as this book was going to press (Toenjes & Dworkin, 2002) questions the analyses that critics like Walt Haney (2000) have offered. Stay tuned.

I don't think [parents] have a clue as to what the test actually consisted of. And I think if parents actually sat down and went through this test and saw what was being done—it's almost laughable. I think they would be appalled.... If someone asked me, "Do you feel the state is, in fact, raising the standards, and is this test a valid, accurate assessment of higher standards?" I could not lie. I would honestly say, "No, I don't feel it is."

Linn (2000) contends that high-stakes tests inevitably produce "inflated notions of achievement" (p. 7). Results on the new global history exam bear out this claim. Interestingly enough, the teachers we interviewed are not sanguine about the high scores their students post. Instead, their comments reflect Stake's (1991) conclusion that teachers "have essentially no confidence in testing as the basis of the reform of schooling in America" (p. 246).

Solutions to the Problems of High-Stakes Tests

So what's the solution? Although some observers (Berliner & Biddle, 1995) question whether there is anything really wrong with America's schools, policymakers seem convinced otherwise. Is the answer even higher stakes? improved tests? more ambitious teaching? The first suggestion seems unlikely: After all, how much higher can policymakers raise stakes? Here, I examine the potential for new tests and ambitious teaching.

The Promise of New Tests?

The problems of high-stakes tests are well documented. Would improved tests help? The answer seems obvious, but may not be.

The technology of testing is much studied (Cizek, 2001) and, with relatively few glitches, produces reliable results when students' performance is compared on the same exam.[7] The incidence of test score pollution, however, undercuts some of this accomplishment. Thomas Haladyna and his colleagues (1991) assert that high-stakes testing is surrounded by a range of activities, some ethical, some not, which damage the relationship between tests and student achievement.[8]

---

[7]The latest "glitch" was CTB/McGraw-Hill's misscoring of almost 9000 New York City students' tests, which resulted in huge numbers of students sent to summer-school remediation. The classic case, however, is the "Lake Woebegone effect" (Koretz, 1988). In nosing around, a West Virginia physician observed that the results on norm-referenced national standardized tests indicated that students in every state were above average. Because norm-referenced tests are predicated on the notion that 50% of the scores must lie below the median, such results smelled funny (Cannell, 1988).

[8]Examples of ethical activities include teaching test preparation skills and developing a curriculum that reflects test objectives. Unethical activities include using programs designed only to boost students' test scores and dismissing low-achieving students on test days. Whether ethical or not, the point Haladyna et al., (1991) stress is that these activities diminish the potential for using high-stakes tests as accurate and useful measures of students' learning.

Haladyna's argument notwithstanding, some observers argue that test questions can be improved. For example, Stuart Yeh (2001) asserts that even multiple-choice questions can be designed to better assess critical thinking. His example of a question using the differing interpretations of the Vietnam War by Frances Fitzgerald and Neil Sheehan presents a genuine task that moves students beyond factual recall. Eva Baker (1994) is less optimistic. Setting out to determine whether radical changes in large-scale tests are possible and realistic, Baker and her colleagues describe the DBQ-like activities they designed. Their efforts fall apart, however, when teachers score the students' essays:

> Four history teachers, handpicked on the basis of their excellent teaching reputations, shared neither explicit nor implicit sets of criteria to judge the quality of students' historical understanding. Judging 85 written explanations, they came to little agreement. (p. 100)

Baker argues that more and better training of scorers can mitigate some of this problem, but when one imagines the testing of hundreds of thousands of students by thousands of teachers, the opportunities for wild scoring fluctuations soar.

Beyond the problems of achieving consistent scores is the authenticity of test questions. Although multiple-choice items have long been suspect, Jill Gradwell, Sandra Cimbricz, and I (Grant, Gradwell & Cimbricz, 2002) question the authenticity of tasks like the DBQ. Using Wiggins and McTighe's (1998) criteria for authentic assessments, we analyzed the DBQ on the first new global history exam. We conclude that although the task has a patina of authenticity, it fails to reflect well the conditions of a genuine historical assignment.

Whether or not new and better test items emerge, the larger issue nags of how test scores are used. Assessment experts caution against using the results of one test to make any decisions about students, much less high-stakes decisions such as who graduates and who doesn't (Linn, 2000). In the end, the key issue is "not whether we should use one kind of test or another but what role testing should play in assessment" (Wiggins, 1993, p. 14).

The (Better) Promise of Good Teaching

Fair enough: Designing better test questions and finding a spot for tests within the wider field of assessment makes sense. But these directions seem like a thin solution to the problem of how to promote greater student learning. So if better tests can't do it, can better teaching?

The answer seems to be, yes. Bubbling along through the last couple of chapters is an emerging consensus that connects ambitious teaching with higher test scores. The problems of what tests measure aside, researchers (Avery, 1999; Newmann et al., 2001; Newmann, Secada, & Wehlage, 1995; Smith & Niemi, 2001) offer evidence of a tight connection between good teaching and higher test scores. The increased use of complex writing tasks, in-depth reading (meaning from sources outside the textbook), student discussion, and learning tools (such as outside speakers, film, computers) strongly correlates with higher scores on the NAEP exams in U.S. history (National Center for Education Statistics, 2002; Smith & Niemi, 2001). Smith and Niemi (2001) conclude that "in history as well as elsewhere, active involvement promotes student achievement" (p. 34). Especially interesting is their finding that good instruction is an even better predictor of strong student test performance than are family and social characteristics. Fred Newmann (1996) concurs: Socioeconomic factors matter, but teachers' pedagogy matters more. "If faced with a choice of only one 'solution' to raise history scores," Smith and Niemi contend, "it is clear that instructional changes have the most powerful relationship to student performance" (p. 38).

The Consequences of High-Stakes Testing

The good news, then, is that teachers can play a powerful role in what their students learn, and that evidence of their learning manifests in higher test scores. If we could be sure that high-stakes testing promoted more ambitious teaching, then the anxieties surrounding the high-stakes environment might be worth it. Unfortunately, there is no evidence for this hope. In fact, cases like that of Paula suggest it's just the opposite: Teachers offer ambitious instruction in spite of rather than because of high-stakes tests (Grant, Derme-Insinna, Gradwell et al., 2002; Grant, Gradwell, Lauricella et al., 2002; McNeil, 2000).

This last point is important, for the gamble on high-stakes tests yields important, if unintended, consequences. Those consequences can include the narrowing of curriculum, the reduction of instruction to test preparation, and the continued disadvantaging of minority and low income students. The work my students and I have done points to yet another consequence: The undermining of ambitious teachers (Grant, Derme-Insinna, Gradwell et al., 2002; Grant, Gradwell, Lauricella et al., 2002). As the evidence mounts that good teaching links to good student test scores, the fact that most teachers perceive that state tests promote recall learning and drill-and-practice teaching means that they feel a steady sapping of their energies. The time, energy, and tension that a new teacher like Paula feels as she juggles competing demands cannot be ignored. Her students do fine on the state tests, but the press of high-stakes conditions feels more burdensome than invigorating. Veteran teachers, by contrast, are just angry that the new global history exam fails to live up to its advanced billing. A teacher who is active in New York state social studies circles sums up the frustrations of many:

> I think teachers throughout the state were appalled when they saw the exam.... I heard that many teachers wrote, when they filled out the evaluation sheet, and they put down comments, that it [the test] was almost like an insult. (Grant, Gradwell, Lauricella et al., 2002, p. 507)

Another veteran teacher recalls her surprise at the exam's simplicity as she distributed it to her students: "You pass them out, and then while they're working on it, you're standing there and going through it and thinking, 'You've got to be kidding me. I mean you [the state] made me nervous for four years prior to this?'" (Grant, Gradwell, Lauricella et al., 2002, p. 507).

Rather than inspire teachers to be more ambitious, then, the new Regents exams in New York and other states (McNeil, 2000) seem to be inspiring a sharp skepticism about the relationship between high-stakes tests and high educational standards. Summing up the feelings of virtually all we interviewed, an experienced teacher notes:

> I think it's a sad, sad case that after two years of studying in great detail and depth that we do, that you have 50 questions and two simple, little essays that someone not even taking the course probably could watch the Discovery Channel a couple of weeks, and get through the essays. I'm not impressed with it at all. (Grant, Gradwell, Lauricella et al., 2002, p. 509)

Such comments inspire a scenario where the state increasingly distrusts teachers and where teachers increasingly distrust the state. McLaughlin (1991) observes that "ironically, accountability schemes that rely on existing testing technology trust the system (the rules, regulations, and standardized procedures) more than they trust teachers to make appropriate, educationally sound choices" (p. 250). Percolating through our studies is a corresponding mistrust. Accused of failing to meet high standards, teachers are aggravated by state efforts that seem to undercut their more ambitious efforts. Ironically, then, high-stakes testing may ultimately drive out the very teachers who are most responsible for their students' academic success.

CONCLUSION

High-stakes advocates like the late Al Shanker argue that "without stakes, reform will not go anywhere: the kids will not take it seriously and neither will the teachers" (Shanker, 1995, p. 149). The commonsense logic embodied in such claims can be powerfully persuasive: Witness the fact that legislation proposed by the Bush administration and overwhelmingly embraced by Congress puts a premium on more testing. Common sense is not always the best sense, however, as the research evidence fails to support testing as lever of reform. High-stakes testing, Linda Darling-Hammond (1991) argues, "cannot be a constructive lever for reform unless we invest in more educationally useful and valid measures of student learning" (p. 229). The good news is that powerful teaching pays off for students. The tricky part is how to support the good teaching that is already occurring and how to nurture that capacity in the classrooms where it is not.

PART IV

Influences on and Prospects for Ambitious Teaching

7

The Influences on Teachers' Classroom Decisions

Percolating through the previous chapters are clues about how and why George Blair and Linda Strait construct their relative practices. The influences these teachers and others perceive and how they make sense of those influences drive this chapter.

Ideas for improving teaching and learning abound. Unfortunately, those ideas tend to be offered in a vacuum, with little awareness of or attention to the complicated lives teachers live. Preservice and practicing teachers deserve more than a set of canned prescriptions. Those of us who work with teachers can help support them as they make ambitious content and instructional decisions, but doing so involves understanding what makes them tick, and that involves examining the influences on the classroom decisions they make.

Determining what counts as an influence and how much authority it has is difficult, however. Although many observers propose simple answers, the research evidence presents a complex picture. The influences on teachers are many, they come from multiple directions, they push in various ways, and they interact such that no influence is purely perceived. In short, sorting out the factors that influence teachers is just as thorny as the other issues dealt with in this book. Thorniness is no reason no to proceed, however, so let's get started.

FRAMING THE STUDY OF INFLUENCES ON TEACHERS

Complicating the study of influences on teachers is how to frame the inquiry. Should we seek out the silver bullet, the one influence or set of influences that explains the greatest number of teacher decisions? Or should we take a shotgun approach, cataloging each and every influence regardless of how significant we think it might be? Or can the apparent influences be grouped and labeled into useful categories?

There is no shortage of silver bullet proposals. Classroom observers long have pitched one or another factor as the principal influence on teachers: The faith state-level policymakers place in high-stakes testing is the most current example. Silver bullets are sexy, but they don't work very well: A single factor may influence some teachers, but there is no evidence that any one factor influences the majority of teachers, and influences them in the same way.

So is the answer to look for the widest array of influences? This approach has some appeal as a survey of influences could provide useful hints. The problem is that a simple list of factors may not explain how those factors influence teachers or to what degree.

A third strategy builds on the second. After surveying the widest array of influences, it makes sense to see if patterns or categories emerge. A number of researchers have taken just this approach. Steve Thornton (1988) notes three groups of influences on the teachers he observed. One group involves the teachers' conception of purpose, that is, their beliefs about why and how they should teach history. The second group of influences revolves around curriculum management. Here, the focus is on the constraints teachers perceive in their work environment. The last group of influences arises from beyond the classroom. These factors, which include the local community and the state social studies curriculum, play some role in how teachers construct their practices. Walter Doyle and Gerald Ponder (1977) also see categories of influence. They argue that the "practicality ethic" drives most teacher decision making, especially in light of innovations. The three categories of influence are *instrumentality* (whether instructional procedures are explicitly delineated and are immediately useful), *congruence* (how well an innovation is perceived to fit with teachers' current practices), and *cost* (perceived benefit vs. perceived investment).

Considering these and other categorization schemes, I see some value in the notion of grouping influences. At the same time, however, my research on elementary, middle, and high school teachers in various school subjects (Grant, 1996, 1998) convinces me that a broader and more inclusive set of categories might be more useful. The three that I offer are *personal, organizational,* and *policy influences*. After analyzing the cases of George Blair and Linda Strait, and the research literature on teachers' decision making, I believe this framework has currency as a way to understand how and why teachers make the content and pedagogical decisions they do. Consequently, I organize the sections that follow around these categories.

But before I do that, let me complicate things a bit. Although the categories of personal, organizational, and policy influences can be isolated and described, I ultimately argue that few teacher decisions reflect purely one category or another. A teacher's preference for the Civil War over the Industrial Revolution or her use of cooperative learning groups instead of a lecture may be based on a policy influence like a state test. Chances are, however, that other factors also play a part. Thus, although understanding teachers' decision making involves sorting through the array of relevant personal, organizational, and policy influences, it also involves being sensitive to instances where those influences interact. Understanding the cross-currents of influence, however, requires some attention to the individual currents. So in the next sections, I use the research literature and examples from the cases of George Blair and Linda Strait to examine, separately, the personal, organizational, and policy influences on teachers, and then to look at the ways in which they interact.

PERSONAL INFLUENCES ON TEACHERS' DECISIONS

Although some influences like state standards and state tests get more press, the role of personal or individual influences on teachers' content and pedagogical decisions is widely acknowledged in the general literature on teaching. Those influences include personal knowledge and beliefs (Eisenhart, Shrum, Harding, & Cuthbert, 1988; Pajares, 1992), dispositions (Buchmann, 1986; Zeichner, 1986), professional experiences (Eisner, 1988; Lieberman & Miller, 1984; Lortie, 1975), personal history and narrative (Carter, 1993; Connelly & Clandinin, 1990; Goodson, 1992), and the function of subject matter knowledge (Shulman, 1986, 1987).

The research on history teachers' decision making reflects some of these general influences. Much of that work focuses, in one way or another, on the importance of teachers' beliefs and on their experiences as learners. Teachers' beliefs can come from many sources and take many forms. The research on history teaching focuses on teachers' beliefs arising from their personal values and lived experiences, their beliefs about teaching and learning in general, and their beliefs about history as a school subject. Teachers' beliefs are a key personal influence, but so too seems to be the impact of teachers' earlier experiences as learners in classrooms.

The Influence of Teacher Beliefs

Teacher beliefs has become a major research area. *Belief* is defined as "a proposition, or statement of relation among things accepted as true," including axioms, rules of practice, and perspectives (Eisenhart et al., 1988, pp. 52–53). This definition hardly narrows things down, but it underscores a couple of important points. One is that beliefs are ideas that teachers *accept* to be true. There is no objectivity requirement here: Beliefs may be grounded in lived experiences, but it is an individual's interpretation of those experiences that makes something a belief. The second point is that beliefs can involve any facet of a teacher's professional life. Beliefs may guide decisions about students, subject matter, administrators, textbooks; the list is endless. The fuzziness of beliefs as an analytic construct plagues many researchers (Pajares, 1992), but as a lens on teachers' thinking and practice, beliefs represent a powerful influence.

Beliefs Based in Values and Experience

One set of beliefs researchers explore involves teachers' personal values and lived experiences. Preservice and inservice education have some effect on teachers' decision making (Yeager & Davis, 1996), but teachers' practices can be affected by a wide range of beliefs, many of which are personal.

Michael Romanowski (1996) offers an candid account of how his personal antinuclear stance played out in his first teaching job in a school near Three Mile Island. Dimly aware of the power plant's importance to the local community, Romanowski fashioned lessons and assignments reflecting his previously held beliefs: "I used various readings and materials that represented the topic from my own 'antinuclear' position, attempting to force students to rethink their views" (p. 291).

The two teachers Elizabeth Sturtevant (1996) profiles demonstrate the classroom impact of beliefs built on lived experience. Among other things, each teacher cites the influence of his spouse (also a teacher) on his instruction. Joe's wife, a third grade teacher, urges him to adopt the whole-language[1] practices she has embraced, such as using Venn diagrams. Dan's wife, also a high school history teacher, encourages him to read and respond more attentively to his students' written assignments. Sturtevant notes that both men are at the early stages of changing their practices. To the extent that they follow through, she argues, the influences on their decisions can be traced back to their spouses.

Beliefs About Teaching and Learning in General

A second grouping of teacher beliefs revolves around how general views of teaching and learning impact teachers' practices. Surveys of teachers' beliefs (Rutter, 1986; Vinson, 1998) show teachers hold a wide array of ideas about teaching and learning in social studies. For example, Anderson, Avery, Pederson, Smith, and Sullivan (1997) demonstrate that teachers' beliefs tend to favor liberal perspectives on citizenship development (e.g., critical thinking and cultural pluralism) over conservative stances (e.g., legalism and assimilationism).

Survey results can map out an array of beliefs, but they do little to show the impact of those beliefs on teachers' practices. Better sources for this phenomena are teacher interviews and classroom observations. In his

---

[1]"Whole language" refers to a movement in English/language arts to put less emphasis on practicing discrete reading and writing skills and more emphasis on reading and writing authentic texts (see, for example, Goodman, 1986).

field study of three high school history teachers, Steve Thornton (1988) demonstrates several instances of curriculum "consonance," where teachers' beliefs result in specific classroom actions. For example, "Carson believes that students should learn to critique their peers' answers, so he structures classroom discussions to facilitate such interchanges" and "Bauer uses the textbook because it is a 'convenient' tool but supplements it with lectures and other materials when he believes the text neglects important issues" (p. 313). Jeff Cornett (1990) asserts that teachers' beliefs contribute to their "personal practical theories" of teaching and learning, which in turn influence their teaching. The high school teacher Cornett studied, Sue Chase, describes a set of beliefs or theories underlying her practice. Those beliefs include *unconditional positive regard* (treating all students well), *empathic understanding* (treating students as individuals and trying to understand what is happening in their lives), *teacher as human* (showing students the teacher's human side), *learning and teaching as fun* (promoting active engagement through discussion), and *organized and systematic presentation of material* (designing and using regular activities and tasks). An example of how these beliefs influence Chase's instruction is her use of review sheets:

> Well, I give review sheets probably because a part of my theory is I don't set myself up as an adversary. There is a body of materials to be mastered and I don't think there should be any secrets about that. Here it is. My job is to give you some explanation, to add to it, to respond to your questions, to be a resource person, and your job is to assimilate and understand, and hopefully to be able to use the material in some way. (p. 259)

Chase's worry about being viewed as an adversary reflects her beliefs that teachers are humans and that teaching and learning ought to be fun. Those beliefs, then, help explain how and why she uses review sheets as she does.

Beliefs About the Nature of History

Researchers are increasingly interested in teachers' beliefs about history as a school subject. Reflecting Shulman's (1986, 1987) attention to the importance of subject matter, these observers (Evans, 1990; Gudmundsdottir, 1990; Wilson & Wineburg, 1993; Wineburg & Wilson, 1991; Yeager & Davis, 1996) offer insights into the influence of teachers' views of history on their classroom pedagogy.

Bruce VanSledright (1996a) portrays a high school teacher, Martha Reese, who prizes the "fact–interpretation" distinction. She believes that teaching and remembering historical facts belong to one dimension of learning history whereas the act of interpretation lies in another. The central role that facts play in Reese's instruction surfaces in the way she envisions the use of textbooks:

I hope that they are using [the textbook] as a source of information not necessarily interpretation.... In fact, I usually give them prefabricated questions based exactly on the textbook because that's the purpose of the exercise—[basic] reading comprehension. The book becomes the authority because the questions are based on the book. (p. 268)

Accumulating historical facts is key to Reese's view of history as a school subject. Unlike many teachers who stop with textbook facts, Reese also believes in the importance of historical interpretation. As a result, she layers on opportunities for students to see, for example, the value of multiple perspectives. For example, after showing a videotape that presents colonial and British views of the Stamp act, Reese challenges students to articulate and explain both stances. She concludes the lesson with a reminder to respect diverse viewpoints: "It's important when studying history to look at different points of view. It's too easy to see it from only this side of the ocean" (p. 270).

Suzanne Wilson and Sam Wineburg (1988) approach the influence of teachers' content area beliefs by studying teachers with different academic backgrounds. All four teach U.S. history, but only Jane has a degree in American history; Cathy majored in anthropology, Fred in international relations and political science, and Bill in American studies. In each case, the teacher's disciplinary background influences his or her classroom practice. For example, Fred's preference for international relations stems from his sense that it offers more general and thematic understandings than does history, which he asserts is simply about facts: "I think history is knowing ... the facts, all the dates. Knowing all the terms, knowing when the conference in Vienna was held or what were the terms of the agreement in World War II" (p. 327). Although historians (e.g., Carr, 1961; Novick, 1988) would blanch at such characterizations, Fred's view of history nevertheless influences his teaching. He covers the traditional history content, but each class begins with an extended treatment of current events, often focusing on international situations. Although different in effect, Jane's disciplinary background also figures prominently in her instruction. Well schooled in U.S. history, Jane draws her students into historical events through thematic units that reflect multiple ideas and multiple instructional strategies. In Jane's hands, "facts were not just told but sung, witnessed, and experienced" (p. 534). Wilson and Wineburg conclude that although different, each teacher's subject matter background "wielded a strong—and often decisive—influence on their instructional decision making" (p. 526).

The Influence of Teachers' Experiences as Learners

Just as teachers' beliefs figure into their classroom practices, so too do their past experiences as learners. Dan Lortie (1975) names the "apprenticeship of observation" as a powerful influence on teachers' broad conceptions of education and on their specific teaching practices. That apprenticeship, Lortie argues, represents a "continuing influence of former teachers" (p. 64) such that "what constituted good teaching then constitutes good teaching now" (p. 66). Lortie demonstrates this influence on teachers regardless of subject matter or grade level.

Bill McDiarmid (1994) offers a useful description of the apprenticeship phenomena in history classrooms. Interested in how prospective teachers think about history as a teaching subject, McDiarmid follows a group of undergraduate history majors through a historiography seminar. The professor for the seminar designs activities pushing students to think about and experience the real work of historians. Those activities include developing a researchable history question, carrying out the research, entertaining multiple viewpoints, writing and supporting a historical argument, and discussing both the progress of their work and their findings with the professor and each other.

Interviewing the students throughout the course, McDiarmid notes their growing understandings of both history and historiography. Expecting a similar change in the students' views about teaching and learning history, McDiarmid reports "We were struck by the extent to which they are prisoners of their own experiences as students" (p. 176). Simply put, most of these prospective teachers said they would set aside the insights they learned in favor of lecturing and emphasizing the recall of facts. In contrast to the workshop method and the emphasis on perspective and interpretation advocated by their professor, students expect to lecture as did their high school and university teachers.

The two veteran teachers in Sturtevant's (1996) study are also influenced by their experiences as learners. Although the impact of their wives figures into their instructional practices, so too does their recalled experiences as students in history classrooms. For example, Joe admits to "stealing" a favored junior high teacher's use of class discussion: "Asking questions ... it's sort of a lecture but in the process of lecturing you're bringing the students into it" (p. 242). A powerful influence, the apprenticeship of observation that factors into preservice teachers' decisions is no less important for veterans.

It will surprise some to learn that preservice teacher education courses are seldom cited as discrete and profound influences on secondary school teachers' practices. Many studies of preservice teachers exist, and some show some positive effects of coursework and field experiences on teacher reflection (Christensen et al., 2001; Dinkelman, 2000), problem-based learning (Hughes, 1997), multicultural education (McCall, 1995), and the use of instructional technology (Mason, 2000). Those studies of practicing teachers that explore the influences on their practices (Grant, 1996; Heilman, 2001; Romanowski, 1996; Sturtevant, 1996) find teachers largely mute about the role of their preservice education. Two conditions temper their dour claim. One is that we simply do not know very much about the transition between learning about teaching and acting as a teacher. Research on preservice *or* practicing teachers fails to capture the evolution, and the influences on that evolution, from one role to the other. The second tempering condition is that no influence develops purely. Professors in preservice programs may hope to provoke their students to more ambitious pedagogies (Segall, 2002; Shermis & Barth, 1982). Remember, however, that every prospective teacher sat in numerous classrooms and watched a range of teachers. Those experiences and the knowledge about teaching that they inspire interact with the ideas preservice teachers learn about in their preparation programs (Angell, 1998; McDiarmid, 1994; Smith, 2000). The result: Any prospective teacher's instruction may owe as much to a significant experience in third grade as it does to a semester-long course in social studies methods.

Personal Influences on George Blair and Linda Strait

The notion of personal influences helps explain the decisions George Blair and Linda Strait make in their civil rights units. Teachers have a good deal of instructional autonomy, so it makes sense that personal knowledge, beliefs, and experiences are among the factors that influence their teaching decisions (Eisenhart et al., 1988; Lortie, 1975; Provenzo & McCloskey, 1996).

Recall that Blair and Strait share several personal traits. Each grew up in working-class environs with parents who promoted education. Each holds two degrees in history, and presumably knows well the subject matter of U.S. history. Each believes he or she learned little of value in teacher preparation courses. And each comes to teaching after a significant nonschool work experience—Blair as an Air Force enlisted man, Strait as a librarian.

The clearest distinctions between these teachers, then, are race and gender. As he is a White male, it would surprise few observers to see Blair treat the civil rights movement in a cursory manner. Those same observers would be hardly surprised that Strait, an African American woman, gives sustained attention to a movement she defines as critical. Race and gender likely figure deeply into each teacher's instructional decisions. But if so, these factors figure just as deeply in *all* the instructional decisions these teachers make, for there is little to distinguish either teacher's civil rights unit from any others they teach. Blair develops a narrative framework based on textbook chapters for each of his units. The Reconstruction unit I observed earlier in the school year had the same characteristics that emerged in his Eisenhower unit—issues woven into a bigger story, a focus on individuals, and teaching as a monologue. Similarly, Strait's civil rights unit exemplified the approach I observed her take in units on immigration and World War II. In each, she constructed a distinct unit, developed a broad range of activities and experiences, and pushed herself and her students into new roles. The point is not that race and class do not matter in the way Blair and Strait construct their civil rights units, but instead that these factors matter no more for that unit than for any other.

The personal influence most directly relevant to each teacher's practice seems to be his or her view of history as a school subject. That factor plays out most directly in the content decisions each teacher makes.

The Influence of George Blair's View of History on His Practice

History, in George Blair's view, is about human stories. Those stories speak to the soaring achievements and dastardly actions of historical actors played out across time and space. Facts and, to a limited degree, interpretations figure into these stories, but it is the power of narrative that defines Blair's view of history as a discipline. The substance of Blair's stories is complex, and reflects what Cornbleth (1998) calls an "imperfect but best" theme: "the recurring image of America as the best country in the world despite past problems, current difficulties, or one or another critique" (p. 628). This theme can be seen in the images of America that Blair holds and how he translates those images to his students. He begins with a reference to World War I and then moves to the civil rights era:

> I think World War One is probably a watershed where we try to stay isolated. But in a very short time, we realize that you can't do it. You are out there and you're a leader and you must, if you have certain value judgments, you must bring those values to the world, and try to make a better place out of it. I think that's one image that we were after. I think another image that we have been trying to deal with in the United States for time immemorial, at least [since] the Civil War, is an equal society, a civil rights society.

Blair's notion of the "best" America, as leader of the world, is tempered by his sense that Americans have far to go to realize these ambitions, especially in terms of civil rights:

> I think those images have remained the same, but my attitudes toward them may change a little bit. Like tolerance; I always thought we were doing pretty well. And as I go through and I look at reality and see what's happening nationwide, I begin seeing, wow, I mean, we're really in some serious trouble here. Very, very serious trouble. So my images of that ... you keep working toward trying to at least be tolerant of people. [But] you wonder if you're going backward. But the idea stays the same.

Like the teachers in Cornbleth's study, and the students in Barton and Levstik's (1998) analysis, George Blair's view of American history is rich in contradictions. His vision of an "equal society, a civil rights society" is undercut by his perception of a growing lack of tolerance and a backsliding away from the social progress.

Blair's belief that history is a spectacular narrative about progress and problems influences his classroom practice in at least two observable ways. One way is in the chronologically-based narrative framework he develops. So strongly held is this belief in narrative that he rejects any interference in the story he wants to tell. Recall his reaction to the state's de-emphasis of the Federal period:

> I find it very difficult to cut things out of American History. I'm sorry, I just find it very difficult. The new course that came out in '89 ... they removed the Federal period of American history. How the hell do you leave out the Federal period of American history? How the hell do you do this? Where's Louisiana, where's Jackson?

Blair's sense of the incoherence of the state's action makes sense when he describes why he will not comply:

> There's something inside of me that says you can't do that. So I teach a survey course and I break my ass getting through it 'cause I have to do an eight-week Constitution unit and that takes eight weeks out of the course. Like somehow we get there. Would I change that? No. I'm not going to change that.

To delete the Federal era would cut into Blair's felt need to "teach the whole course. Colonialism to Clinton." And he refuses.

A second way George Blair's beliefs about history influence his practice can be seen in his use of lecture. Much of what passes for lecture in American classrooms is really a combination of lecture, recitation, and class discussion. A good example is John Price, one of the teachers featured in Wineburg and Wilson's (1991) study. Price's voice dominates the class period, but his is not the only voice as he invites students to answer his questions and to pose their own questions and conjectures. This is not the case in Blair's classroom. There, he holds center stage much as a university professor might in an auditorium filled with undergraduates. Students are there to listen and take notes as Blair delivers the day's lesson. So important is the coherence and presentation of Blair's narrative, he invites no interruption. Those narratives are, to my ear, skillfully constructed and rendered as Blair weaves together a broad range of people, places, and events. This is no co-constructed history, though, as students play only the role of audience.

The Influence of Linda Strait's View of History on Her Practice

Beliefs about history also influence Linda Strait's classroom decisions. Understanding those beliefs helps explain some of the differences between her practice and George Blair's.

The substance of Strait's view of history reflects Cornbleth's (1998) theme of "multiple America," the sense that U.S. history represents a "multifaceted America more like a prism than a pane of glass" (p. 632). Although Strait does not ignore historical facts, she promotes the value of perspective—that different actors may hold very different perceptions of an event, and that those perceptions interplay with the "facts." This complex view of history emerges as Strait describes her belief that there is always more than one "side" to an historical account:

> What I try to convey is that America is multifaceted. That there—it's not *just* White America anymore. I don't know if it ever was *just* that, but that's how it was always taught in the history books. So, I'm trying to let them see that there's another side, and it's ever increasing, that other side of the diversity in America, and we have got to see it, recognize it, and start working together.

Strait's beliefs in a "multiple America" underscore the sense that "various participants and subsequent onlookers are seen to view events differently, and these differences are seen as legitimate if not equally compelling" (Cornbleth, 1998, p. 632).

This conception of history impacts Linda Strait's practice in two ways. The first is the amount of time she devotes to the civil rights movement. If she considered only the dictates of the Regents test and the state curriculum, an 8-day unit makes little sense, for the civil rights movement does not figure prominently in either policy. Most any era could serve her needs, but the complexities of the civil rights era provide a natural and expansive context for Strait's interest in multiple perspectives. The second way that Strait's view of history influences her practice is in her emphasis on social history. Textbooks and most teachers tend to focus on political and economic events. Strait does not discount this content, as, for example, her lecture notes cover the major civil rights actors and legislation. Nevertheless, much of her unit focuses on social history or the "lives of ordinary people in all their richness" (Appleby et al., 1994, p. 84). The two videotapes, the roundtable discussion and the skating-rink simulation, and the class readings of "40 Lives for Freedom" and "Hate Crimes—Summer, 1991" emphasize the roles and experiences of people unlikely to appear on a standardized state test. Make no mistake: Strait's students learn about the people, places, and events that make up standard accounts of the U.S. civil rights movement. They get more than that, however, as Strait introduces them to the wider fabric of people and history.

The Influence of Personal Factors on Teachers' Decision Making

Policymakers, test developers, in-service instructors, textbook authors, and university professors all hope to capture teachers' attention. Their efforts are not all in vain. But the examples of George Blair, Linda Strait, and their peers in the research literature suggest that other, more individual, influences matter too. And they are complicated. First, personal factors are not of a single type: They represent diverse experiences that may be formal and informal, in and out of school, and current and past. Second, personal influences may push teachers in different directions. Some, like the "apprenticeship of observation" are seen as conservative, whereas others, like the belief in "multiple America," can see viewed as progressive. Finally, a single type of influence can be interpreted in different ways. George Blair and Linda Strait both view history in general, and the civil rights movement in particular, as important. How they translate their views into practice, however, is dramatically different.

So powerful are personal influences that Romanowski (1996) claims, "The knowledge that students have the opportunity to learn hinges on the manner in which teachers approach their subject matter" (p. 293). He may be stating the case a bit too strongly, but the authority of personal influences on teachers' decision making can not be ignored.

ORGANIZATIONAL INFLUENCES ON TEACHERS' DECISIONS

In understanding teachers' classroom practices, personal influences merit attention. The bureaucratic system under which schools operate means that teachers generally work in isolation from other adults, that oversight of their work is weak, sporadic, and unsystematic, and that teacher autonomy is the norm (Doyle & Ponder, 1977; Lipsky, 1980; Lortie, 1975). In these conditions, personal factors are likely to fill institutional gaps. Still, no teacher works in a vacuum. A second category of influences on teachers' decisions, then, can be described as organizational.

The relevant dimensions of organizational influence include the impact of institutional cultures (Hargreaves, 1994; Sarason, 1982; Tyack & Cuban, 1995), organizational structures (Bolman & Deal, 1991; Chubb & Moe, 1988; Meyer & Rowan, 1978), and the nature of schools as bureaucratic organizations (Cohen & Spillane, 1992; Lipsky, 1980). Still others cite the influence of organizational players such as students and teaching peers (Lortie, 1975) and school and district administrators (Spillane, 1993).

The research specific to teaching and learning history reflects two types of organizational influence. One type features the influence of teachers' relationships with individuals and groups across a range of sites: classroom, school, and district. These people include students, teaching colleagues, principals, and district administrators. Of these relationships, the influence of students consumes the bulk of the research. The second type of organizational influence highlights the context of schooling. This context includes organizational norms and structures. Of this research, which is far less than the first category, it is the structures of schools that are most explored.

The Influence of Teachers' Relationships

The relationships teachers have with their students, colleagues, principals, and other administrators can influence their classroom decisions. Of those relationships, however, it is students who seem to have the most direct and powerful impact.

Relationships With Colleagues and Administrators

Teachers are surrounded by people, and yet teaching is often described as a lonely profession. This label stems from the lack of interaction that teachers, especially high school teachers, have with other adults. With children for six or more hours a day, teachers interact with colleagues and administrators infrequently and for small amounts of time. The influence of other adult contacts on teachers' decision making, then, is necessarily conditioned by the rarity of its occurrence.

From a small-scale survey, Stodolsky and Grossman (1995) report that social studies teachers, unlike their math and science peers, display little consensus around or coordination of the content they teach. Reporting on a nationwide survey, Rutter (1986) notes that social studies teachers spend little time talking and collaborating with their teaching colleagues. The infrequency with which teachers attend professional development activities, visit other classrooms, and plan lessons together, Rutter argues, contributes to feelings of isolation, stagnation, and alienation.

These feelings can be distressing, especially to new history teachers who expect to learn from and with their colleagues (Grant, 2000). More often than not, teachers find themselves feeling alone. Hoping to learn more about how to respond to the new global history state curriculum and test, a novice teacher pans the district-level sessions she attended, but she assigns much of that responsibility to her colleagues:

> We went to the district-wide [inservices]. They [the inservice leaders] always tried to be very positive, but the overwhelming number of teachers who are so negative about this assessment always wins out. It basically becomes a complaining session and you really aren't focusing on what the whole meeting was about anyway. (p. 7)

It is not surprising that teacher frustrations might boil over during a meeting, but the lack of attention this teacher's colleagues pay to substantive issues reflects a lost opportunity. Such opportunities can be created, however, if teachers craft ways to work with one another. A high school teacher describes a budding relationship with another new teacher as they discuss the DBQ on the state test: "I just wrote [a DBQ] a few weeks ago with a colleague," she said, "It is a lot easier to bounce off the ideas with somebody" (p. 7). Although she gets no administrative support for collaboration, this teacher chose to build a relationship with a colleague that could become an important influence on her teaching.

If the impact of teaching colleagues is rarely mentioned in the research, neither is that of school and district administrators (McNeil, 1988; Sturtevant, 1996). Moreover, although there is some evidence that the influence of colleagues can be positive, there is no similar evidence with respect to administrators. A high school teacher describes the impact of an on-going argument with his principal over the use of a history textbook:

> The administration has insisted that I use the textbook. They find that I'm too controversial and I present too many ideas and the textbook is a way of simply assuring that the kids are going to learn what they have to learn.... I do use a textbook and they have worksheets, but that doesn't mean that we're going to follow the textbook chronologically. We just jump around the textbook and find other aspects of that that will fit into the pattern that I am involved in. (Evans, 1990, p. 114)

Although this situation could be variously interpreted, it illustrates how a principal can influence the actions a teacher takes.

Relationships With Students

Teachers cite students as an important classroom influence far more than they do colleagues and administrators. Given the structure of the school day and who teachers most interact with, this conclusion makes considerable sense. How teachers respond to their students, however, is not always predictable, as teachers may make accommodations for or surrender to student pressures. Moreover, teachers may consider and then reject students' influences, carrying on with their intended practices.

Teachers can accommodate their students either directly or indirectly (Cornett, 1990; Rossi & Pace, 1998; Sturtevant, 1996). Teaching children of diverse backgrounds, Joe realizes that his students are variously able to meet his expectations. Rather than lower those expectations, Joe works with each student as needed. One student, Annie, credits Joe's extra efforts for her improved grades: "He taught me a way of studying," she said (Sturtevant, 1996, p. 243). Dan illustrates a more indirect means of accommodating students. "I really do like them," he said, "and I want them to be comfortable" (p. 246). Sturtevant's classroom observations of Dan's class support his dispositions as he works to create an "exceptionally caring attitude toward his students" (p. 246). The teachers Cornett (1990) and Rossi and Pace (1998) profile serve as examples of teachers who act both directly and indirectly in response to their sense of their students' needs.

Understanding student needs and working to accommodate them is an obvious way that teachers' decisions are influenced by their students. A less obvious reaction occurs when teachers seem to surrender to students' actions. Sedlak et al. (1986) describe the classroom "bargains" teachers make where they exchange lowered academic expectations for better student behavior. Labeling a similar phenomenon, "defensive teaching," McNeil (1988) describes it as "choosing methods of presentation and evaluation that [teachers] hope will make their workload more efficient and create as little student resistance as possible" (p. 158). Of the six barriers to higher order thinking that Joe Onosko (1991) identifies, two illustrate teachers' capitulation to students: Teachers cite large numbers of students and low expectations of students' abilities as prime reasons for not teaching ambitiously. Managing large numbers of students across the school day can be difficult (Sizer, 1984), but teachers' perception that students lack sufficient motivation, knowledge, and capacity to think deeply can be equally debilitating (Onosko, 1991). Despite evidence to the contrary (e.g., Keating, 1988), some teachers believe that students labeled "lower ability" are completely incapable of higher order thinking. A high school teacher defends his decision to avoid more active teaching and learning activities as inappropriate for "these" students:

> Given the constraints that are inherent in teaching lower ability students I am satisfied with the materials, content, skills, and teaching techniques that I use…. I think it is unrealistic for anyone to expect consistent higher order thinking from these students…. These students usually think and operate on a very concrete level … basically I would need to teach Advanced Placement students. (Onosko, 1991, p. 352)

This teacher's view of students drives his practice: With students capable only of "concrete" thinking, it is "unrealistic" for him to teach in more ambitious ways. He could do so, he reasons, only if they morphed into Advanced Placement students.

Romanowski (1996) describes another way that teachers yield to student pressures. Recall that his "antinuclear" beliefs lead him to construct instructional activities promoting that view. When students reacted negatively, he notes, "I quickly realized that a 'me against them' classroom atmosphere was developing" (p. 291). Under mounting pressure from his students and their parents, Romanowski backed off:

> I decided to omit the previous year's supplemental lessons on nuclear power. I limited my presentation to the textbook's portrayal. Furthermore, I elected to remain silent regarding my own "antinuclear position" and attempted to develop a more "objective" presentation of the issues. (p. 292)

Romanowski reports that he continued to ask some challenging questions of his students, but in the main, "controversial topics were avoided" (p. 292). He is not alone. Another teacher he interviewed talks about her decision to avoid challenging her students:

> I just give them the facts. I just think that when you are looking at a controversial issue, I can say what my opinion would be, but I try not to. I try to remain neutral and not to impose my views, I give them the basic facts, and then let them choose and draw conclusions. I try to avoid challenges. (p. 306)

Student (and community) pressures can be substantial, and the urge to capitulate to them can be overwhelming. Teachers do have a third option, however. Rather than accommodate or surrender, they can resist. This resistance may take a couple of different forms.

One form of resistance is hinted at in Romanowski's (1996) continued questioning of his students' views on nuclear power. He accedes to the pressure students and their parents unleash, but he does not acquiesce completely. Nor do many of the other teachers he studied. One teacher describes how he takes the strong Christian beliefs of his students and the community into consideration but does not let those beliefs coerce his instructional decisions:

> I think it is important to challenge what the students think they believe. For example, in the case of the New Deal I use various sources that raise issues like socialism, redistribution of wealth, the welfare system, you know, things like that. These are somewhat opposite to what they (students) believe.... Discussing these makes them rethink positions or shows the inconsistency in their thinking. (p. 303)

Another teacher portrays his resistance more explicitly: "It's white-bread, middle-class America, you know; it really is. I think that's even more reason why to provide some outside things to force the kids to think a little more critically" (p. 302).

The teachers Romanowski (1996) describes represent their resistance to student influences largely around political issues. Another way in which teachers challenge their students' expectations involves academics. Although many of the teachers Onosko (1991) studied point to students as a barrier to more ambitious teaching, some actively resist this conclusion. One teacher castigates his colleagues who hold such views:

> Low level kids spend years on recall because "they still don't know enough"—BS! ... All learning and thinking should begin with high level questions.... When students are actively pursing whole, meaningful tasks, they will naturally use all the skills in Bloom's taxonomy. (p. 353)

Another teacher fights students' beliefs about themselves: Sensitive to his students' conviction that they are incapable of anything more that rote learning, this teacher challenges rather than capitulates to their press to go easy:

> Most students like to think, in all levels. They resist more in writing than orally. Many have been trained to regurgitate history and they need to be retrained,

so there may be initial resistance, but it can be overcome through teaching. Resisters will moan and groan as you push them, but eventually they'll thank you for it.... I roll with the students who are thinking. It does become contagious.... It's really up to the teacher to make thinking a pleasurable experience. (p. 354)

This teacher and those described by other researchers (see, for example, Cornbleth, 1990; Heilman, 2001; Ladson-Billings, 1994) demonstrate the power of teachers to understand the beliefs, knowledge, and experiences their students bring to class. Understanding these things, however, is not the same as surrendering to them. Instead, these teachers push their students to greater understandings by building on their native ideas.

The Influence of Organizational Norms and Structures

If the people in a school setting can influence teachers' practices, so too can the prevailing organizational norms and structures. Although the research in this area specific to history teachers is pretty thin, the few studies available coincide with the larger literature on a number of points. One of those points is that the influences on teachers are many, consisting of a wide range of institutional norms and structures. Norms include expectations of how "noisy" classrooms can be, how grades are determined, and which textbooks will be used and how. Structures include how the school day is organized and how students are slotted for classes. The second point is that teachers may respond to these norms and structures in various ways. Teachers, like all street-level bureaucrats (Lipsky, 1980), make a wide range of decisions that may or may not reflect institutional pressures.

Organizational Norms

The decentralized nature of schools as organizations has been long noted (Cohen & Spillane, 1992; Meyer & Rowan, 1978). That decentralization underscores the development of particular norms or regularities (Sarason, 1982). Among those norms is the value of teacher autonomy. Teachers work in bureaucratic systems, yet the influence of those systems does not reach evenly or consistently into each classroom (Meyer & Rowan, 1978; Rowan, 1990). Teachers have little choice over some matters, such as the students they teach and the standardized tests they administer. But other matters—how they group students, what messages they draw from tests—are firmly in their domain (Lortie, 1975; Lipsky, 1980). Other school norms include teacher authority over students and teacher isolation from their colleagues.

Catherine Cornbleth (1990) describes how teachers go about setting their classroom norms, or ground rules, in the beginning of the school year. Those norms include the kind of bargains just discussed. A seventh grade social studies teacher, for example, announces, "If you don't aggravate me, I won't aggravate you.... As long as you do what I tell you, we'll get along fine" (p. 65). Cornbleth points out that such norms "were supported and encouraged by the school administration and documents such as the staff and student handbooks" (p. 69). She goes on to note that the "apparent consensus regarding school goals and practices served to realize and maintain them" (p. 69).

A different kind of organizational norm plays out as a barrier to higher order thinking in Onosko's (1991) study. Teacher isolation, he observes, is inherent in most school cultures: Teachers are expected to operate as "separate galaxies in a vast universe of instruction" (p. 359). Illustrating this norm, a teacher recalls his surprise in learning that a colleague was working on a K–12 curriculum for social studies: "Here we've been teaching for 20 years and have never really shared these main ideas behind our teaching. We've taught in the same building, but really don't know what one another is doing" (p. 359). The principal effect of this "Lone Ranger syndrome" is an "an atmosphere of individualism, noncommunication, and at times competition" (p. 359).

These outcomes may not directly affect student learning in the classroom, but Onosko (1991) believes that they undercut collaborative efforts to make teaching and learning a more vibrant part of teachers' conversations and that they leave teachers who are enacting more ambitious pedagogies feeling unsupported. This last point speaks to the cost of trying new instructional approaches. Doyle and Ponder (1977) assert that teachers are more willing to adopt innovative practices if they believe that their school communities value such efforts. This is not to say that teachers in more isolated school settings will not enact classroom changes, but it does mean that such changes are more likely to develop and to be sustained in schools where the norms encourage them.

Organizational Structures

Changing school norms and cultures is difficult work (Fullan & Stiegelbauer, 1991). Easier is changing school structures (Tyack & Cuban, 1995). American schools have provided fertile ground for new arrangements of teachers, students, and content. From basic skills to Advanced Placement courses, from ungraded to graded classrooms, and from segregated to desegregated schools, experimenting with institutional structures has been steady work (Elmore & McLaughlin, 1988).

James Ladwig and Bruce King (1992) analyze the changes made in the social studies departments of four high schools and the impact of those changes on students' higher order thinking. At Shaw High School, the structural changes center on teaming social studies and English teachers and providing them with a common planning time for one of two already established history courses. Teaching teams and common planning times are also part of the restructuring at Nelson High School, as is the creation of a block schedule. Creating integrated humanities (English and history) courses and a more systematic schedule of teacher professional development are the major differences at Carter High School, where teams of teachers teach the new courses on a block schedule. Finally, at Williams High, the social studies department divides itself into grade-level teams who take responsibility for designing appropriate courses and assessments for students in each grade. Teachers on each grade-level team are given common planning time and allowed to create different kinds of courses based on flexible modular schedule.

Ladwig and King (1992) find that the higher order thinking opportunities students have vary considerably by the school structure adopted, with the Williams plan offering the most possibilities. The authors see as problematic, however, the conclusion that organizational structures (and restructuring) necessarily contribute to more ambitious classroom practices. Although Williams outscores the other three schools, it does not score as high as some traditionally structured schools. In fact, none of the generally believed structural changes such as common planning time or team teaching is positively correlated with more advanced thinking opportunities across all four restructured schools. In short, the structures around teachers many change, but their teaching may not.

Where Ladwig and King did find powerful learning opportunities, it was programmatic rather than organizational changes that mattered. Programmatic efforts include curriculum development that expressly promotes more ambitious teaching and learning and efforts to build a department consensus around such practices. Ladwig and King conclude that theirs is not an argument against restructuring so much as it is an argument for more attention to curriculum and pedagogy.

In contrast to Ladwig and King (1992), Linda McNeil (2000) argues that organizational structures can support powerful teaching and learning. McNeil asserts that magnet schools, especially ones that free teachers from the morass of district and state controls, can foster and sustain creative teachers. The educational mission at Pathfinder, one of the schools McNeil profiles, presumes that all children are gifted and talented in one way or another and so deserve the most ambitious opportunities to learn that teachers can muster. To effect that mission, teachers and students are trusted to seek out and examine important questions and to do so in rigorous and thorough fashion. Embodying these ideas is Ms. McDonnell, a history teacher, who "conveyed absolute confidence that her students could learn and conducted class accordingly" (p. 73). Freed from a stultifying list of curricular facts, teachers like McDonnell pursue ideas and instructional strategies rarely found in more conventional classrooms. Similar stories are told by other participants in fundamental school restructuring (see, for example, Meier, 1996).

Organizational Influences on George Blair and Linda Strait

Just as George Blair and Linda Strait share a number of personal characteristics, so too do they share a work space. Westwood High, designed as an open-space school, forces elements of community on its teachers. The few solid walls mean that teachers can hear and see into their peers' classrooms. The department "office," located in the middle of the classroom wing, is bounded by movable partitions. Within the office space, student desks are arranged in a large, open rectangle, one desk per teacher. Along the partitioned walls is a full-sized desk for each teacher. Most teachers work at the student desks where conversation is continuous.

The conversation consists mostly of social talk—weekend and vacation plans, good-natured jabs at one another, stories about family members, off-the-cuff reviews of television shows, movies, and sports events. Far less common is conversation about teaching and learning. Perhaps because they might overhear, students are discussed in quiet side conversations. Grading is sometimes addressed in the whole group, as is where a teacher is in the curriculum. But teaching practices, ideas about students as learners, and curriculum goals are rarely if ever mentioned. The formal department meetings I observed typically focused on logistical concerns—who would proctor which Regents exams, where extra copies of textbooks were located, which forms had to be completed by what dates.

The departmental community to which George Blair and Linda Strait belong is largely a social one. Members seem to like one another, and arguments almost never surface. These are people who get along by going along. And one part of going along is not talking about their craft. Blair and Strait both talked expansively to me about their teaching, their students, their content, but they do not have these conversations with one another. Close in physical proximity, Blair, Strait, and their colleagues are isolated professionally.

As a result of this context, neither teaching colleagues nor administrators play any direct role in how Blair and Strait construct their civil rights units. Department norms and structures play more subtle roles, with the autonomy that comes from professional isolation probably the biggest result. Strait reports a hassle over grading with her previous principal, but neither she nor Blair feels particularly constrained by the people and context in which they teach.

The exception is their students. Of the many potential organizational influences on Blair and Strait, it is their students who seem to wield the most impact. And yet, although there are no discernible differences among the students who sit in each teacher's class, how their influence plays out is vastly different.

The Influence of Students on George Blair's Practice

Like most teachers, George Blair expects his students will learn how to read and write, to endure college lectures, to become good human beings, and to do well on the Regents test. Blair believes his subject-matter knowledge and teaching approach are more than adequate to help students achieve these goals. How and why he constructs his practice as he does, however, owe much to his sense of the students in front of him.

Put simply, George Blair does not believe his students know very much. Despite their 2 years of U.S. history in seventh and eighth grade, he claims they come to him ill-prepared:

> Seventh and eighth they get this two-year program. They're 12 years old. I mean they don't know up from down anyway. When they come here they don't have the faintest idea.... You want a kid to remember a couple of things from seventh and eighth grade to eleventh grade? You've got to be kidding me. They went through three years of puberty. Do you know what they're thinking about? They're not thinking about the Wilmot Proviso. And to say there's carryover, that's absolutely asinine.

Ill-informed, Blair's students are also ill-equipped to think on their own:

> I'd say I don't think the kid can make the generalization from this time to an historical event or general ideas of life or the flow of society or the flow of history, or the flow of psychology, the flow of people, the flow of culture.

Blair's perceptions of his students' deficiencies play out in two features of his instructional practice: storytelling and note giving. He constructs narratives for each of the units he teaches because he believes students cannot see the big picture of the subject matter at hand. If they are to ever understand the story of the civil rights era, it will be because he has given them one to remember. He provides chapter notes on the overhead because he senses that students cannot synthesize the important details from their textbook and because these notes will help students recall the story grammar—the actors, settings, plot lines, and outcomes—of each narrative. "I want them to pick up the major points that are in the book," he said, "[but] I don't think they have the historical background to understand what the important points are in the chapter and what is not important, so the notes I hope point out what I think the important points are in the chapter." Believing them to be unable to "pick up the major points" or to craft these points into a coherent narrative, Blair does this work and then offers his students the benefits of his labor.

George Blair appears to have the subject-matter knowledge to help his students develop a deep understanding of history. His note giving and storytelling, however, suggest he holds a thin view of his students as learners.

As he constructs his pedagogy, then, Blair mixes a rich sense of people, actions, and events with the notion that his students will not understand these things unless they are spoon-fed.

The Influence of Students on Linda Strait's Practice

Linda Strait sees the students who come to her class very differently than does her colleague. And the way she perceives those differences plays out both in her general practice as well as her civil rights unit.

Strait constructs a range of activities and assessments for each unit, in large part because she believes all students can learn. Not all students learn the same way, however, as different learning experiences will engage different students. "I am of the belief that all students can learn," she said, "just in different ways, and different styles." Although simply put, this sense of students ripples throughout Strait's teaching practice, most notably in the range of classroom activities that she designs for each unit. Whether for Reconstruction, immigration, or World War I, Strait constructs diverse in and out of school learning tasks.

Experiences with students, however, significantly impact the way Linda Strait reconstructed this year's civil rights unit, in terms of both activities and ideas. Strait believes her students need to deal with tough issues like race, and she would like to take this thorny issue on head first. Two years ago she used a series of activities garnered during a prejudice reduction workshop to develop a unit that focused exclusively on African Americans. The results, she reports, were disastrous:

> The students were resistant to hearing about it [racism.... They said that I was creating the problem by bringing it up, and we don't need to be doing stuff like this. [They said] I make it worse when I'd bring out the stuff, and make people hateful of each other, and they said, "You're causing the problem."

Strait said she felt "so bad" that she put the activities away. Although this experience chilled her, she was not dissuaded from dealing with race. Acknowledging that her head-on approach "seems to offend too many people" and encourages them to become "resistant," Strait decided to take a different approach in her U.S. history class this year.

That different approach is to blend the experiences of African Americans with those of other minority groups. The result is a unit where students explore the African American push for equal rights in the context of similar efforts by other nonmajority groups. Strait deals with racial issues in other units throughout the school year. Her principal vehicle, however, is the civil rights unit.

Strait feels conflicted about her decision. On the one hand, she is pleased with the way the unit played out. She dealt with many of the issues she wanted to, and her students seemed to embrace rather than resist her efforts. Her new unit, she asserts, "softens the approach to [racism]." Although many teachers would be satisfied with this compromise, Strait is not. "I want to go right at it full force," she said, "It's not my nature to just ease into it like that. And so it's restraining on me." Unsure that she can ever meet both her needs and her students', Strait concludes, "I guess there has to be a balance."

The Influence of Organizational Factors on Teachers' Decision Making

Aspects of this discussion of organizational influences seem surprising. One surprise involves those individuals and groups not mentioned as influential. For example, school board members, teachers' union officials, and figures outside the education system (e.g., politicians) go unmentioned. Although principals cite these groups as influential (National Center for Education Statistics, 1995), teachers do not. Other groups, like teaching colleagues, are far less mentioned than one might expect. Although Lortie (1975) and others report colleagues as a common influence, colleagues appear to matter little in history teachers' decision making. Lortie was right on another score, however: The egg-crate organization of schooling, where each teacher and her students are effectively sealed off, remains largely intact. Teachers' interactions are primarily with their students; few teachers have much regular, substantive interaction with adults.

Less surprising is how strongly students figure into teachers' decisions. Although some observers might argue that teachers should simply plan the best lessons they can and then expect students to accommodate, the examples given here suggest otherwise. The views that teachers like George Blair and Linda Strait hold of their students impact their instruction in both general and particular ways.

Like personal influences, organizational factors are many and complex. Teachers' practices are sensitive to the people they encounter and to the norms and structures that characterize the contexts in which they teach. Also common is the sense that organizational factors can be seen as opportunities and constraints. With organizational influences, however, comes an important distinction: Teachers may interpret and act upon the same influence in very different ways. Thus, depending on the teacher, any factor may be perceived as an opportunity or as a constraint.

A case in point is the influence of students. Recall the discrepancy in the views expressed by teachers on the capability of low-achieving students to do critical thinking (Onosko, 1991). Although one teacher views his students as incapable of sustained thinking ("I think it is unrealistic for anyone to expect consistent higher order thinking from these students"), another claims the opposite ("When students are actively pursing whole, meaningful tasks, they will naturally use all the skills in Bloom's taxonomy"). Like Linda Strait and George Blair, these two teachers teach the same students, and yet they perceive them in entirely different ways.

Further complicating our understanding of influences is the ongoing development of Linda Strait's civil rights unit. On the one hand, she views her students' collective insensitivities toward racism as a constraint on her preference to "go right at it full force." At the same time, she likes many of the activities she developed for the new, "balanced" unit. In this context, then, Strait's students are both opportunity and constraint.

Linda Strait's civil rights unit exemplifies one last point about influences: They can change over time. The influence of her students seems to have had three incarnations, each of which compelled different actions. First, thinking her students were simply unaware of the enduring legacy of racist thought and action, Strait tackled the issue head on through the experiences of African Americans. Second, thinking her students unappreciative of her initial classroom efforts, she scrapped her original unit. Then, thinking that they need to see African American experiences with racism in a broader context, she developed a unit reflecting a more inclusive approach. Influences, then, can be perceived as weak or strong, and as opportunity or constraint. They can also be perceived as mutable, changing in both direction and impact over time.

POLICY INFLUENCES ON TEACHERS' DECISIONS

The power of personal and organizational factors would seem to define the field of influence on teachers' classroom decisions. With the rise of standards-based curricula and high-stakes testing, however, policy influences also must be considered.

Several observers speak to the general nature of policy as an influence (or not) on teachers' instructional decisions (Cuban, 1990; Firestone, Mayrowetz, & Fairman, 1998; McLaughlin 1990). Others (Cohen & Spillane, 1992; Porter, Floden, Freeman, Schmidt, & Schwille, 1988; Spillane, 1993) collapse several policy influences under the heading of "instructional guidance systems." Still others note the influence of specific policy factors such as curriculum frameworks (Grant, 1997a, 1997b; Jennings, 1996; Porter, 1989), textbooks (Cohen & Ball, 1990; Stake & Easley, 1978), and tests (Corbett & Wilson, 1991; Firestone et al., 1998).

The research on history teachers generally follows the range of factors just mentioned. In particular, researchers have looked at the role of textbooks, curriculum, and tests. Because I give sustained attention to the impact of testing in chapter 6, I focus here on the impact of textbooks and curriculum standards.

The Influence of Textbooks on Teachers' Practices

Strong is the influence of textbooks on teachers' decisions, or so many believe (Armento, 1986; Garcia, Powell, & Sanchez, 1991; Morrissett, Hawke,

& Superka, 1980; Sewall, 1988). A distinction rarely made, however, is between use and influence. To be sure, textbooks are widely used in classrooms, but so are pencils. What if any *influence* textbooks have over
teachers' decisions is not well understood.

Textbook analyses pervade the research literature (Wade, 1993), and it
will surprise no one to learn that reviewers deride them as "biased, superficial, or poorly written" (p. 233). Some analysts hint that students internal-
ize the messages textbooks broadcast (e.g., Anyon, 1979; Commeyras &
Alvermann, 1994; Tyson-Bernstein, 1988). Other researchers question this
assumption, however. Tony Sanchez (1997) studies the influence of textbook coverage on White students' knowledge and attitudes toward African Americans. In an experiment, White students exposed to a more
thoughtful and thorough treatment of African American experiences show
no significant knowledge or attitude gains over their peers who receive
more limited coverage. Textbooks may routinely frustrate and bore students (Beck et al., 1991; Paxton, 1997), but they do not necessarily change
what students know and believe.

If textbooks' influence on students is more potential than real, so too is
that influence on teachers. Part of the evidence for this claim comes
from studies that suggest teachers use textbooks neither as much nor
as exclusively as some would maintain. Harriet Tyson-Bernstein (1988)
claims that textbooks are "the de facto curriculum of the public
schools, as well as the de facto mechanism for controlling teachers" (p.
11). Tyson-Bernstein's confident assertion, however, is not borne out in
the research literature. In his close study of nine teachers, Romanowski
(1996) observes that texts typically fill the role of "supplemental
source," providing background and classroom activities to the lectures
and discussions teachers organize. Teachers use the chapter organization of their textbook to frame the course of study, but they "considered
moving beyond the textbook and utilizing additional sources to be an
important aspect of good teaching" (p. 301). As one teacher notes: "I
think the main thing about the textbook is that I use them where they
can be used, but, for gosh sakes, you have to do more than that. You've
got to use more than the textbook" (p. 300).

Evidence that teachers push beyond textbook teaching is plentiful
(Grant, 1996; Gudmundsdottir, 1990; Rossi, 1995; Rossi & Pace, 1998;
Wineburg & Wilson, 1991). McNeil (1988) points out, however, that back-
ing off the use of textbooks may not mean abandoning tight control over
course content. Teachers, McNeil notes, stress the "efficiency of presentation" by "maintaining tight control over course content, eliminating almost
all reading assignments or written work" (p. 166). The instruction that results is not textbook bound, but neither is it the kind of ambitious instruction that reformers desire.

As bad as they are, textbooks seem less like a powerful influence than a
prosaic fixture of school classrooms. Evidence of their use is not evidence
of their impact. Teachers use textbooks as tools to enable (or not) their in-

struction. The direction their instruction takes, however, seems to be minimally affected by the texts teachers use.[2]

The Influence of Curriculum Standards

Since *A Nation at Risk* (National Commission on Excellence in Education, 1983), policymakers have expressed faith in new curriculum standards. Picking up on that hope, advocates of systemic reform (e.g., Fuhrman, 1993a; Smith & O'Day, 1991) urge state-level action on curriculum frameworks as a key component of improving teachers' instruction.[3] These curriculum frameworks, Smith and O'Day (1991) argue are the "basic drivers" of and "first step" toward real instructional change (p. 247). If new curriculum standards induce changes in classrooms, then it makes sense to think about curriculum as an influence on teachers' practices.

The zeal behind new curriculum standards is hard to understand, however, given the research literature. That literature, both in general (e.g., Bowe, Ball, & Gold, 1992; Grant, 1998; Hertert, 1996; Lusi, 1997; Porter, 1989) and specific to history teaching (e.g., Grant, 1997b, 2000; Thornton, 1988; Wineburg & Wilson, 1991), offers little support for curriculum guidelines as a powerful influence on teachers' classroom decisions.

Curriculum standards or guidelines, especially for history courses, typically prescribe a list of content to teach. In history, that means lists of people, places, events, documents, and the like arranged in chronological order, such as the New York state U.S. History and Geography curriculum (New York State Education Department, 1999), or by theme, such as the National Council for the Social Studies (1994) publication *Expectations of Excellence*. Guidelines may be offered by state departments of education or professional organizations, but they can also be developed by nationally sponsored groups such as the National Center for History in the Schools (1996) or by district or even school-level committees. In any case, curriculum standards are just that—descriptions of the content to be taught. Instruction is rarely mentioned, and never discussed in detail (Grant, 1995b). For example, the authors of the Bradley Commission curriculum guidelines justify their inattention to instruction this way: "Because our resources and time were too limited to become heavily involved in pedagogical techniques or improved teacher training, the Bradley Commission concentrated on curriculum" (Bradley Commission, 1989, p. 19). Although it is difficult to imagine good pedagogy without good instruction,

---

[2]Although he did not study teachers' responses, Peter Dow's (1991) fine chronicle of the development of the *Man: A Course of Study* project offers insights into the problematic nature of trying to change teachers' practices through textbooks.

[3]Systemic reform is the notion that schooling problems must be attacked at the system, rather than at the classroom, level. In that vein, systemic reformers support state-level efforts that offer new, and closely aligned, curriculum guidelines, new testing programs, and the like (Fuhrman, 1993; O'Day & Smith, 1991).

curriculum reformers seem content to focus on *what* rather than *how* teachers ought to teach.

But maybe it does not matter, for teachers report that they give little attention to curriculum proposals anyway. Susan Stodolsky and Pam Grossman (1995) find that not only do social studies teachers feel they have "almost total control over the teaching techniques they use in their own classrooms" (p. 237), but they also believe they have "rather high degrees of curricular control and autonomy" (p. 240). The teachers in Elizabeth Sturtevant's (1996) study "verified that they were not evaluated on whether the curriculum guide was followed specifically; in fact, both indicated that they rarely looked at it" (p. 237).

These findings are consistent with those my colleagues and I have come to in our study of New York global history teachers (Grant et al., 2001; Grant, Derme-Insima, Gradwell et al., 2002; Grant, Gradwell, Lauricella et al., 2002). The principal change in the state global history curriculum was a shift from a cultural and regional study of the world to a chronological, history-based study. Few teachers are happy with this change, but virtually all have made the shift. The more we inquired, however, the less dramatic the change seems to be. Rather than influence teachers to make radical shifts in their content decisions, most teachers say that the new curriculum represents only a change in emphasis. As an experienced teacher notes, "It's [the new global curriculum] probably more like rather than different from the previous approach in many ways" (Grant et al., 2001, p. 113).

I return to the issue of new curriculum standards in chapter 8. For now, however, I want to emphasize the point that curriculum, in whatever form and from whatever source, seems to be a relatively weak influence on teachers' practices. Teachers in states like New York that have a long history of state-level curriculum documents do pay attention to those documents, especially when a new policy is announced. But doing something differently does not necessarily mean that a real change has occurred. So the situation can develop where the content that teachers teach is arranged differently due to a curricular shift, but the impact of the shift is negligible.

Policy Influences on George Blair and Linda Strait

New York state education leaders have long taken an active role in developing curriculum and tests, but not in choosing textbooks. Linda Strait and George Blair have a district-level U.S. history curriculum, but it mirrors that of the state in that it represents a straightforward chronology of key people, places, and events. When they talk about the "curriculum," it is the state policy to which they refer. Similarly, there are district-level tests, but it is only the Regents exam that matters: At the time of this study, students earned a Regents diploma or a local diploma depending on which test, the Regents exam or the Regents Competency Test, they passed. Unlike other states such as Texas and California, state-level policymakers do not choose the textbooks New York teachers use. In some schools, textbook decisions are made by departments, teams of appointed teachers, or school and district administrators. At Westwood, textbook decisions are left to each teacher. Thus, Blair and Strait solicit samples and choose among them the textbooks they use.

Having discussed the impact of the state Regents test on George Blair's and Linda Strait's teaching in chapter 5, I turn here to the influence of textbooks and the state curriculum. Both considerations figure into their respective practices, but in seemingly minor ways.

The Influence of Textbooks and Curriculum on George Blair's Practice

Just as the state test is one of the factors George Blair considers, so too are the state curriculum and his chosen textbook.

Both influences, textbook and state curriculum, figure into Blair's organization and presentation of U.S. history. The state curriculum serves as a backdrop to his overall course planning. The textbook serves both as a specific outline for his course and as the source of his test questions and overhead notes of each chapter.

Blair believes that the state has a legitimate and important role in developing curriculum content. But he expresses an important caveat: It is other teachers who need this direction, not him:

> I would like to see a little more direction from the State [for other teachers]....
> There are other people who don't [know how to teach] when there are no controls. I've seen it. I saw it at the middle school when we were talking about exploratory kinds of education in the '70s and the '80s, and I watched people go in helter-skelter directions. And everybody thinks they're doing the right thing, and I find it very difficult to be critical, but I sure as hell can say, well maybe these people need some herding, you know they've gotta get direction. They gotta be, not in lock step, but there's gotta be direction.

Having seen colleagues fail to provide a coherent course of study, Blair believes state policymakers should assert a firmer hand in directing the U.S. history curriculum. Blair's yearly course of study generally follows the state prescription, but where his and the state's views deviate, as in the example of the Federal period, Blair does not hesitate to assert his authority. Of the state curriculum, he notes, "I don't use much of it to be very candid with you. I can teach whatever I want to. There is no one who watches." He adds, "I have been teaching U.S. History for years on and off, and the changes that have come don't really affect me that much. And to be very candid, I haven't seen anything that I can't sidestep yet." So although Blair does not challenge directly the state's presumption of curricular authority, he has no problem doing so in practice.

Blair's textbook is a more regular presence in his teaching. Unlike Linda Strait, who organizes her teaching units in big topical chunks, Blair's units follow the textbook's chapter organization. He does not cover every chapter, nor does he give equal attention to each, but he translates the chronological framework of the book into the yearly course plan he develops. More directly, Blair pulls his overhead notes and his test questions from the textbook pages:

> When I put the test together, it comes out of the book, it comes out of the notes. And there will be things in the book that I have not covered, but I will put them in the test to make sure they're reading the book, but I'm just trying to point out the high points of the chapter.

Although visible, the presence of a textbook guarantees no particular influence, for Blair exercises considerable control over which of the authors' points make it into his notes and test questions. His selections represent "the things that I think are important, that you should know." The text provides the fodder from which he draws, but Blair sorts that fodder into groupings that fit his needs.

The state history curriculum and the textbook he uses both figure into George Blair's instruction, but neither seems to exert a directional influence on the decisions he makes. This is not to say that they are unimportant, but rather that their importance may be tempered by the vision of history that Blair holds.

The Influence of Textbooks and Curriculum on Linda Strait's Practice

The state curriculum and her textbook play a slightly different role in Linda Strait's teaching. But as in her colleague's classroom, neither influence seems especially strong.

As a new teacher, Strait checked the state curriculum fairly often. Now in her fifth year, she does so less frequently and typically only when she is redesigning a unit. She finds the document generally unhelpful, however, as the breadth of content described means that ideas are weakly developed. "The curriculum is just too broad," she observes, "There's just too much there." Knowing that she cannot teach the entire curriculum well, Strait feels forced to make choices about what content to include and how much emphasis to give it. And when she must decide, her personal views about the content play out. Asked how she constructed a unit on Native Americans, Strait describes the interplay between the state curriculum and her own sense of the material:

> I think my own whims and personal feelings decide that. One of the things, I believe, that's in the New York State syllabus is for them to be more understanding and empathetic with different groups other than their own, and to

> respect other cultures. It seems like whenever something like that falls into place, I naturally move toward that and I enjoy it. So I think a lot of my own personal feelings come into play as to what I emphasize and what I don't.

In this example, Strait uses the state curriculum to support her predilection toward teaching about different groups. The language of understanding and empathy in the curriculum does not induce her instructional decisions, but it does support them.

Teaching about different groups also underlies Strait's choice of textbooks. "That's why I thought that textbook was the ideal one," she said, "'Cause I wanted everything that I taught to touch on ... all of the different people that are in the United States today." She is no longer satisfied with her choice: It fails to go into the depth that she thought it did. So she uses it sporadically, both for background information and, at times, for the end-of-chapter questions. What she does not do, however, is follow the textbook mindlessly. In the case of the civil rights unit, she selects sections of multiple chapters to serve her teaching goals:

> I skip all over the place, and I eliminate some chapters also.... And when I did the civil rights [unit], I was taking it way—because—well, they did it sort of in chronological order, and I had to go back, because I did it conceptually. So I really didn't follow that book at all.

Underscoring the minimal influence of the textbook on Strait's teaching are the many other resources she uses to build the conceptual matter of her units. Documentaries, magazine articles, and the like are more than supplements to the textbook readings; they provide key content from which Strait expects her students to draw in their thinking and writing.

Although somewhat different in effect, curriculum and textbooks influence Linda Strait's decision making as minimally as they do George Blair's. These factors are not irrelevant, but neither do they strongly and decisively impact either teacher's practice.

The Influence of Policy Factors on Teachers' Decision Making

In some ways, I stole my own thunder by discussing the role of testing in chapter 6. That feature of the educational system is now so pervasive as to seemingly redefine the nature of schooling and the influences on teachers' decision making. And yet, the research evidence mitigates that claim: Testing may be a more powerful influence than other policy factors such as textbooks and curriculum guides, but to most teachers tests are just one more influence on their practice (Cimbricz, 2002; Firestone et al., 1998).

Again, there are some surprises in the research on policy influences. The most salient is that textbooks, curriculum standards, and tests are not as powerful as many observers believe (e.g., Fuhrman, 1993; Smith & O'Day,

1991). These factors crop up in teachers' talk and in their classrooms, but muted is their importance in directing teachers' decision making.

Other patterns carry over from the earlier reviews of personal and organizational influences. First, teachers face multiple policy influences rather than a single one. Second, their perceptions of those influences can vary, sometimes significantly, from one teacher to another. Third, teachers' perceptions of policy factors can change over time.

There is one more point to be made about influences in this section: Influences push teachers in no obvious directions, and in that sense, they may be more potential than predictable. The cases of George Blair and Linda Strait are instructive here, for in their responses to textbooks, tests, and curriculum, we see a range of behaviors, a number of which could be interpreted as out of character. For example, we might have predicted that Strait, as a relatively new teacher, would follow the state curriculum meticulously and that Blair, as a relatively traditional teacher, would use the textbook as his bible. Moreover, the units that each teacher constructed might lead us to predict that Blair would give substantially more attention to the state Regents exam than Strait would. And yet, closer examination shows that none of these seemingly safe predictions bears out. Textbooks, tests, and curriculum have the potential to influence teachers' instruction, but they offer no guarantees that they will matter much at all.

THE INTERACTION OF INFLUENCES

Mapping the array of personal, organizational, and policy influences is illuminating. Teachers may act as "gatekeepers" of the teaching and learning students experience (Thornton, 1991), but they do so in complex contexts (Cornbleth, 1989, 2002). Teachers make hundreds of decisions every day, and many of those choices reflect their individuality. Yet there are constraints: Teachers "are not free to choose methods, content, or classroom organization for psychological, social, or personal reasons alone" (Buchmann, 1986, p. 531). Their views of subject matter, the colleagues and students they work with, the textbooks and curriculum frameworks they use, these and other factors influence teachers in myriad ways. But they do not do so in a singular, insulated fashion (Adler, 1984; Thornton, 1988). Instead, as we see throughout the examples given earlier, influences interact.

Consider some brief examples. Romanowski's (1996) story of how he modified his antinuclear beliefs and classroom decisions based on the reaction of his students and their parents demonstrates how personal and organizational factors can interact. We see a similar interaction in Linda Strait's construction and reconstruction of her civil rights unit; her ideas and her students' ideas work back and forth until the unit takes on a "balanced" look. Examples of how organizational and policy factors interact can be seen in the teacher Evans (1990) profiles who uses the textbook "insisted" on by his principal and, conversely, in the autonomy afforded George Blair and Linda Strait in their decisions around which textbooks they will use and how.

In other cases, we see all three categories of influence at play. A quick illustration can be seen in Martha Reese's case (VanSledright, 1996a). Recall that Reese explains her use of textbooks this way:

> I hope that they are using [the textbook] as a source of information, not necessarily interpretation.... In fact, I usually give them prefabricated questions based exactly on the textbook because that's the purpose of the exercise—[basic] reading comprehension. The book becomes the authority because the questions are based on the book. (p. 268)

I first used Reese's words to illustrate the importance of her view of history. In that context, I highlighted the distinction she makes between facts and interpretation, a key element of one's sense of history. Given the ensuing discussion, however, we can now see this quote as an instance where personal, organizational, and policy factors interact. In short, her view of the differences between historical fact and interpretation (personal) impacts the kind of texts she chooses (policy) and the ways in which she uses those texts. Key to that interaction, however, is Reese's implied view of students (organizational): Students need to see facts and interpretations as separate, and they can do so if she chooses resources that help make this distinction clear. She chooses the textbook to present students with the facts; she chooses other sources, such as the videotape explaining the different Revolutionary perspectives of the colonists and the British, to demonstrate differing interpretations.

In Martha Reese's case, different influences work in agreeable combinations: Her views of history cohere with the views she holds of students and with her use of classroom resources. Because influences are multiple, however, less agreeable interactions are also possible. For as currents of influence interact, cross-currents can develop, alternatively pushing and pulling teachers in multiple and conflicting directions.

A good example of this phenomena is Paula, the Global History teacher described in chapter 6. Consider these four quotes:

> I think the curriculum should have gone in a very different direction, and maybe even if they wanted to change it from the more social science approach I would have liked to have seen it go to some kind of thematic approach where history, great themes of history, and teachers would be free to pick out examples of those themes and teach those themes, not necessarily in chronological order.... That seems to me more how history really is written, how historians write, and it seems more meaningful to me certainly and, I think, to kids as well.

> I just feel this sense of breathlessly running through a curriculum, never having an opportunity to relax enough to do that, to bring the materials [primary source documents] in and work with kids, take the time to work with kids through those materials. Because clearly it would take lots of time, and if I've

got to get through World War II in two weeks, you know, I just don't know how to, how I could do that at this point.

I think when I'm doing it [using documents] for the way I'd like to do it, I have an idea of the response I'm looking for, but if [the students] come up with something that is different from what I was expecting but it makes sense and they can back up with some reasoning, then that's acceptable. But if I were using it for the state test-taking skill thing, then there would be one response, and if they didn't get that, then it would be wrong.

I feel a pressure to drill certain kids on methods of passing a test.

Read with the idea of multiple influences in mind, the currents of personal, organizational, and policy influences jump out. Paula's personal view of history runs toward the notion of great themes that cut across chronological eras. Some might disagree with her broad claim that this is "how historians write," but one senses that she sees history as less about historical particulars than about historical patterns and issues. Paula's view of history runs counter to the direction she believes is expressed in the state curriculum and testing policies. Those documents promote a sense of history bound up in surface-level detail. That detail makes curriculum and test question writing easier, but it undermines the power of historical analysis. The conflict between Paula's personal views and those she sees in the state policies is mediated by yet a third influence: her sense of what her students bring to class. Paula sees the potential her students hold to understand multiple perspectives and to make real and important sense of history, especially through the use of primary source documents.

If the distinct personal, organizational, and policy currents are visible, so too are the cross-currents: As Paula's sense of her students figures into the mix of her personal views of history and of the new state curriculum and test, trouble brews. Each set of influences is strong, but the directions in which they push conflict. She resolves this conflict, because she has to, but the results—drilling students on test questions, rushing through important events, and searching for documents that support her aims and the state's—frustrate her. The tension she feels, caught between these competing influences, is palpable:

Generally I think it's forced me to teach history in a way that I'm philosophically at odds with, in a way that I don't think kids are going to remember or care about, and I feel obligated to do that because of this test at the end.

Influences need not always collide, but with so many in circulation in and around teachers' classrooms, the potential is always there.

IMPLICATIONS

The notion that teachers' decisions reflect currents and cross-currents of influence fits with much of what we know about schools and classrooms and the people who teach and learn within them. Human beings are complex characters, so understanding what drives them is messy. Some factors seem relatively easy to discern, but most are complicated largely because it is rare for a single influence to dominate. Most often, multiple influences are evident, and although some times those influences cohere, they can just as often conflict.

This analysis points to at least three interrelated implications. One concerns the relationship between influence and authority. A second involves the role of teachers as gatekeepers. The last implication asks about the possibilities for ambitious teaching.

One implication of an interactional view of influences highlights the relationship between influence and authority. An interactional perspective helps describe and explain teachers' instructional decisions, but no theory explains all behavior. Among the attendant uncertainties is how the constructs of influence and authority are related. In this chapter, I describe a range of personal, organizational, and policy factors, and through examples, I discuss the degree of influence or authority each carries. This analysis becomes complicated, however, because factors that seem authoritative in one situation or to one teacher seem less so in other cases. Instead of applying uniformly and consistently, influences are fluid, situational, and contingent, so the authority of any one influence is sensitive to context and time and the other influences at hand. What counts as an influence and what weight an influence carries are meaningless in the abstract. Instead, what teachers pay attention to (i.e., what counts as an influence) and the significance they assign it (i.e., what is authoritative) are contextualized decisions that reflect a complex interpretation of individual and social currents. The result: The hope for precise definitions, calculations, and predictions of the factors that influence teachers is naive.

If the relationship between influence and authority is murky, so too is the teacher's role in all this. No single view seems satisfactory. Those who would situate all authority in the power structures of schools misunderstand the part that teachers' knowledge, beliefs, and experiences play in the decisions they make. Those who hold the reverse view are just as short-sighted: Teachers' personal preferences are bounded by the contexts in which they work. Teachers help shape those contexts, but they do not control them. A more useful view is the one Thornton (1991) offers in his conception of teachers as curricular and instructional gatekeepers. That view provides the needed space to see the external (organizational and policy) and internal (personal) influences on teachers in the same field of vision. Teachers ultimately make most of the classroom decisions that affect their students. Those decisions reflect a good measure of each teacher's knowledge, beliefs, and experiences, so understanding, for example, a teacher's view of history is likely to tell us something significant about the instructional decisions he or she makes. But not everything. For gatekeeping implies that influences reside on both sides of the gate. If some of those influences are personal, others reflect the organizational and policy contexts in which the teacher operates. When the influences that emerge from those contexts cohere, then the job of gatekeeper is relatively easy. Influences, like air currents, can clash, however. It is in those situations that the role of gatekeeping takes on a special importance.

And in the U.S. system of schooling, conflicts are inevitable, especially when teachers choose to teach ambitiously. Some features of American education represent the best in democratic and progressive intentions; the drive to ensure equal access to public education is but one. Those features stand in some contrast, however, to what many see as a generally conservative tone (Apple, 1979; Giroux, 1981). That tone manifests in numerous ways: standardized curriculum and standardized tests, preference given to compliant students and compliant teachers, mediocre teaching and mediocre learning. Teachers who challenge this status quo, whether by pressing union issues, questioning administrative dictates, or teaching in ambitious ways, can expect criticism from some quarters, including their own colleagues. But because schools are complex contexts and because there is an enduring rhetoric around schools as places for building strong minds and active citizens, teachers who push the boundaries can find room for and encouragement of their efforts. Thus, constraints and opportunities, currents and cross-currents, can surface across the school day.

Teachers who choose to teach conservatively face an easier path than those who choose to push hard themselves and their students. With even a modest effort, the former can expect little challenge or resistance or reward. Ambitious teachers can expect all three.

8

Promoting Ambitious Teaching and Learning

Although broad agreement exists on the need to improve teaching and learning, how to make that happen is a complex question. High on most reformers' lists are new curriculum, improved assessments, restructured schools, and expanded teacher professional development. In some ways, the jury is still out on each of these possibilities: Positive features of each can be detected, but none has fulfilled its promise. Ambitious teaching and learning seem both within our collective grasp and just out of our reach.

The notion of "ambitious" teaching and learning has been percolating throughout the preceding chapters. I have used a number of synonyms for this adjective—good, powerful, skilled, thoughtful—but have left it undefined until now because I wanted its several facets to emerge through the cases of George Blair and Linda Strait and my review of the relevant research literatures. With this background, and before I turn to a discussion of those reforms intended to promote change, I now define this key construct. At heart, ambitious teaching and learning lies within the relationships David Hawkins (1974) defines as I (teacher), thou (learners), and it (subject matter) and Lee Shulman (1987) summarizes as pedagogical content knowledge. In short, ambitious teaching and learning occur when smart teachers, curious students, and powerful ideas come together.

I begin this chapter by reviewing the possibilities for and problems of the major reforms advocated in curriculum, tests, schooling, and professional development. I argue that although each has useful elements, none is a panacea. I conclude that the only safe bet, the only means to teaching and learning that is real, deep, and lasting, is to invest in good teachers and powerful ideas.

THE PROSPECTS FOR AMBITIOUS TEACHING
AND LEARNING

It seems as if the United States has been in education reform mode forever. Yet the talk about new tests, new school structures and the like is only the latest manifestation of an age-old impulse (Tyack & Cuban, 1995). Reforming education has been "steady work" (Elmore & McLaughlin, 1988) even if the results have not. In the first years of the most recent reform effort, beginning with the *Nation at Risk* report (National Commission on Excellence in Education, 1983), reformers tinkered with existing regulations, increased the number of student graduation credits, and revised the requirements for teacher certification. These efforts may have had some salutary effects (Mirel & Angus, 1994), but they left untouched most elements of teaching and learning. These policies led to "great bookkeeping," but made "little pedagogical sense" (Kirp & Driver, 1995, p. 590).

The wave of reforms that began building in the 1990s honed in on school subject matters. New policies such as the California frameworks in mathematics and language arts, the National Council of Teachers of Mathematics curriculum standards, and the National Center for History in the Schools content standards pitched curriculum reform as the key to more ambitious teaching and learning.

Reflecting the ascendance of constructivist thought, the new curriculum policies challenge the prevailing views that knowledge consists of discrete, sequential, and fixed bits of information; that good teaching is didactic and emphasizes drill, practice, and evaluation; and that learning is a passive process, a reflex of teaching. The new policies promote the view that knowledge is constructed as individuals interact with ideas and one another; that good teaching is guiding or facilitating learning; and that learning is an active construction, where students develop understandings reflecting both new information and the ideas, experiences, and theories they bring with them. In addition, reformers confront the notion that ambitious teaching and learning should be reserved for only the brightest students. Although past reforms alternately aimed low or only at selected students, the new proposals express a promising, if problematic, objective: higher academic standards for all students.[1]

On the heels of curriculum reform have come new tests and new proposals to restructure schools, features of which are known as "systemic reform" (Smith & O'Day, 1991). Arguing that past reforms have resulted in an education system that is "uncoordinated, piecemeal, fragmented, project-centered, and irrational" (Fuhrman, 1993, p. 15), systemic reformers promote the establishment of coherent and coordinated policies begin-

---

[1]The basic-skills reforms of the 1970s pushed academic standards downward, making "minimum competency" the goal. The subject-matter reforms of the 1950s and '60s pushed strong academic goals, but only for the nation's top students.

ning with new curriculum guidelines and developing through new state-level tests and more creative school structures (e.g., site-based school management) (O'Day & Smith, 1993).

More recently, reformers have turned to professional development, *capacity building* in policy talk, as a central feature of any sustainable reform movement (Chrispeels, 1997; Gould, Bornstien, & Florentine, 1997). In this view, teacher learning is seen as fundamental to changing traditional classroom practices (Sykes & Darling-Hammond, 1999).

None of these policy prescriptions are cheap, either in terms of money or time or energy. And given the track record of educational reform, the potential for real results from the current efforts is just that: potential. Excellent classroom teachers exist, and students in those classes benefit far more than do their peers. How to promote opportunities for more teachers and students to reach deeply into ideas is not just a noble goal: If the education system in the United States is to avoid collapsing into a morass of for-profit schools, charter schools, and the like, then Americans are going to have to be convinced that their children are being well served. Curriculum, assessment, structural, and teacher capacity-building efforts are promoted as ways to better serve children. In the sections that follow, I review the research around these efforts, by describing the key features and assumptions of each reform, and commenting on the promise and problems of each as a means of promoting ambitious teaching and learning.

The Prospects for New Curriculum Standards

In chapter 7, the research I reviewed on the influence of curriculum guidelines offers a mixed view: Although history teachers are more attentive to state policies than national reforms, they do not view curriculum standards from any source as a profound influence on their teaching. Such conclusions do not bode well for new standards-setting efforts. But new curricula, if perceived as promoting a robust approach to teaching and learning, could support and extend the practices of teachers currently or willing to try teaching ambitiously.

The Assumptions Behind New Curriculum Standards

Although some states have long been in the curriculum guideline business, most others have joined in only in the last 20 years or so. New York policymakers have produced generations of long and specific lists of social studies content to be taught at each grade level. By contrast, until the 1990s, the entire K–12 social studies curriculum in Maine consisted of a single paragraph.

History teachers in both New York and Maine now have lengthy curriculum standards documents that reflect a number of assumptions (Grant,

1995b). One of those assumptions is that such guidelines offer an image of what is possible. Standards like those proposed by the National Center for History in the Schools push far beyond the minimum competency policies adopted by states like Texas and Florida in the late 1970s. As a result, these documents promote a wider and richer scope of teachable ideas. A related assumption is that new curriculum standards provide both impetus and support for instructional changes. If powerful ideas are represented in new curriculum policies and if those policies bear the state's seal of approval, then teachers should find them compelling. A third assumption is that new curriculum guides might provide a context that encourages teachers to talk and plan together. To the extent that they support ambitious teachers and unsettle their more staid colleagues, new curriculum policies can inspire substantive conversations about teaching, learning, and subject matter.

Curriculum Standards as a Vehicle for Ambitious Teaching and Learning

If any of the preceding assumptions hold true, then the potential rises for new curricula to induce and support ambitious teaching and learning. Unfortunately, the research base on if and how new state and national curriculum efforts impact teachers' practices is thin and not very encouraging.

The *Man: A Course of Study* (MACOS) project developed in the 1960s under the leadership of Jerome Bruner (1966) is one of a handful of innovative curriculum projects offered in the social studies. Bruner and his colleagues created an inquiry-driven program for upper elementary age students that used social science methods to examine world cultures. Despite wide praise from professional organizations, MACOS died a quick death in the classroom. Part of the problem was political: Conservative critics fixated on a couple of units and denounced the entire project as promoting secular humanism and un-American standards (Dow, 1991). Also problematic was how MACOS was introduced to teachers. Bruner operated under the assumption that teachers would automatically and enthusiastically embrace a well-designed curriculum project. He was wrong. Neither the curriculum nor the limited professional development that accompanied it persuaded the bulk of classroom teachers to give up their traditional practices (Shaver, 1979).

The other inquiry-driven curriculum projects offered under the New Social Studies label (Fenton, 1967; Haas, 1977) met a similar fate. For example, Edwin Fenton and his colleagues produced a lovely set of textbook curriculum materials, complete with primary source documents, for high school U.S. history (Fenton et al., 1970). As with MACOS, some teachers embraced these materials; the majority turned their backs.

The failure of these earlier curriculum projects casts doubt on current efforts to promote more ambitious teaching and learning. Recent survey research shows that secondary-level history teachers are significantly less likely to know about reforms in their subject matter than are their math and science colleagues (Littman & Stodolsky, 1998). They may know about curriculum changes at the state level, but they report little if any understanding of or interest in the national debate over teaching and learning history (Cornbleth & Waugh, 1995; Nash, Crabtree, & Dunn, 2000). Moreover, even when history teachers know of reform proposals, they say they make far fewer changes in their teaching than do their school-level peers.

Interview studies of 9th- and 10th-grade New York teachers, (Grant et al., 2001; Grant, Derme-Insinna, Gradwell, et al., 2002; Grant, Gradwell, Lauricella et al., 2002) support these conclusions. The shift from a cultural-focused global studies curriculum to a chronological, global history curriculum presumably was intended to promote a profound shift in teachers' classroom practices. The teachers interviewed are making changes: They are reorganizing their content from a cultural to a chronological approach, such that, for example, instead of teaching a comprehensive unit on the political, economic, and social development of Chinese culture, teachers are now discussing events in Chinese history as they occur within a broad chronological and world history framework. Few teachers think this is a good idea: Interspersing events from around the world into a time-based frame strikes them as too big a conceptual load for their students. Chronology is a key historical perspective, but in these teachers' view, it is too weak for young learners. An experienced teacher points to the problems his students encounter as they try to make sense of disparate world events:

> I think chronological is a tough approach.... Kids are not good with dates, they're not good with making connections. And when you're flip-flopping to different regions of the world, you really don't realize that you are talking about the same time period. (Grant et al., 2001, p. 113)

If few teachers think the shift to chronology is a good idea, even fewer see this as a radical change. Most express the view offered by a veteran teacher who sees the change as one of emphasis rather than substance:

> I don't think it was that big of a deal in the change. I think the curriculum is still basically the same, but you have a different emphasis now. We did more with timelines and trying to get students to understand that during one period, this was happening in Europe, and this was happening in China, so you had to change things around a little bit, but I think that for the most part it's still the same course, but you have a historical perspective more than a regional perspectives.... As far as the curriculum goes, I think it was just a little bit of a change. (Grant et al., 2001, p. 113)

Only one of the 16 teachers we interviewed said that she has made any dramatic changes in the units she teaches. A novice teacher, she sees the new curriculum as bigger and more unwieldy than the old one. With too much to teach and too little time, she chooses to eliminate study of the Aztecs, Incas, and Mayans. Expecting to hear many more stories of hard curriculum choices, we were surprised that this was the one example we encountered.

The new global history curriculum inspires no great changes in teachers' instructional or assessment practices either. A couple of teachers told us that they are using their textbooks and lectures more often. One said that he has cut back on some research projects. Teachers are including more state test-like items on their classroom assessments, but they attribute that behavior to the new state test rather than to the new history curriculum.

New York teachers' classroom decisions reflect some attention to the new state-level content standards. Curriculum guidelines, however, exist more as potentials than as straitjackets. Standards, whether new or old, are open to interpretation and are more suggestive than prescriptive (Grant, 1995b). So despite some protests to the contrary (Cornett, 1990), teachers can and do make important decisions about the content they teach. The bulk of the research casts teachers in an active and transformative curriculum role (e.g., Evans, 1990; Rossi, 1995; Rossi & Pace, 1998; Thornton, 1988). The results can vary from the pedantic (McNeil, 1988) to the powerful (Wineburg & Wilson, 1991), but in any case, the real decisions about classroom curriculum reflect teachers' gatekeeping.

Reasonable people can disagree about whether or not state and national curriculum policies support ambitious teaching and learning, and whether or not teachers should, as a rule, resist them. The research evidence is clear: Curriculum standards, in and of themselves, are a weak influence on teachers' practices. And so, although ambitious teachers might see them as supportive, new curriculum guidelines seem like an unlikely source of robust change in most classrooms.

The Prospects for Revised Tests

State-level policymakers, and the test developers they hire, deserve some credit for taking seriously the critiques of standardized testing. Ten years ago, open-ended items like document-based questions either did not exist on history tests or appeared only in specialized cases such as the Advanced Placement exam. Test development has a long way to go to silence the critics, but the efforts made to date deserve recognition.

The construction of better test questions is only one issue, however. Even more important are the ways in which tests and test scores are used. In chapters 6 and 7, I argue that tests are an uncertain influence on teachers' classroom practices. Because, if anything, tests seem to promote more conservative teaching, slim is the hope that new tests can be a powerful lever for ambitious teaching and learning.

The Assumptions Behind New Tests

The purposes tests serve are several. They include measuring students' abilities and achievements, grouping students for instruction, and evaluating students' progress and teachers' effectiveness (Haladyna et al., 1991; Messick, 1988). Purposes are not the same thing as assumptions, however: What tests can do, is not necessarily what they are supposed to do.

The assumptions behind using tests include efficiency, fairness, and accountability (Clarke et al., 2000; Koretz, 1988; Madaus & Kellaghan, 1992a, 1992b; Mathison, 1997). The notion that tests are efficient rests on the idea that in a couple of hours or less, students' abilities, achievements, and their progress can be measured and scored. The New York global history course of study takes 2 years to complete; decisions about which students pass the course are based on a 3-hour exam. The assumption of fairness involves issues like the precision of test design and scoring, and in the presumed value of objectivity. The design of test questions speaks to the scientific nature of assessment, whereas the statistical analysis of students' responses addresses the accuracy of calculations. If all students must take and pass the same objectively developed and precisely scored exam, then the process is presumed to be fair. The third assumption promotes accountability. Traditionally, this assumption has applied most directly to students: Knowing that they will be tested, students presumably will take seriously the material taught.

The assumptions of efficiency, fairness, and accountability are well established. More recent test-based assumptions focus on teachers and their classroom practices. These assumptions include the idea that tests drive teachers' practices, and that tests can leverage classroom change (see, for example, Amrein & Berliner, 2002; Cimbricz, 2002; Firestone et al., 1998; Grant Derme-Insinna, Gradwell, et al., 2002; Grant, Gradwell, Lauricella et al., 2002; Noble & Smith, 1994; Smith, 1991). As states aim for more elaborate curriculum standards, so too do they aim for more rigorous exams. Combining new tests with higher stakes, policymakers assume that teachers will heed the messages that tests broadcast and will make changes to enrich their teaching and to ensure higher student test scores.

Tests as a Vehicle for Ambitious Teaching and Learning

Retrofitting tests with the assumptions about teachers and teaching makes sense: If tests hold real power over teachers, then they should be an effective vehicle for change. Assumptions do not always bear fruit, however, and high-stakes tests are an unfortunate example of this truism.

Without repeating the arguments and examples developed in chapter 6, I do want to pick up on the issue of testing leading to ambitious teaching and learning. Simply put, there is no research evidence that demonstrates a causal connection between tests and good teaching. There is a lot of *talk* about why tests are needed. The late head of the American Federation of Teachers, Al Shanker (1995), argues that "as long as students are given no reason to work, it is hard to see how any reform, however ingenious or creative, will achieve what is needed" (p. 147). Chester Finn (1995) concurs: Reforms will fail, Finn argues, without "a meaningful examination or assessment system tied to those [national] goals" (p. 121).

Shanker's and Finn's arguments seem sound, yet they are arguments without evidence: Neither cites a single study demonstrating a causal relationship between new tests and ambitious teaching and learning. The reason is simple: There are none. After reviewing the existing research on state testing and teachers' thinking and practice, Sandra Cimbricz (2002) concludes that although the wider testing literature includes many advocacy pieces like Shanker's and Finn's, "empirical support of the claim that state testing positively influences teachers' thinking and practice ... seemed to vanish" (p. 6). Audrey Amrein and David Berliner (2002) make an analogous argument for the effect of high-stakes, state-level tests on student learning. Amrein and Berliner review the testing programs and results in 18 states with high-stakes testing programs and then compare those results with students' performance on nationally normed tests such as the SAT, NAEP, and AP exams. They conclude that no causal connection exists between tests and increased student learning:

> Both the uncertainty associated with high-stakes testing data, and the questionable validity of high-stakes tests as indicators of the domains they are intended to reflect, suggest that this is a failed policy initiative. High-stakes testing policies are not now and may never be policies that will accomplish what they intend. (p. 41)

Taken together, the Cimbricz (2002) and Amrein and Berliner (2002) studies challenge the presumption that new tests will promote ambitious teaching and learning. The faith that policymakers and the public place in tests seems quite remarkable in this light. It also seems myopic. The public has an excuse: Although arguments not unlike Cimbricz's and Amrein and Berliner's have been made for some time in professional journals,[2] until recently the problems of state-level testing have not made their way into the popular press. Policymakers are less off the hook. Researchers have long known that policymakers rarely read their work (Cohen & Garet, 1975), so it is not hard to believe that policy can reflect unfounded assumptions. What seems less excusable, however, is that policymakers have failed to explore whether or not their efforts are having the desired effects. Unintended consequences are still consequences. Policymakers can be

---

[2]See the special section of *Phi Delta Kappan* edited by Anne Lieberman (1991) for a prelude to the conclusions Cimbricz (2002) and Amrein and Berliner (2002) reach.

excused for initiating bad policy if they are acting on the best information at the time. Inexcusable, however, is maintaining bad policy and arguing that it works.

The Prospects for Restructured Schools

If new curricula and tests are weak vehicles for promoting ambitious teaching and learning, where else might policymakers turn? Many observers (e.g., Fullan & Stiegelbauer, 1991; Little, 1982; Provenzo & McCloskey, 1996; Rosenholtz, 1991) believe the answer lies in changing the context of schooling. These authors emphasize the need to transform school structures—the rules, norms, schedules, grade arrangements, and the like—that influence how teachers and students move through the school day. Traditionally, these reforms have involved how students are grouped by grade level and ability, how school-level decisions are made, what class schedules teachers and students follow, and what constitutes a unit of study (Tyack & Cuban, 1995).

Two more recent reforms propose block scheduling and mentoring teachers. The first refers to the practice of redesigning the traditional structure of 45-minute class periods to provide up to 90-minute blocks of instructional time. Teacher mentoring involves the pairing up of experienced and novice teachers in a form of apprenticeship. Among the virtues of each reform is its promise as means to more ambitious teaching and learning.

In chapter 7, I argue that although several organizational influences can be detected, teachers pay more attention to some than to others, and that the most consistently mentioned influence is students. This is not to say that teachers can disregard their school context, but it does mean that reforms like block scheduling and mentoring will have real meaning only to the extent that they strike deeply at the heart of the student–teacher relationship. The available research suggests that neither does.

The Possibilities of Block Scheduling

Block scheduling addresses the choppiness of the typical secondary school day (Adams & Salvaterra, 1997). Dividing that day into six to nine class periods of 45 minutes lessens the confinement of fidgety bodies and minds. But this practice also hampers sustained instructional activity. Every teacher knows the frustration of an end-of-period bell that rings just as students and ideas are clicking. With more time, the thinking goes, teachers can do more extended activities such as presentations, mock trials, and simulations, and can delve more deeply into issues (Rettig & Canady, 1996). The authors of the National Commission on Time and Learning (1994) conclude that increasing the amount of instructional time teachers and students have together may be the most important reform of schooling ever.

The Realities of Block Scheduling

A popular idea, block scheduling plans exist in at least half of the high schools in the United States (Gruber & Onwuegbuzie, 2001). Yet the enthusiasm for this effort is tempered by the existing research. The potential for block scheduling enabling more ambitious teaching and learning may be there, but the evidence thus far presents a mixed picture.

A fair amount of data supports the salutary effect of block schedules on students' attitudes toward and participation in school (Gruber & Onwuegbuzie, 2001). Conflicting evidence, however, surfaces around the academic windfall from this approach. Several reports (DiRocco, 1999; Hess, Wronkovich, & Robinson, 1999; McGorry & McGorry,1998) show that block-scheduled students surpass their traditionally scheduled students on most academic measures, and other investigations (Dibiase & McQueen, 1999; Queen, Algozzine, & Eaddy, 1996) illustrate greater than expected success for block-scheduled social studies students in final course averages and on standardized tests. At the same time, contradictory findings surface (Cobb, Abate, & Baker, 1999; Georgia Department of Education, 1998; Gruber & Onwuegbuzie, 2001). These researchers find either that traditionally scheduled students outperform block-scheduled students, or that there are no statistically significant differences between the two groups.

The inconsistent student achievement results associated with block scheduling mirror the mixed feelings teachers have about it, especially on first encounter. Teachers typically struggle in their initial efforts to reconfigure their class time (Queen et al., 1996). More importantly, many are never able to break out of traditional modes of instruction: Instead of lecturing for 45 minutes, they now lecture for 90. This need not be the case, however. Martin Ediger (1998) offers a vision of what ambitious teaching can look like in a block scheduling format. The expanded time period allows the teacher he observed to lead an inquiry lesson into life in the Middle East that would either be impossible or unwieldy in a traditional schedule. Ediger notes, however, that although traditional teaching methods can be effective under block scheduling, the full effect of this reform is lost if teachers do not expand both their thinking and their practices.

Bryant and Bryant (2000) point to a key issue related to the promise of block scheduling as a means of promoting more ambitious teaching and learning: "Block scheduling remains only another time-management tool unless classroom teaching/learning interactions also change" (p. 9). A new class schedule, then, is no quick fix. It can encourage and enable thoughtful teaching and learning, but only to the extent that the teachers seize the initiative.

The Possibilities of Mentoring Teachers

The argument about instructional time notwithstanding, other reformers tackle a different enduring problem: the induction of novice teachers.

"Trial by fire" and "sink or swim" are but two expressions for the abrupt way in which new teachers enter the profession (Lortie, 1975). Student teaching is, for most teachers, only the first brief taste of life on the other side of the desk. In their first days, newly minted lawyers do not try murder trials, brand new architects are not put in charge of major commissions, and tenderfoot physicians do not face a full schedule of delicate operations. Novices in each of these professions serve lengthy apprenticeships under knowing mentors. Teachers do not. With some coursework and a few weeks of practice teaching, they walk into exactly the same kinds of classrooms that their most experienced peers do. Many survive, but survival often means getting from one day to the next without a growl from students, colleagues, or the principal. In this atmosphere, bargaining for good behavior and defensive teaching flourish (McNeil, 1988; Sedlak et al., 1986).

Advocates of teacher mentoring look to other professions for useful apprenticeship models. What they find are longer induction periods and closer working relationships with experienced colleagues.

Mentoring can mean many things (Poetter, McKamey, Ritter, & Tisdel, 1999) because the roles of mentor and protégé depend on organizational definitions, expectations, and contexts. At heart, mentoring refers to the relationship between an experienced teacher and an inexperienced one. Although personal dynamics are bound to surface, professional issues are expected to dominate the conversations: Mentors guide, question, support, and critique their protégés' content choices, instructional decisions, understandings of students, classroom management, assessment designs.

A key assumption behind the mentoring model is that mentors guide but do not dominate their protégés. Effective mentors do not do the work for their charges, nor do they expect them to follow in lockstep fashion. Among the complexities of teaching and learning is the demand for split-second decision making in hundreds of situations each day (Jackson, 1968). Good mentors help their protégés by listening as they talk through how they size up problematic situations, what options they consider, and what they think about the results of their actions. Rather than simply categorize a novice's decisions and actions as good or bad, or lecture the novice about what he or she should have done, wise mentors ask questions, pose alternatives, and urge reflection, all in the belief that novices learn more when they deliberate on their thinking and actions rather than memorize a laundry list of do's and dont's.

A second assumption behind mentoring is that although the protégé is expected to gain the most from the relationship, a mentor may also profit as he or she comes to see teaching and learning through the beginner's lens (Orland, 2001; Poetter et al., 1999; Tauer, 1998). The focus of any mentoring situation has to be on the novice, for it is his or her development that characterizes the relationship. But also important is the corollary development that mentors experience if they too reflect on and modify their classroom practices.

The Realities of Mentoring Teachers

Both of these assumptions bear on the promotion of ambitious teaching and learning. As with block scheduling, however, the burden is on each teacher to make the most of a mentoring relationship.

On the protégé side of mentoring, the research is mixed about the potential for thoughtful teaching. Even in the studies that show growth in novice teachers' thinking and teaching (Bullough, Young, & Erickson, 2002; Evertson & Smithey, 2000; Gilles, Cramer, & Hwang, 2001), there is a persistent emphasis on survival (Moir & Gless, 2001; Spinder & Biott, 2000). Of course, if teachers do not survive their first years, the issue of ambitious teaching and learning is moot. Still, it is too often the case that survival equates with conventional approaches to teaching, learning, and subject matter. Moreover, patterns of thought and behavior established early on can be hard to upend (Moir & Gless, 2001; Yeager & Wilson, 1997).

In their experimental field study, Carolyn Evertson and Margaret Smithey (2000) demonstrate the benefits novice teachers can incur from relationships with thoughtful mentors.[3] The protégés of such mentors "showed increased evidence of developing and sustaining more workable classroom routines, managed instruction more smoothly, and gained student cooperation in academic tasks more effectively" (p. 300). A long-term interview study of first-year teachers' mentored experiences undertaken by Carol Gilles, Mary Cramer, and Sang Hwang (2001) confirms Evertson and Smithey's sense that novices' focus on day-to-day growth. Survival, in the sense of managing the role of teacher, the intricacies of discipline and classroom management, and the demands of schooling, is foremost in the interviewees' minds. As one novice put it: "I often feel like I'm in a rowboat with hundreds of kids and no oars. I know I've got to get them to land, but how?" (p. 92).

The smooth management of classroom life is not unimportant, but less well understood in Evertson and Smithey's (2000) study is the mentor teachers' impact on the novice teachers' impulse to teach in ambitious ways. Similarly, Gilles and her colleagues (2001) find survival concerns far exceed concerns about "meeting the needs of all my students," the category in this study that is closest to ambitious teaching and learning. The authors note, however, that these mentored first-year teachers moved more quickly to concerns about their students' needs than previous studies have shown.

Research into the mentor's role also highlights the potential for both ambitious and conventional teaching (Feiman-Nemser, 2001). Thomas Poetter and his colleagues (1999) describe the positive side of men-

---

[3]The emphasis here is on "thoughtful," for the mere availability of a mentor is not enough. Instead, the mentor's knowledge and skill as a teacher of teachers are crucial (Evertson & Smithey, 2000).

toring. Each of the three mentors they interviewed cites the experience as valuable because it helped him or her see teaching in a new way. For example, Christina and her protégé, Nathalie, worked together to research and explore ideas about inclusion, the practice of involving all students in regular education classrooms regardless of their disabilities. The relationship grew into a collaboration when Christina found herself thinking and acting in unfamiliar ways, such as observing colleagues teaching, seeking out research articles, and sharing her concerns with Nathalie. The relationship encountered bumps along the way, but in the end, Christina asserts that the experience as mentor fueled her growth as a teacher:

> I think it's always easier when you have someone to collaborate with rather than just doing the research on your own and coming up with your own ideas. I think you grow much more when you have someone to share your ideas with. If I hadn't had Nathalie this year, I probably would have given up. But she has been the light for me. At times when I was down, she kept me going. (p. 118)

The benefits to Christina, the mentor, support her revitalization as a teacher. Missing from this account and most others, however, is a sense of if and how mentor teachers ratchet up their own instructional practices. Tauer (1998) notes that although mentors see their relationships with protégés as positive, the impact on their own teaching and professional lives is enigmatic at best. In short, mentoring relationships may benefit mentors and novices in important ways, but whether those ways include more powerful teaching is unclear.

Like block scheduling, mentoring has the potential to promote ambitious teaching and learning. For novices, guided entry into classrooms and regular conversations about instructional practice could foster thoughtful teaching. Opportunities to reflect on one's own practices through the experiences of a novice also could inspire more powerful teaching by mentors. The research literature confirms the positive feelings mentors and protégés hold, but definitive evidence of mentoring as an inducement for richer teaching and learning has yet to materialize. A mentoring relationship, like a block schedule, can become a rich experience if acted on by energized teachers. Short of that, the potential may go unrealized.

Efforts to reform teaching and learning through restructuring schools show no sign of abating. In addition to block scheduling and teacher mentoring, reformers advocate team teaching (Ladwig & King, 1992), magnet schools (McNeil, 2000; Riley, Wilson, & Fogg, 2000), and smaller classes and schools (Meier, 1996). These efforts may support ambitious teaching and learning, but none is an effective and widespread catalyst for dramatic change. Good teachers will seize on these efforts, but policymakers can not count on restructuring alone to prod less able teachers.

The Prospects for Expanded Professional Development

In an oft-cited piece, Brian Rowan (1990) observes that control strategies like curriculum policies, textbook adoptions, and standardized testing may have a global effect on teachers' practices. But because these efforts do not concern the core elements of teaching and learning, they rarely have any profound or sustained effect. Many school observers agree, and they conclude that real classroom change will occur only when the professional development of teachers becomes a central feature of educational policy.

Professional development of teachers goes by many names—staff development, capacity building, inservice—and takes many forms—afternoon workshops, conference presentations, summer institutes. Common across these labels and manifestations is a consensus that teachers view most professional development with disdain. And well they should: The standard inservice program is weakly conceived and poorly delivered (Grossman, Wineburg, & Woolworth, 2001; Lieberman, 1995; Little, 1993; Novick, 1996). Moreover, the mix of messages broadcast from one professional development session to another can seem incoherent and only distantly related to teaching and learning (Grant, 1997a). So important are these problems that Smylie (1995) argues, "We will fail ... to improve schooling for children until we acknowledge the importance of schools not only as places for teachers to work but also as places for teachers to learn" (p. 92).

The research on professional development as a means to improved teaching and learning offers mixed results. Traditionally conceived professional development continues, and it continues to get poor reviews. Other forms of professional development are emerging, and although they too can be problematic, they show some potential for impacting teachers' practices. The good news is that powerful opportunities for teachers to learn do exist; the bad news is that teachers are generally on their own to find and take advantage of these opportunities.

The Assumptions Behind Expanded Professional Development

Most of the assumptions behind professional development seem obvious. First, the changing interpretations of disciplines like history and the growing research on wise practices demand that teachers become lifelong learners. Just as doctors must keep pace with new understandings in their field, so too must teachers in theirs. Second, professional development ought to present teachers with the best of current thinking. Teaching and learning are complex, so it makes sense that professional development focuses on key elements at the heart of that interaction. Finally, teachers must take an active role in their own learning. Much of the pedagogy practiced by professional developers is abysmal, and teachers are justified in ignoring it. That said, the volume of professional development opportunities is staggering. Teachers have to be choosy about where they spend their time and money, but there is much to be gained if they take the initiative and choose wisely.

Rowan (1990) synthesizes these assumptions this way: If teachers' practices need to change, then attention should center on core issues of teaching and learning; and if teachers are going to learn how to think and teach differently through professional development opportunities, then the nature of those opportunities—the content taught, the pedagogy employed—must change. Linda Darling-Hammond and Milbrey McLaughlin (1996) add that capacity building must be the central assumption that professional developers hold: "Capacity building policies view knowledge as constructed by and with practitioners for use in their own contexts, rather than something conveyed by policymakers as a single solution for top-down implementation" (p. 203).

Professional Development as a Vehicle for Ambitious Teaching and Learning

Of the many reforms of teaching and learning, it is professional development that seems most likely to effect real and sustained changes. Investing in teachers makes considerable sense, as good teaching is highly correlated with good test scores (Smith & Niemi, 2001). Whether professional developers can deliver on their promises, however, is questionable.

Linda Darling-Hammond (1996) argues that traditional models of professional development provide teachers with little of value. What is needed, she asserts, is a new "infrastructure of reform," which focuses on the "development of institutions and environmental supports that will promote the spread of ideas and shared learning about how change can be attempted and sustained" (p. 204). Some of those structures exist outside of schools (Darling-Hammond, 1996; Lieberman, 1995; Lieberman & Grolnick, 1996; Novick, 1996). They include school–university partnerships, teacher-to-teacher and school-to-school networks, and involvement in district, state, and national activities and organizations. Other structures can develop within schools. Examples include support for action research projects and peer reviews of teachers' practices (Darling-Hammond, 1996; Lieberman, 1995; Smylie, 1995)

Whether within or outside schools, several characteristics define successful professional development experiences. Hilda Borko and Ralph Putnam (1996) review a number of professional development programs and conclude that the valuable ones share three characteristics. First, effective professional development focuses on the substance of teaching and learning. If teachers are to become more ambitious through professional development, then professional developers must help teachers grow in their conceptions of subject matter, pedagogy, and sub-ject-specific pedagogy. Borko and Putnam see the "expansion of teach-ers' knowledge base as a central goal" (p. 58), and they argue that that knowledge base needs to include development of greater subject matter knowledge, openness to constructivist ideas about learning, and under-standing of children's ways of thinking. The second characteristic of good professional development programs is that they mirror that which is expected to develop in teachers' classrooms: If reformers want to see ambitious teachers acting on constructivist assumptions, then the pro-fessional development teachers experience needs to model those be-haviors. Moreover, teachers attempting to change their practices need support and supervision as they try out those changes in their class-rooms. The third attribute of powerful professional development is a cadre of professional developers who are sensitive to the knowledge, be-liefs, and experiences brought by the teachers sitting in front of them. If understanding students' prior knowledge is important for adult teachers of children, so too is it important for adult teachers of teachers. What teachers already know and believe *may* get in the way of their learning to teach differently—the apprenticeship of observation, for example, does not go away just because professional developers wish it would. But teachers will not embrace more ambitious pedagogies unless they speak to teachers' lived experiences. As Darling-Hammond (1996) observes, "like students, teachers learn by doing, reading, and reflecting; collabo-rating with other teachers; looking closely at students and their work; and sharing what they see" (p. 204). Joe Onosko and Bob Stevenson (1991) add one more condition: Powerful professional development en-gages teachers in higher order thinking, such as authentic problem solv-ing. The point here is simple: If teachers have not been engaged in a genuine learning experience, it will be difficult for them to design similar experiences for their students and to know what to do when students run into difficulties.

Unfortunately, most professional development opportunities fail to meet these criteria. As New York policymakers unveiled the new state cur-riculum standards in social studies, I attended various sessions designed to introduce teachers to the standards (Grant, 1997a). A variety of profes-sional development sessions, however, is not the same thing as good pro-fessional development sessions. In analyzing the data I collected, I was struck by the mixed messages broadcast, and by a sense of frustration among the teacher-participants. The many, and often conflicting, mes-sages that session leaders offered cut to the heart of the new standards: Al-though the "what" of teaching was the ostensible focus, helping teachers think about the content to be taught was only part of what developed, and often not a very important part. In fact, when one teacher asked how the new curriculum document would affect him, the session leader said mat-ter-of-factly, "It won't" (p. 270). Instead of emphasizing content, the profes-sional developers directed their comments to instruction and assessment.

Although the standards say almost nothing directly about teaching, leaders of the sessions I attended routinely talked about the need for teachers to change their instruction. "Teachers have to do things differently," said one leader (p. 270). Even more common than instruction, however, were messages about assessment. New state tests were years away, but leaders of the curriculum standards sessions stressed the importance of testing. A state education department spokesperson said that tests "help grow change in the system" and a social studies district supervisor noted that real classroom change would come "if we change the tests" (p. 271).

Teachers attending these sessions expressed limited enthusiasm for the new standards; they expressed nothing but frustration with the sessions themselves. The mix of messages they perceived left most with the sense that state policymakers were unsure what direction they wanted teachers to take. As one teacher noted, "[The curriculum framework] sounds like a bunch of double-talk to me.... It doesn't amount to anything. I see no meat here. I see nothing I can get hold of" (Grant, 1997a, p. 275). Teachers were even less impressed with the professional development sessions they attended. Summing up many of their peers' experiences, one teacher said, "Did they inform me of anything?" whereas another commented, "If we taught like that, we'd be fired" (p. 277).

None of the teachers I interviewed said they expected to make profound changes in their classroom practices as a result of the new curriculum or of the professional development sessions they attended. Most left those sessions more confused and annoyed than when they came in. They did not disagree that the teaching and learning in their classrooms could be improved, they simply did not think they had been helped. As one teacher noted her frustrations:

> I don't think you can learn how to do it [teach in new ways] in five staff development days.... Somebody needs to teach us how to do that. And it's gonna take time.... We don't have the faintest idea how to do it. (Grant, 1997a, p. 279)

When I asked teachers how professional development might be improved, most hesitated. They mentioned taking classes and having more time to prepare for courses and to share ideas and materials with colleagues. Perhaps because of their poor previous experiences and knowing the constraints of the school day, these teachers seemed to have as much trouble imagining what useful professional development might look like as they did in imagining how to ratchet up their own teaching.

There are exceptions, however. Although not overwhelming in number, there are cases of teachers for whom professional development stimulates their growth as ambitious teachers (Bickmore, 1993; Christensen et al., 2001; Wineburg & Wilson, 1991; Wilson & Wineburg, 1993). The case of Emily (Riley et al., 2000) is typical. In her first social studies job as an eighth-grade U.S. history teacher, Emily taught students labeled "low ability." Her traditional approaches of lecture and textbook assignments bored her and her students. Seeking help from colleagues proved futile:

> After about two weeks, I realized that these cute, eager kids were getting a glazed look, and I went to another teacher and asked, "What else are you doing?" She said, "Get used to it. This is how they all are and you've got the really low-level students." ... Anything I would try to do [later] that was innovative, I was told, "Your kids can't do that." There was no point in reading historical fiction because "they won't read." (p. 362)

Many young teachers might have taken this advice. Emily did not: "I think that got my dander up, and I was determined that these kids would learn.... I began to put together whatever I could to make my classroom more interactive, where they were grouping and enjoying learning, and learning more than just the facts" (p. 362). Emily's determination came from a source deep within, but it was nurtured by some of the professional development opportunities that she sought out. Those opportunities included her own independent reading and applying for grants to develop classroom projects.

Understanding Emily's experience, like that of other history teachers in the research literature, is important for three reasons. One reason is for the professional development activities she does not cite: late-afternoon workshops, half-day district inservices, and the like. Although standard fare on many professional development menus, these kinds of sessions rarely encourage and support ambitious teaching and learning. Emily finds ways to learn what she wants to learn, but those ways lie outside the typical professional development experience. This point leads to the second reason Emily's case is instructive: It is Emily who determines what she wants to learn and how she will learn it. Professional development programs are generally designed for large numbers of teachers by people who believe they know what teachers need. This one-size-fits-all approach may be efficient, but it seldom meets the needs of individual teachers. Emily knows what she needs to learn and she figures out where to go in order to do so. The last reason Emily's case is important is that it speaks to the power of persistence. Emily might have waited for an administrator to ask her what she wanted to learn; she might have volunteered this information at a faculty meeting. Given her colleagues' tendency to ignore "low-level" students, however, it is unlikely that Emily's interests were widely shared. Undeterred, she pushed on: "It was wonderful watching the 'lower-level' kids do what the 'smart' kids were doing and watching them blossom" (Riley et al., 2000, p. 363). Resources in the form of books and grant programs were available to help Emily make the classroom changes she desired, but those opportunities would have lain fallow without Emily's determination to upgrade her practice. Professional development opportunities offer possibilities. It is up to teachers, individually and together, to make those possibilities real.

One way teachers can take more control over their own professional development is through teacher networks (Lieberman, 1995; Lieberman & Grolnick, 1996). Networks, which can be formal or informal and live or computer linked, offer teachers occasions for "directing their own learning; allowing them to sidestep the limitations of institutional rules, hierarchies, and geographic locations; and encouraging them to work together with many different kinds of people" (Lieberman & Grolnick, 1996, p. 8). These efforts represent a kind of "conversational community" (Grant & VanSledright, 1992; VanSledright & Grant, 1991) where the discussions may draw on any area of teacher's classroom lives—instruction, curriculum, students, administrators—and cross both personal and professional boundaries.

Interested in promoting ambitious teaching and learning among practicing teachers, Pam Grossman, Sam Wineburg, and Stephen Woolworth (2001) began building a network or "teacher community" of English and social studies teachers (with a special education and an English as a second language [ESL] teacher), all from an urban high school.[4] The group meets twice monthly to read in the areas of English and history and to create an interdisciplinary curriculum. A key feature of this effort is the largely free-form agenda. Grossman and her colleagues came to the teachers not to sell them on the latest cooperative learning strategy or collection of primary sources documents, nor did they come to harangue teachers about the importance of higher order thinking: "We had no set agenda for the teachers other than a desire to provide opportunities for continued learning and interactions around the subject matter of history and English" (p. 950). This collective venture has produced bumps—arguments over understandings of ideas, illusions of consensus, shifting factions—as well as breakthroughs—surprising realizations, opportunities for sharing deepseated beliefs, and tolerance for risk taking. The account of this adventure illuminates both the promise and the problems of looking deeply at subject matter, teaching, and learning.

Professional development holds promise for real and sustained movement toward ambitious teaching and learning. Realizing that promise is problematic, if for no other reason than the poverty of teachers' past experiences. The breadth of opportunities available suggests that almost every teacher can find something of value. But separating the valuable from the superfluous is no small task, especially when teachers are often required to attend more of the latter than the former. Moreover, teachers may feel isolated when it comes to learning about and then enacting more challenging practices. Finally, as with other reforms, professional development may be more effective in supporting than in prompting ambitious teaching and learning. Efforts like the teacher community Grossman,

---

[4]See Rust (1999) for an account of a similar project with elementary school teachers.

Wineburg, and Woolworth (2001) are building may be places where teachers can reflect on and upgrade their teaching. At this point, however, the promise exceeds the reality.

A REASON TO BE CONCERNED: THE COMPLEX NATURE OF PROMOTING AMBITIOUS TEACHING AND LEARNING

Lee Shulman (1983) describes the horrors that policymakers envision:

> For many of the policymakers, the vision is of teachers who do not teach, or teach only what they please to those who please them ... whose low expectations for the intellectual prowess of poor children lead them to neglect their pedagogical duties toward the very groups who need instruction most desperately; or whose limited knowledge of the sciences, mathematics, and language arts results in their misteaching the most able. (p. 484)

To this nightmare, Shulman adds that of teachers:

> Teachers harbor their own nightmares.... They are subject to endless mandates and directives emanating from faceless bureaucrats pursuing patently political agendas. These policies not only dictate frequently absurd practices, they typically conflict with the policies transmitted from other agencies, from the courts, or from other levels of government. Each new policy further erodes the teacher's control over the classroom for which she is responsible. (p. 485)

Anyone who has worked on educational policy recognizes the potential for misunderstanding, misinterpretation, and misapplication as teachers interpret new initiatives. Anyone who has taught recognizes the confusion, frustration, and anxiety that develop when outsiders get involved in school practices (Grant, 1995a).

The problem of using policy as a means of promoting ambitious teaching and learning is well established (Rowan, 1990; Tyack & Cuban, 1995). Educational policy is a blunt tool that seems to work best when addressing broad schooling inequities (Green, 1983). The fine, complex work of teaching and learning, however, seems to lie well beyond the rhetorical reach of policy and policymakers (Grant, 1998; Rowan, 1990).

Other problems crop us as well, for ambitious teaching and learning cuts across the grain of U.S. schooling in several ways. The goal of ensuring that every child has an opportunity to learn in powerful ways is widely embraced. Realizing that goal, however, gives rise to at least three problems beyond the ineffectiveness of policy reforms.

Teachers as Objects and Agents of Change

One of those problems is the nature of teachers as both objects and agents of reform (Warren, 1989). Teachers become the object of reform when policymakers assume that teachers' practices contribute to students' poor academic performance. Improvements will come, they assume, when teachers change their pedagogy to reflect reform-minded proposals. Fair enough, but the irony is that teachers are also the instrument of any real change. Policymakers and professional developers can help teachers transform their pedagogical practices, but they cannot do it for them. Teaching practices change largely when teachers decide to change them. As Guskey (1996) notes, "Teachers are the ones chiefly responsible for implementing change" (p. 118).

Guskey's (1996) observation puts the point on a key issue: Ambitious teaching and learning develop when teachers choose to pursue those goals. There is no end of resources to help teachers teach thoughtfully. The source of that impulse, however, lies primarily within each classroom teacher. Researchers are a long way from understanding what influences teachers, but the effects of what they hold dear are visible every day. Teachers like Linda Strait and Emily work from entirely different motivations than do most of their colleagues. They gatekeep the ideas and activities their students experience just as much as their less ambitious peers do, and their efforts are not always successful. What distinguishes these teachers, however, is the drive to push themselves and their students beyond the routine. If that drive is widely missing in teachers, reformers have few tools to stimulate it.

Few Models of Ambitious Teaching and Learning

A compounding problem for those who advocate more ambitious teaching and learning is the dearth of good models. In this book, I describe the practices of several powerful teachers. I do so in the hope that preservice and practicing teachers who aim high will see that they are not alone.

Unfortunately, the modal history teacher is much closer to the stereotype. Large- and small-scale studies routinely point to a deadness within classroom activity (Cuban, 1984; Cusick, 1983; Goodlad, 1984; McNeil, 1988). Teachers talk, write on the board, and grade tests; students respond to questions, write in their notebooks, and answer test items. Patterns develop, and a sort of banal and reciprocal comfort emerges: Teachers do not challenge students and students do not challenge their teachers. The cases of powerful teaching in this book challenge this portrayal, but they do not overpower it.

Teachers anxious to upgrade their teaching work against the odds. First, the professional development sessions they attend feature insipid ideas and poor pedagogy. Teachers can learn important things through professional development activities, but they typically see few models of thoughtful teaching. Second, the norms of high school departments put a premium on isolating teachers from one another and on silence about substantive issues of teaching and learning. Teachers intent on ratcheting up their understanding of history, students, and teaching find few exemplary teachers willing to let them observe or to engage them in on-going conversations. Finally, although the rhetoric of new curriculum standards, tests, and restructuring plans promotes ambitious teaching and learning, it fails to deliver. Authors of curriculum standards ignore teaching altogether; authors of test questions send mixed messages about what is valued; and restructuring plans tinker around the edges of teachers' practices, but rarely get to the heart.

There are exceptions to each of the claims just made, but the fact stands: Teachers desirous of, but not skilled at or comfortable with, more robust approaches to teaching and learning can count on little support or encouragement. And if this conclusion holds, it is no leap to assume that teachers satisfied with lower expectations of themselves and their students will see little impetus to change.

An Ill-Structured Reward System

A third concern surrounding the prospects for ambitious teaching and learning revolves around the ill-structured reward system for good teaching.

The rewards for teaching ambitiously are two, and both fall under the category of what Lortie (1975) calls "psychic rewards," or the task-related satisfactions that grow as one exerts more effort. One of those rewards involves the gains students make when challenged to do more than they (or anyone else) expect. Recall Emily's words: "It was wonderful watching the 'lower-level' kids do what the 'smart' kids were doing and watching them blossom" (Riley et al., 2000, p. 363). Feeding off students' appreciation is a second kind of psychic reward: the self-satisfaction that teachers experience when they push themselves, knowing that what they attempt is risky, but ultimately better for kids.

Tempering these rewards are colleagues' and administrators' reactions and a minimum of incentives. Colleagues and administrators may support the efforts of ambitious teachers, but the typical responses range from indifference to pity. Because most teachers work in isolation and because teaching and learning are so rarely discussed, ambitious teachers often sense indifference from their peers, principals, and district administrators. As long as students are not disruptive of other classes, intrepid teachers' efforts generally are ignored. New teachers' trials are especially vulnerable to being ignored or pitied as the work of the naïve. One can imagine the patronizing look Emily's colleague offered as she reminded Emily to "get used to it. This is how they [low level students] all are" (Riley et al., 2000, p. 362). Whether reflecting an enduring frustration, professional jealousy, or lost hope, such comments denigrate thoughtful teaching. So too does a principal's passing remark about classes being too noisy and a superintendent's inservice harangue that ignores the link between good teaching and higher test scores. Teachers who hope for professional respect and congratulations are quickly disabused of such notions.

Accompanying the absence of professional praise are limited incentives to go beyond the status quo. Teachers, as group, typically resent programs that identify and label colleagues as "master" teachers, or that provide financial benefits for distinguished teaching. The "unstaged" nature of careers in classroom teaching (Lortie, 1975) means that advancement is often seen as possible only if teachers leave for administrative posts.

Teachers who push beyond traditional practices face a rocky road (Cohen, 1988). Not only are there few incentives (and some active disincentives) to enrich their teaching, but the rewards they can identify—student appreciation and the attendant self-satisfaction—are tenuously linked. Many a teacher has tried and failed in his or her initial attempts to raise the academic bar. Students, comfortable with generally low expectations of their abilities, often resist instruction that is both more engaging and more demanding (Stevenson, 1990). With confidence shaken by an activity gone awry, it takes a determined teacher to reflect on the lessons learned and to try again. When students respond positively (and they invariably do once they trust their teachers' good intentions), then teachers' satisfied smiles emerge. Those smiles can be long in coming, however: The uncertainties of ambitious teaching are not for the faint of heart, the weak-willed, or the impatient. Rebuffed in their initial efforts and unsupported by the people and system around them, it is not hard to understand why many teachers pack up their ambitious plans and put them away.

A REASON TO BE OPTIMISTIC:
GOOD TEACHERS AND POWERFUL IDEAS

Those with hopes for a revitalized teaching force have cause for gloom. None of the current reform measures—curriculum, tests, restructuring, or professional development—is a panacea; teaching and learning are too complex to respond immediately and radically to any one impulse. Moreover, the regularities of schooling—teacher isolation, professional indifference, and the lack of incentives— combined with the lack of good models and the ironic view of teachers as objects *and* agents of reform sap the prospects for ambitious teaching and learning. Sure, the pessimists will say, there are instances of teachers rising above the fray, but they are far more the exception than the rule.

It's a hard argument to dispute. And yet, within that argument grows the seed of optimism. For seen from a different vantage, the exceptions undercut the rule. I take no Pollyanna-ish position here. All is not roses in high schools, and that so many teachers pursue pedantic ends is sorely disappointing. But the fact remains: Teachers can construct interesting classroom lives for themselves and their students, and that possibility underscores the potential for meaningful change.

Interpreting Policies to Support Ambitious Teaching and Learning

One reason to be optimistic is that the reform policies of the last several years serve the goals of ambitious teaching and learning. They may do so in largely rhetorical ways, they may send conflicting messages, and they may not persuade every teacher, but teachers with even the slightest interest in ramping up their instruction can draw support from the policies around them.

Policymaking can be a hard thing to watch. (A veteran state legislator once told me that there are two things one should never witness first hand: sausage making and policymaking.) Whim, fads, personal experience, and pressure groups can play as big a role in the policymaking process as do reason, research, and forethought. The results rarely satisfy anyone, and often are open to wide-ranging interpretations (Cohen & Garet, 1975; Green, 1983; Kingdon, 1984).

Since the *Nation at Risk* report (National Commission on Excellence in Education, 1983), policymakers have hit their stride. National reports, state-level requirements, local implementation plans—each competes with the others for teachers' and the public's attention. Diverse in scope and means, these efforts aim, at least rhetorically, at improving teaching, learning, and assessment. Like all texts, reform-minded policies can be variously interpreted. Understanding what policymakers *intended* might be interesting on some level, but what happens with policies once they hit the ground is what matters.

Where policies hit the ground is in the classroom, so how teachers interpret reforms is important. Kirst and Walker (1971) note that teachers have a "pocket veto" over any new idea crossing the classroom threshold. The evidence suggests that many use that veto to protect their past practices. And yet the ability to veto an idea carries with it the corresponding ability to accept and act on that same idea. Teachers may not interpret new policies as supporting ambitious instruction (recall Paula's reaction to the new state global history curriculum and test), but they could. So although reform-minded policies may not induce many teachers to take up the cause, they can offer support for teachers working in that direction (Grant, 1998).

Schooling and Ambitious Teaching and Learning

A second reason to be optimistic about the potential for richer teaching and learning is the organization of schooling. Although many of the norms and regularities of the school day seem to undercut ambitious teaching, the decentralized nature of most schools offers room for growth.

Those who criticize schools as conservative, status-preserving bureaucracies have much evidence on which to draw (Apple, 1979; Giroux,

1981). Long-established patterns of power and privilege mean that schools are less able to challenge prevailing political, economic, and social conditions than they are to preserve them. Those patterns extend into the professional lives of teachers, as navigating one's way through extant norms, structures, and relationships can be difficult. Although one might expect history teachers to be more inclusive and embracing of their colleagues than their English, science, or math peers, the opposite seems to be true (Stodolsky & Grossman, 1995). Moreover, the reward system in most schools typically promotes cautious teaching and modest learning (Cusick, 1983; McNeil, 1988; Provenzo & McCloskey, 1996).

Unappreciated by their colleagues and unrewarded by the bureaucracy, teachers taking ambitious steps in their teaching may see little incentive to continue. And yet, any number of teachers do continue. They do so by redefining the rewards of practice away from peer and administrator acknowledgements to the self-satisfaction of seeing better than expected student gains and brighter than expected student smiles. These teachers know that the isolation and silence that surround their professional lives cushion their practices, allowing them to push themselves and their students in profitable directions. The constraints of schooling that teachers perceive can seem very real and very limiting (Cornbleth, 2002). Ambitious teachers perceive differently.

The Research Base for Ambitious Teaching and Learning

One last reason for optimism is the growing research base that demonstrates the power in ambitious teaching and learning. In the preceding chapters, and more fully in the research on which I draw, there is ample evidence that good teaching and learning can and does exist.

Think back to the accomplished teachers profiled in these pages. Different in age, gender, race, and region, they share key features. Ambitious teachers know their subject matter well. Whether through coursework or their own study, these are teachers who see value in and think hard about history. It is not simply the subject that they teach; it is one of the reasons they teach. Ambitious teachers also know their students well. The parts of that knowing include understanding the kinds of lives students lead, understanding something of how they think and perceive the world, and understanding that they are capable of far more than they and most others believe. Good teachers know when to push and when to support, when to praise and when to prod their students toward the realization that learning consists of struggle as much as triumph. And ambitious teachers know how to create space for themselves and their students in an environment that may never appreciate either of their efforts. Without minimizing the potential for constraining influences, these teachers understand how to use the existing situations to best advantage.

It is not by chance that the teachers I profile describe conflicts with others. Those conflicts may be with colleagues, principals, parents, and even whole communities. And they can seem overwhelming. The road to ambitious teaching and learning is far more like a steep mountain trail than a newly-paved freeway. Both are paths leading in particular directions and offering particular advantages and disadvantages. The special challenges of ambitious teachers are many, but with special challenges come special rewards: The view from the freeway can never equal that from the mountain.

℘   Ↄ

In the end, then, the one safe bet for any real, deep, and lasting change is to invest in good teachers, for they will persist even when the forces around them disapprove. There are many ways to support such teachers. Understand, however, that different teachers will read different meanings into any of the opportunities offered.

Understand also that teachers will gatekeep these opportunities with their students, so what is inside the gatekeeper's head is at least as important as what is outside. The best curriculum, textbook, instructional activity, and the like are useless in the hands of a dull teacher, whereas a good history teacher can do wonders with ideas alone. As noted earlier, ambitious teaching and learning occur when smart teachers, curious students, and powerful ideas come together. There is much that administrators, policymakers, and the public can do to support this relationship, but without it, nothing of consequence will occur. The students (and the ideas) are out there. Let's see what we can all do to give them good teachers.

References

Adams, D., & Salvaterra, M. (1997). Structural and teacher changes: Necessities for successful block scheduling. *High School Journal, 81*, 98–106.

Adler, S. (1984). A field study of selected student teacher perspectives toward social studies. *Theory and Research in Social Education, 12*, 13–30.

Amrein, A., & Berliner, D. (2002). High-stakes testing, uncertainty, and student learning. *Educational Policy Analysis Archives, 10*(18). Available online at http://epaa.asu.edu/epaa/v10n18.html

Anderson, C., Avery, P., Pederson, P., Smith, E., & Sullivan, J. (1997). Divergent perspectives on citizenship education: A Q-method study and survey of social studies teachers. *American Educational Research Journal, 34*, 333–364.

Anderson, J., Reder, L., & Simon, H. (1996). Situated learning and education. *Educational Researcher, 25*(4), 5–11.

Angell, A. (1998). Learning to teach social studies: A case study of belief restructuring. *Theory and Research in Social Education, 26*(4), 502–529.

Anyon, J. (1979). Ideology and United States history textbooks. *Harvard Educational Review, 49*(3), 361–386.

Apple, M. (1979). *Ideology and curriculum*. Boston: Routledge and Kegan Paul.

Appleby, J., Hunt, L., & Jacob, M. (1994). *Telling the truth about history*. New York: W. W. Norton.

Armento, B. (1986). Research on teaching social studies. In M. C. Whitrock (Ed.), *Handbook of research on teaching* (pp. 942–951). New York: Macmillan.

Avery, P. (1999). Authentic assessment and instruction. *Social Education, 63*(6), 368–373.

Baker, E. (1994). Learning-based assessments of history understanding. *Educational Psychologist, 29*(2), 97–106.

Banks, J. (1994). *Multiethnic education: Theory and practice* (3rd ed.). New York: Simon & Schuster.

Barr, R., Barth, J., & Shermis, S. (1977). *Defining the social studies*. Arlington, VA: National Council for the Social Studies.

Barton, K. (1997a). "Bossed around by the queen": Elementary students' understanding of individuals and institutions in history. *Journal of Curriculum and Supervision, 12*(4), 290–314.

Barton, K. (1997b). "I just kinda know": Elementary students' ideas about historical evidence. *Theory and Research in Social Education, 25*(4), 407–430.

Barton, K. (2001). "You'd be wanting to know about the past": Social contexts of children's historical understanding in Northern Ireland and the USA. *Comparative Education, 37*(1), 89–106.

Barton, K., & Levstik, L. (1996). "Back when God was around and everything": Elementary children's understanding of historical time. *American Educational Research Journal, 33*(2), 419–454.

Barton, K., & Levstik, L. S. (1997, March). *Middle graders' explanations of historical significance*. Paper presented at the American Educational Research Association, Chicago.

Barton, K., & Levstik, L. (1998). "It wasn't a good part of history": National identity and students' explanations of historical significance. *Teachers College Record, 99*(3), 478–513.

Barton, P., & Coley, R. (1998). *Growth in school: Achievement gains from the fourth to eighth grade*. Princeton, NJ: Educational Testing Service.

Beals, M. (1994). *Warriors don't cry: A searing memoir of the battle to integrate Little Rock's Central High*. New York: Pocket Books.

Beard, C. (1934). *The nature of the social sciences in relation to objectives of instruction*. New York: Charles Scribner's Sons.

Beatty, A., Reese, C., Persky, H., & Carr, P. (1996). *U. S. history report card.* Washington, DC: U.S. Department of Education, Office of Educational Research and Improvement.

Beck, I., McKeown, M., Sinatra, G., & Loxterman, J. (1991). Revising social studies text from a text-processing perspective: Evidence of improved comprehensibility. *Reading Research Quarterly, 26*(3), 251–276.

Becker, C. (1932). What is evidence? The relativist view. *American Historical Review, 37,* 3–23.

Bedwell, L., Hunt, G., Touzel, T., & Wiseman, D. (1984). *Effective teaching: Preparation and implementation.* Springfield, IL: Charles C. Thomas.

Bennett, C., & Spaulding, E. (1992). Teaching the social studies: Multiple approaches for multiple perspectives. *Theory and Research in Social Education, 20*(3), 263–292.

Berkin, C., Brinkley, A., Carson, C., Cherny, R., Divine, R., Foner, E., Morris, J., Wheeler, A., & Wood, L. (1995). *American voices: A history of the United States.* Glenview, IL: Scott Foresman.

Berliner, D. C., & Biddle, B. J. (1995). *The manufactured crisis: Myths, fraud, and the attack on America's public schools.* Reading, MA: Addison-Wesley.

Bickmore, K. (1993). Learning inclusion/inclusion In learning: Citizenship education for a pluralistic society. *Theory and Research in Social Education, 21*(4), 341–384.

Bodnar, J. (1994). *Remaking America: Public memory, commemoration, and patriotism in the twentieth century.* Princeton, NJ: Princeton University Press.

Bolman, L., & Deal, T. (1991). *Reframing organizations: Artistry, choice, and leadership.* San Francisco: Jossey-Bass.

Boorstin, D., & Kelley, B. (1994). *A history of the United States.* Needham, MA: Prentice Hall.

Booth, M. (1980). A modern world history course and the thinking of adolescent pupils. *Educational Review, 32,* 245–257.

Borko, H., & Putnam, R. (1996). Expanding a teacher's knowledge base: A cognitive psychology perspective n professional development. In T. Guskey & M. Huberman (Eds.), *Professional development in education* (pp. 35–65). New York: Teachers College Press.

Bowe, R., Ball, S., & Gold, A. (1992). *Reforming education and changing schools: Case studies in policy sociology.* London: Routledge.

Bradley Commission. (1989). Building a history curriculum: Guidelines for teaching history in schools. In P. Gagnon (Ed.), *Historical literacy: The case for history in American schools* (pp. 16–47). New York: Macmillan.

Brophy, J. (1992). Fifth-grade U.S. history: How one teacher arranged to focus on key ideas in-depth. *Theory and Research in Social Education, 20*(2), 141–155.

Brophy, J., & Good, T. (1986). Teacher behavior and student achievement. In M. C. Whitrock (Ed.), *Handbook of research on teaching* (3rd ed., pp. 328–375). New York: Macmillan.

Brophy, J., & VanSledright, B. (1997). *Teaching and learning history in elementary schools.* New York: Teachers College Press.

Brown, A. (1994). The advancement of learning. *Educational Researcher, 23*(8), 4–12.

Brubaker, D., Simon, L., & Williams, J. W. (1977). A conceptual framework for social studies curriculum and instruction. *Social Education, 41,* 201–205.

Bruner, J. (1960). *The process of education.* New York: Vintage.

Bruner, J. (1966). *Toward a theory of instruction.* Cambridge, MA: Belknap Press.

Bruner, J. (1986). *Actual minds, possible worlds.* Cambridge, MA: Harvard University Press.

Bruner, J. (1990). *Acts of meaning.* Cambridge, MA: Harvard University Press.

Bruner, J. (1996). *The culture of education.* Cambridge, MA: Harvard University Press.

Bryant, C., & Bryant, R. (2000). Social studies in the block schedule: A model for effective lesson design. *The Social Studies, 91*(1), 9–16.

Buchmann, M. (1986). Role over person: Morality and authenticity in teaching. *Teachers College Record, 87*(4), 529–541.

Bullough, R., Young, J., & Erickson, L. (2002). Rethinking field experience: Partnership teaching versus single-placement teaching. *Journal of Teacher Education, 53*(1), 68–80.

Burroughs, S. (2002). Testy times for social studies. *Social Education, 66*(5), 315–319.

California Board of Education. (1988). *History–social science framework for the California public schools.* Sacramento: California Department of Education.

Camilli, G., Cizek, G., & Lugg, C. (2001). Psychometric theory and the validation of performance standards: History and future perspectives. In G. Cizek (Ed.), *Setting performance standards: Concepts, methods, and perspectives* (pp. 445–476). Mahwah, NJ: Lawrence Erlbaum Associates.

Cannell, J. (1988). Nationally normed elementary achievement testing in America's public schools: How all 50 states are above the national average. *Educational Measurement: Issues and Practices, 7*, 5–9.

Carr, E. (1961). *What is history?* New York: Vintage.

Carter, K. (1993). The place of story in the study of teaching and teacher education. *Educational Researcher, 22*(1), 5–12.

Cheney, L. (1987). *American memory.* Washington, DC: National Endowment for the Humanities.

Chrispeels, J. (1997). Educational policy implementation in a shifting political climate: The California experience. *American Educational Research Journal, 34*, 453–481.

Christensen, L., Wilson, E., Anders, S., Dennis, M. B., Kirkland, L., Beacham, M., & Warren, E. (2001). Teachers' reflection on their practice of social studies. *The Social Studies, 92*(5), 205–208.

Chubb, J., & Moe, T. (1990). *Politics, markets, and America's schools.* Washington, DC: Brookings Institution.

Cimbricz, S. (2002). State testing and teachers' thinking and practice: A synthesis of research. *Educational Policy Analysis Archives, 10*(2). Available online at http://epaa.asu.edu/epaa/v10n2.html

Cizek, G. (Ed.). (2001). *Setting performance standards: Concepts, methods, and perspectives.* Mahwah, NJ: Lawrence Erlbaum Associates.

Clarke, M., Madaus, G., Horn, C., & Ramos, M. (2000). Retrospective on educational testing and assessment in the 20th century. *Journal of Curriculum Studies, 32*(2), 159–181.

Cobb, R., Abate, S., & Baker, D. (1999). Effects on students of a 4 x 4 junior high school block scheduling program. *Educational Policy Analysis Archives, 7*(3), 1–20. Available online at http://epaa.asu.edu/epaa/v 7n3.html

Cohen, D. (1988). Teaching practice: Plus que ca change ... In P. Jackson (Ed.), *Contributing to educational change: Perspectives on research and practice* (pp. 27–84). Berkeley, CA: McCutchan.

Cohen, D., & Ball, D. (1990). Relations between policy and practice: A commentary. *Educational Evaluation and Policy Analysis, 12*(3), 249–256.

Cohen, D., & Barnes, C. (1993). Pedagogy and policy. In D. Cohen, M. McLaughlin, & J. Talbert (Eds.), *Teaching for understanding: Challenges for policy and practice* (pp. 207–239). San Francisco: Jossey-Bass.

Cohen, D., & Garet, M. (1975). Reforming educational policy with applied social research. *Harvard Educational Review, 45*(1), 17–43.

Cohen, D., McLaughlin, M., & Talbert, J. (1993). *Teaching for understanding: Challenges for policy and practice.* San Francisco: Jossey-Bass.

Cohen, D., & Spillane, J. (1992). Policy and practice: The relations between governance and instruction. In G. Grant (Ed.), *Review of research in education* (Vol. 18, pp. 3–49). Washington, DC: American Educational Research Association.

Collingwood, R. G. (1946). *The idea of history.* Oxford: Clarendon Press.

Commeyras, M., & Alvermann, D. (1994). Messages that high school world history textbooks convey. *The Social Studies, 85*, 268–274.

Connelly, F. M., & Clandinin, D. J. (1990). Stories of experience and narrative inquiry. *Educational Researcher, 19*(4), 2–14.

Corbett, H. D., & Wilson, B. (1991). *Testing, reform, and rebellion.* Norwood, NJ: Ablex.

Cornbleth, C. (1990). *Curriculum in context.* London: Routledge.

Cornbleth, C. (1998). An American curriculum? *Teachers College Record, 99*(4), 622–646.

Cornbleth, C. (2002). What constrains meaningful social studies teaching. *Social Education, 63*(3), 186–190.

Cornbleth, C., & Waugh, D. (1995). *The great speckled bird: Multicultural politics and education policymaking.* New York: St. Martin's.

Cornett, J. (1990). Teacher thinking about curriculum and instruction: A case study of a secondary social studies teacher. *Theory and Research in Social Education, 18*(3), 248–273.

Cronbach, L. (1963). Evaluation of course improvement. *Teachers College Record, 64,* 674–683.

Cronon, W. (1992). A place for stories: Nature, history, and narrative. *The Journal of American History, 78,* 1347–1379.

Cuban, L. (1984). *How teachers taught: Constancy and change in American classrooms, 1890–1980.* New York: Longman.

Cuban, L. (1990). Reforming again, again, and again. *Educational Researcher, 19*(1), 3–13.

Cuban, L. (1991). History of teaching in social studies. In J. Shaver (Ed.), *Handbook of research on social studies teaching and learning* (pp. 197–208). New York: Macmillan.

Cusick, P. A. (1983). *The egalitarian ideal and the American high school.* New York: Longman.

Darling-Hammond, L. (1991). The implications of testing policy for quality and equality. *Phi Delta Kappan, 73*(3), 220–225.

Darling-Hammond, L. (1996, May). *The current status of teaching and teacher development in the United States.* Paper presented at the Invitational Conference on Teacher Development, American Educational Research Association, Washington, DC.

Darling-Hammond, L., & Falk, B. (1997). Using standards and assessments to support student learning. *Phi Delta Kappen, 79*(3), 190–199.

Darling-Hammond, L., & McLaughlin, M. (1996). Policies and support professional development in an era of reform. In M. McLaughlin & I. Oberman (Eds.), *Teacher learning: New policies new practices* (pp. 202–219). New York: Teachers College Press.

Dewey, J. (1902/1969). *The child and the curriculum.* Chicago: University of Chicago Press.

DiBiase, W., & McQueen, A. (1999). Middle school social studies on the block. *The Clearing House, 72,* 377–384.

Dickinson, A., Lee, P., & Rogers, P. (1984). *Learning history.* London: Heinemann.

Dinkelman, T. (2000). An inquiry into the development of critical reflection in secondary school teachers. *Teaching and Teacher Education, 16*(2), 195–222.

DiRocco, M. (1999). How an alternating-day schedule empowers teachers. *Educational Leadership, 56,* 82–84.

Doppen, F. H. (2000). Teaching and learning multiple perspectives: The atomic bomb. *The Social Studies, 91*(4), 159–169.

Dorn, S. (1998). The political legacy of school accountability systems. *Educational Policy Analysis Archives, 6*(1). Available online at http://epaa.asu.edu/epaa/v6n1.html

Dow, P. (1991). *Schoolhouse politics: Lessons from the Sputnik era.* Cambridge, MA: Harvard University Press.

Doyle, W., & Ponder, G. (1977). The practicality ethic in teacher decision–making. *Interchange, 8*(3), 1–12.

DuBois, W. E. B. (1903/1989). *The souls of black folk.* New York: Bantam.

Dyson, A. H. (1999). Transforming transfer: Unruly children, contrary texts, and the persistence of the pedagogical order. In A. Iran-Nejad & P. D. Pearson (Eds.), *Review of research in education 24* (pp. 141–172). Washington, DC: American Educational Research Association.

Ediger, M. (1998). Block of time in teaching the social studies. *Journal of Instructional Psychology, 25*(2), 139–144.

Egan, K. (1988). *Teaching as story-telling: An alternative approach to teaching and the curriculum.* London: Routledge.

Egan, K. (1989). Layers of historical understanding. *Theory and Research in Social Education, 17*(4), 280–294.

Ehman, L. (1980). The American school in the political socialization process. *Review of Educational Research, 50*(1), 99–119.

Eisenhart, M., Shrum, J., Harding, J., & Cuthbert, A. (1988). Teacher beliefs: Definitions, findings, and directions. *Educational Policy, 2,* 51–70.

Eisner, E. (1988). The primacy of experience and the politics of method. *Educational Researcher, 20,* 15–20.

Elmore, R., & McLaughlin, M. (1988). *Steady work: Policy, practice, and the reform of American education.* Santa Monica, CA: Rand.

English, F. (1980). *Improving curriculum management in the schools.* Washington, DC: Council for Basic Education.

Epstein, T. (1998). Deconstructing differences in African-American and European-American adolescents' perspectives on U.S. history. *Curriculum Inquiry, 28*(4), 397–423.

Evans, R. (1988). Lessons from history: Teacher and student conceptions of the meaning of history. *Theory and Research in Social Education, 16*(3), 203–225.

Evans, R. (1989). Teacher conceptions of history. *Theory and Research in Social Education, 17*, 210–240.

Evans, R. (1990). Teacher conceptions of history revisited: Ideology, curriculum, and student belief. *Theory and Research in Social Education, 28*(2), 101–138.

Evans, R. (1992). Misunderstanding social studies: A rejoinder to Whelan. *Theory and Research in Social Education, 20*(3), 313–317.

Evertson, C., & Smithey, M. (2000). Mentoring effects on proteges' classroom practice: An experimental field study. *Journal of Educational Research, 93*(5), 294–304.

Feiman-Nemser, S. (2001). Helping novices learn to teach: Lessons from an exemplary support teacher. *Journal of Teacher Education, 52*(1), 17–30.

Fell, B. (1976). *America B. C.: Ancient settlers in the new world*. New York: Quadrangle/New York Times Book Co.

Feltovich, P., Spiro, R., & Coulson, R. (1993). Learning, teaching, and testing for complex conceptual understanding. In N. Frederikson, R. Mislevy, & I. Bejarq (Eds.), *Test theory for a new generation of tests* (pp. 181–217). Hillsdale, NJ: Lawrence Erlbaum Associates.

Fenton, E. (1967). *The new social studies*. New York: Holt, Rinehart & Winston.

Fenton, E., Kownslar, A., Blackwell, V., Bryan, S., Campbell, D., Fleckenstein, J., Foster, E., Jirak, I., & Penna, A. (1970). *The Americans: A history of the United States*. New York: American Heritage.

Finn, C. (1995). Who's afraid of the big, bad test? In D. Ravitch (Ed.), *Debating the future of American education: Do we need national standards and assessments?* (pp. 120–144). Washington, DC: Brookings Institution.

Firestone, W., & Mayrowetz, D. (2000). Rethinking "high stakes": Lessons from the United States and England and Wales. *Teachers College Record, 102*(4), 724–749.

Firestone, W., Mayrowetz, D., & Fairman, J. (1998). Performance-based assessment and instructional change: The effects of testing in Maine and Maryland. *Educational Evaluation and Policy Analysis, 20*(2), 95–113.

Flavel, J. H. (1974). The development of inferences about others. In T. Mischel (Ed.), *Understanding other persons* (pp. 66–116). Totowa, NJ: Rowman and Littlefield.

Foster, S. (1999). Using historical empathy to excite students about the study of history: Can you empathize with Neville Chamberlain? *The Social Studies, 90*(1), 18–24.

Foster, S., & Yeager, E. (1999). "You've got to put together the pieces": English 12-year-olds encounter and learn from historical evidence. *Journal of Curriculum and Supervision, 14*(4), 286–317.

Fournier, J., & Wineburg, S. (1997). Picturing the past: Gender differences in the depiction of historical figures. *American Journal of Education, 105*, 160–185.

Frederiksen, N. (1984). The real test bias. *American Psychologist, 39*, 193–202.

Freeman, D., Kuhs, T., Porter, A., Knappen, L., Floden, R., Schmidt, W., & Schwille, J. (1980). *The fourth grade mathematics curriculum as inferred from textbooks and tests*. East Lansing, MI: Institute for Research on Teaching, Michigan State University.

Freire, P. (1972). *Pedagogy of the oppressed*. New York: Herder and Herder.

Fuhrman, S. (1993a). *Designing coherent education policy: Improving the system*. San Francisco: Jossey-Bass.

Fuhrman, S. (1993b). The politics of coherence. In S. Fuhrman (Ed.), *Designing coherent education policy: Improving the system* (pp. 1–34). San Francisco: Jossey-Bass.

Fuhrman, S. (Ed.). (2001). *From the capitol to the classroom: Standards-based reform in the states*. Chicago: University of Chicago Press.

Fullan, M., & Stiegelbauer, S. (1991). *The new meaning of educational change* (2nd ed.). New York: Teachers College Press.

Gage, N. L. (1986). *Hard gains in the soft sciences: The case of pedagogy*. Bloomington, IN: Phi Delta Kappa.

Garcia, J., Powell, R., & Sanchez, T. (1991). Multicultural texts as tools: Teachers as catalysts. *Ethnic Forum, 11*, 18–30.

Georgia Department of Education. (1998). *Brief summary of block scheduling findings*. Atlanta, GA.

Gilles, C., Cramer, M., & Hwang, S. (2001). Beginning teacher perceptions of change: A longitudinal look at teacher development. *Action in Teacher Education, 23*(3), 89–98.

Giroux, H. (1981). *Ideology, culture, and the process of schooling*. Philadelphia: Temple University Press.

Glatthorn, A. (1987). *Curriculum leadership*. Glenview, IL: Scott, Foresman.

Goodlad, J. (1984). *A place called school*. New York: McGraw-Hill.

Goodman, K. (1986). *What's whole in whole language?* Portsmouth, NH: Heinemann.

Goodson, I. (1992). *Studying teachers' lives*. New York: Teachers College Press.

Gould, J., Bornstien, H., & Florentine, K. (1997). Building capacity for systemic reform at the high school level. *Journal of Staff Development, 18*, 14–18.

Grant, S. G. (1995a). Nightmares and possibilities: A perspective on standards-setting. *Social Education, 59*(7), 443–445.

Grant, S. G. (1995b). Teaching history: Curricular views from California and the United Kingdom. *Journal of Social Studies Research, 19*(2), 17–27.

Grant, S. G. (1996). Locating authority over content and pedagogy: Cross-current influences on teachers' thinking and practice. *Theory and Research in Social Education, 24*(3), 237–272.

Grant, S. G. (1997a). Opportunities lost: Teachers learning about the New York state social studies framework. *Theory and Research in Social Education, 25*(3), 259–287.

Grant, S. G. (1997b). A policy at odds with itself: The tension between constructivist and traditional views in the New York state social studies framework. *Journal of Curriculum and Supervision, 13*(1), 92–113.

Grant, S. G. (1998). *Reforming reading, writing, and mathematics: Teachers' responses and the prospects for systemic reform*. Mahwah, NJ: Lawrence Erlbaum Associates.

Grant, S. G. (2000). Teachers and tests: Exploring teachers' perceptions of changes in the New York state testing program. *Educational Policy Analysis Archives, 8*(14), 1–16. Available online at http://epaa.asu.edu/spaa/v8n14.html

Grant, S. G. (2001a). It's just the facts, or is it? An exploration of the relationship between teachers' practices and students' understandings of history. *Theory and Research in Social Education, 29*(1), 65–108.

Grant, S. G. (2001b). An uncertain lever: Exploring the influence of state-level testing in New York State on teaching social studies. *Teachers College Record, 103*(3), 398–426.

Grant, S. G., Derme-Insinna, A., Gradwell, J. M., Lauricella, A. M., Pullano, L., & Tzetzo, K. (2001a). Teachers, tests, and tensions: Teachers respond to the New York state global history exam. *International Social Studies Forum, 1*(2), 107–125.

Grant, S. G., Derme-Insinna, A., Gradwell, J. M., Lauricella, A. M., Pullano, L., & Tzetzo, K. (2002). Juggling two sets of books: A teacher responds to the new global history exam. *Journal of Curriculum and Supervision, 17*(3), 232–255.

Grant, S. G., Gradwell, J. M., & Cimbricz, S. (2002, November). *A question of authenticity: Examining the document based question on the New York state Global History and Geography Regents exam*. Paper presented at the National Council for the Social Studies, Phoenix, AZ.

Grant, S. G., Gradwell, J. M., Lauricella, A. M., Derme-Insinna, A., Pullano, L., & Tzetzo, K. (2002). When increasing stakes need not mean increasing standards: The case of the New York state Global History and Geography exam. *Theory and Research in Social Education, 30*(4), 488–515.

Grant, S. G., & VanSledright, B. (1992). The first questions of social studies: Initiating a conversation. *Social Education, 56*(3), 141–143.

Grant, S. G., & VanSledright, B. (1996). The dubious connection: Citizenship education and the social studies. *The Social Studies, 87*(2), 56–59.

Grant, S. G., & VanSledright, B. (2001). *Constructing a powerful approach to teaching and learning in elementary social studies*. Boston: Houghton Mifflin.

Green, T. (1983). Excellence, equity, and equality. In L. Shulman & G. Sykes (Eds.), *Handbook of teaching and policy* (pp. 318–341). New York: Longman.

Greene, S. (1994). The problems of learning to think like a historian: Writing history in the culture of the classroom. *Educational Psychologist, 29*(2), 89–96.

Grissmer, D., & Flanagan, A. (1998). *Exploring rapid achievement gains in North Carolina and Texas*. Washington, DC: National Educational Goals Panel.

Grossman, P., Wineburg, S., & Woolworth, S. (2001). Toward a theory of teacher community. *Teachers College Record, 105*(6), 942–1012.

Gruber, C., & Onweugbuzie, A. (2001). Effects of block scheduling on academic achievement among high school students. *High School Journal, 84*(4), 32–42.

Gudmundsdottir, S. (1990). Curriculum stories: Four case studies of social studies teaching. In C. Day & M. Pope (Eds.), *Insights into teacher thinking and practice* (pp. 107–118). London: Falmer.

Guskey, T. (1996). Professional development in education: In search of the optimum mix. In T. Guskey & M. Huberman (Eds.), *Professional development in education: New paradigms and practices* (pp. 114–131). New York: Teachers College Press.

Haas, J. (1977). *The era of the new social studies*. Boulder, CO: ERIC Clearinghouse for Social Studies/Social Science Education and Social Science Education Consortium.

Haladyna, T., Nolen, S., & Haas, N. (1991). Raising standardized achievement test scores and the origins of test score pollution. *Educational Researcher, 20*(5), 2–7.

Hall, E. (1970). A conversation with Jean Piaget and Barbel Inhelder. *Psychology Today, 3*(12), 25–32, 54–56.

Hallam, R. (1970). Piaget and thinking in history. In M. Ballard (Ed.), *New movements in the study and teaching of history* (pp. 162–178). Bloomington: Indiana University Press.

Hallam, R. N. (1969). Piaget and the teaching of history. *Educational Research, 12*, 3–12.

Hallden, O. (1994). On the paradox of understanding history in an educational setting. In B. S. Leinhardt (Ed.), *Teaching and learning in history* (pp. 27–46). Hillsdale, NJ: Lawrence Erlbaum Associates.

Haney, W. (2000). The myth of the Texas miracle in education. *Educational Policy Analysis Archives, 8*(41). Available online at http//epaa/asu.edu/epaa/v8n41.html

Haney, W., Madaus, G., & Lyons, R. (1993). *The fractured marketplace for standardized testing*. Boston: Kluwer.

Hargreaves, A. (1994). *Changing teachers, changing times: Teachers' work and culture in the postmodern age*. New York: Teachers College Press.

Hawkins, D. (1974). I, thou, and it. In *The informed vision: Essays on learning and human nature* (pp. 48–62). New York: Agathon Press.

Heilman, E. (2001). Teachers' perspectives on real world challenges for social studies education. *Theory and Research in Social Education, 29*(4), 696–733

Hertert, L. (1996). Systemic school reform in the 1990's: A local perspective. *Educational Policy, 10*(3), 379–398.

Hertzberg, H. (1988). Are method and content enemies? In B. Gifford (Ed.), *History in the schools* (pp. 13–40). New York: Macmillan.

Hess, C., Wronkovich, M., & Robinson, J. (1999). Measured outcomes of learning under block scheduling. *NASSP Bulletin, 83*(611), 87–95.

Heubert, J., & Hauser, R. (1999). *High stakes: Testing for tracking, promotion, and graduation*. Washington, DC: National Academy Press.

Hirsch, E. D. (1987). *Cultural literacy: What every American needs to know*. Boston: Houghton-Mifflin.

Holt, T. (1990). *Thinking historically: Narrative, imagination, and understanding*. New York: College Entrance Examination Board.

Hughes, A. (1997). Toward a more thoughtful professional education for social studies teachers: Can problem-based learning contribute? *Theory and Research in Social Education, 25*, 431–445.

Hunter, M. (1976). *Improved instruction*. El Segundo, CA: TIP.

Jackson, P. (1968). *Life in classrooms*. New York: Holt, Rinehart, & Winston.

Jacobs, E. (1999). *Cooperative learning in context*. Albany, NY: SUNY Press.

Jenness, D. (1990). *Making sense of social studies*. New York: Macmillan.

Jennings, N. (1996). *Interpreting policy in real classrooms: Case studies of state reform and teacher practice*. New York: Teachers College Press.

Johnson, D., & Johnson, R. (1991). *Learning together and alone: Cooperative, competitive, and individualistic learning*. Englewood Cliffs, NJ: Prentice Hall.

Johnson, D., Johnson, R., & Holubec, E. (1993). *Circles of learning: Cooperation in the classroom*. Edina, MN: Interaction Books

Joyce, B., & Weil, M. (1986). *Models of teaching*. Englewood Cliffs, NJ: Prentice Hall.

Keating, D. (1988). *Adolescents' ability to engage in critical thinking*. Madison, WI: National Center on Effective Secondary Schools.

Keedy, J., Fleming, T., Wheat, D., & Gentry, R. (1998). Students as meaning-makers and the quest for the common school: A micro-ethnography of a US history classroom. *Journal of Curriculum Studies, 30*(6), 619–645.

Kellaghan, T., Madaus, G., & Airasian, P. (1982). *The effects of standardized testing*. Boston: Kluwer-Nijhoff.

King, A., & Brownell, J. (1966). *The curriculum and the disciplines of knowledge*. New York: John Wiley & Sons.

Kingdon, J. (1984). *Agendas, alternatives, and public policies*. Boston: Little, Brown.

Kirp, D. L., & Driver, C. E. (1995). The aspirations of systemic reform meet the realities of localism. *Educational Administration Quarterly, 31*(4), 589–612.

Kirst, M., & Walker, D. (1971). An analysis of curriculum policy-making. *Review of Educational Research, 41*(5), 479–508.

Klein, S., Hamilton, L., McCaffrey, D., & Stecher, B. (2000). What do test scores in Texas tell us? *Educational Policy Analysis Archives, 8*(49), 1–15. Available online at http://epaa.asu.edu/epaa/v8n49.html

Kohn, A. (2000). *The case against standardized testing: Raising the scores, ruining the schools*. Portsmouth, NH: Heinemann.

Koretz, D. (1988). Arriving in Lake Woebegon: Are standardized tests exaggerating achievement and distorting instruction? *American Educator, 12*(2), 8–15, 46–52.

Koretz, D. (1995). Sometimes a cigar is only a cigar, and often a test is only a test. In D. Ravitch (Ed.), *Debating the future of American education: Do we need national standards and assessments?* (pp. 154–166). Washington, DC: Brookings Institution.

Kornhaber, M., Orfield, G., & Kurlaender, M. (2001). *Raising standards or raising barriers? Inequality and high-stakes testing in public education*. New York: Century Foundation Press.

Kuhn, T. (1970). *The structure of scientific revolutions* (2nd ed.). Chicago: University of Chicago Press.

Kurfman, D. (1991). Testing as context for social education. In J. Shaver (Ed.), *Handbook of research on social studies teaching and learning* (pp. 310–320). New York: Macmillan.

Ladson-Billings, G. (1994). *The dreamkeepers: Successful teachers of African Americans children*. San Francisco: Jossey-Bass.

Ladwig, J., & King, M. B. (1992). Restructuring secondary social studies: the association of organizational features and classroom thoughtfulness. *American Educational Research Journal, 29*(4), 695–714.

Lampert, M. (1985). How do teachers manage to teach? Perspectives on problems in practice. *Harvard Educational Review, 55*(2), 178–194.

Larson, B. (2000). Classroom discussion: A method of instruction and a curriculum outcome. *Teaching and Teacher Education, 16*(5), 661–677.

Lee, P. J. (1984). Historical imagination. In A. Dickinson, P. Lee, & P. Rogers (Eds.), *Learning history* (pp. 85–116). London: Heinemann.

Leinhardt, G. (1994). History: A time to be mindful. In G. Leinhardt, I. Beck, & C. Stainton (Eds.), *Teaching and learning in history* (pp. 209–255). Hillsdale, NJ: Lawrence Erlbaum Associates.

LeMahieu, P. (1984). The effects on achievement and instructional content of a program of stduent monitoring through frequent testing. *Educational Evaluation and Policy Analysis, 6*(2), 175–187.

Leming, J. S. (1994). Past as prologue: A defense of traditional patterns of social studies instruction. In M. Nelson (Ed.), *The future of social studies* (pp. 17–23). Boulder, CO: Social Science Education Consortium.

Levstik, L. (1986). The relationship between historical response and narrative in a sixth-grade class. *Theory and Research in Social Education, 24*(1), 1–19.

Levstik, L. (1989). Historical narrative and the young reader. *Theory Into Practice, 28*(2), 114–119.

Levstik, L. (1993a). Building a sense of history in a first-grade classroom. In J. Brophy (Ed.), *Advances in research on teaching* (Vol. 4, pp. 1–31). Greenwich, CT: JAI.

Levstik, L. (1993b). I wanted to be there: The impact of narrative on children's historical thinking. In M. Tummell & R. Amnon (Eds.), *The story of ourselves* (pp. 65–77). Portsmouth, NH: Heinemann.

Levstik, L. (1995). Narrative constructions: Cultural frames for history. *The Social Studies, 86*, 113–116.

Levstik, L., & Pappas, C. (1987). Exploring the development of historical understanding. *Journal of Research and Development in Education, 21*, 1–5.

Lieberman, A. (1991). Accountability as a reform strategy. *Phi Delta Kappan, 73*(3), 219–220.

Lieberman, A. (1995). Practices that support teacher development: Transforming conceptions of professional learning. *Phi Delta Kappan, 76*(8), 591–596.

Lieberman, A., & Grolinck, M. (1996). Networks and reform in American education. *Teachers College Record, 98*(1), 7–45.

Lieberman, A., & Miller, L. (1984). *Teachers, their world, and their work*. Alexandria, VA: Association for Supervision and Curriculum Development.

Linn, R. (2000). Assessments and accountability. *Educational Researcher, 29*(2), 4–16.

Lipsky, M. (1980). *Street level bureaucracy: Dilemmas of the individual in public services*. New York: Russell Sage Foundation.

Little, J. (1982). Norms of collegiality and experimentation: Workplace conditions of school success. *American Educational Research Journal, 19*(3), 325–340.

Littman, C., & Stodolsky, S. (1998). The professional reading of high school academic teachers. *Journal of Educational Research, 92*(2), 75–84.

Lortie, D. (1975). *Schoolteacher*. Chicago: University of Chicago Press.

Lusi, S. F. (1997). *The role of state departments of education in complex school reform*. New York: Teachers College Press.

Lyle, S. (2000). Narrative understanding: Developing a theoretical context for understanding how children make meaning in classroom settings. *Journal of Curriculum Studies, 32*(1), 45–63.

Madaus, G. (1988). The influence of testing on the curriculum. In L. Tanner (Ed.), *Critical issues in curriculum: 87th Yearbook of the NSSE, Part 1* (pp. 100–120). Chicago: University of Chicago Press.

Madaus, G., & Kellaghan, T. (1992a). Curriculum evaluation and assessment. In P. W. Jackson (Ed.), *Handbook of research on curriculum* (pp. 119–154). New York: Macmillan.

Madaus, G., & Kellaghan, T. (1992b). A national test or testing system: Issues for the social studies comunity. *Social Education, 56*(2), 89–91.

Mason, C. (2000). Online teacher education: An analysis of student teachers' use of computer-mediated communication. *International Journal of Social Education, 15*(1), 19–38.

Mathison, S. (1997). Assessment in social studies: Moving toward authenticity. In E. W. Ross (Ed.), *The social studies curriculum* (pp. 213–224). Albany, NY: SUNY Press.

McCall, A. (1995). Constructing conceptions of multicultural teaching: Preservice teachers' life experiences and teacher education. *Journal of Teacher Education, 46*, 340–350.

McDiarmid, G. W. (1994). Understanding history for teaching: A study of historical understanding of prospective teachers. In M. Carretero & J. Voss (Eds.), *Cognitive and instructional processes in history and social sciences* (pp. 159–185). Hillsdale, NJ: Lawrence Erlbaum Associates.

McGorry, E., & McGorry, S. (1998). Intensive scheduling: A hybrid model for the junior high. *Clearing House, 71*, 149–152.

McIntosh, P. (1992). White privilege and male privilege: A personal account of coming to see correspondences through work in women's studies. In M. L. Andersen & P. H. Collins (Eds.), *Race, class, and gender* (pp. 76–81). Belmont, CA: Wadsworth.

McKee, S. (1988). Impediments to implementing critical thinking. *Social Education, 52*, 444–446.

McKeown, M., & Beck, I. (1994). Making sense of accounts of history: Why young students don't and how they might. In G. Leinhardt, I. Beck, & C. Stantion (Eds.), *Teaching and learning in history* (pp. 1–26). Hillsdale, NJ: Lawrence Erlbaum Associates.

McKinney, C. W., & Jones, H. J. (1993). Effects of a children's book and a traditional textbook on fifth-grade students' achievement and attitudes toward social studies. *Journal of Research and Development in Education, 27*(1), 56–62.

McLaughlin, M. (1990). The Rand Change Agent study revisited: Macro perspectives and micro realities. *Educational Researcher, 19*(9), 11–16.

McLaughlin, M. (1991). Test-based accountability as a reform strategy. *Phi Delta Kappan, 73*(3), 248–251.

McNeil, L. (1988). *Contradictions of control*. New York: Routledge.

McNeil, L. (2000). *Contradictions of school reform: Educational costs of standardized testing*. New York: Routledge.

Mehrens, W., & Phillips, S. E. (1986). Detecting impacts of curricular differences in achievement test data. *Journal of Educational Measurement, 23*(3), 85–96.

Meier, D. (1996). *The power of their ideas*. New York: Beacon.

Messick, S. (1988). Assessment in the schools: Purposes and consequences. In P. Jackson (Ed.), *Contributing to educational change: Perspectives on research and practice* (pp. 107–125). Berkeley, CA: McCutchan.

Meyer, J., & Rowan, B. (1978). The structure of educational organizations. In M. W. Meyer Associates (Eds.), *Environments and organizations* (pp. 78–109). San Francisco: Jossey-Bass.

Miller, S. (1995). Teachers' responses to test-driven accountability pressures: "If I change, will my scores drop?" *Reading Research and Instruction, 34*(4), 332–351.

Mirel, J., & Angus, D. (1994). High standards for all? The struggle for equality in the American high school curriculum, 1890–1990. *American Educator, 18*(1), 4–42.

Moir, E., & Gless, J. (2001). Quality induction: An investment in teachers. *Teacher Education Quarterly, 28*(1), 109–114.

Morgan, T. (1993). *Wilderness at dawn*. New York: Simon & Schuster.

Morrissett, I., Hawke, S., & Superka, D. (1980). Project SPAN: Analysis and proposals for the 1980s. *Social Education, 44*(7), 560–569.

Nash, G., Crabtree, C., & Dunn, R. (2000). *History on trial: Culture wars and the teaching of the past*. New York: Vintage.

National Center for Education Statistics. (1995). *Who influences decision making about school curriculum: What do principals say?* (Issue Brief (IB–4–95)). Washington, DC: US Department of Education.

National Center for Education Statistics. (1999). *What happens in classrooms? Instructional practices in elementary and secondary schools, 1994–95*. Washington, DC: U. S. Department of Education.

National Center for Education Statistics. (2002). *U.S. history highlights: The nation's report card 2001*. Washington, DC: US Department of Education, Office of Educational Research and Improvement.

National Center for History in the Schools. (1994). *National standards for United States history*. Los Angeles: Author.

National Center for History in the Schools. (1996). *National standards for history, basic edition*. Los Angeles, CA: Author.

National Commission on Excellence in Education. (1983). *A nation at risk*. Washington, DC: US Government Printing Office.

National Commission on Time and Learning. (1994). *Prisoners of time*. Washington, DC: Author.

National Council for Social Studies. (1994). *Expectations of excellence*. Washington, DC: Author.

Newmann, F. (1990). Higher order thinking in teaching social studies: A rationale for the assessment of classroom thoughtfulness. *Journal of Curriculum Studies, 22*(1), 41–56.

Newmann, F. (1996). *Authentic achievement: Restructuring schools for intellectual quality*. San Francisco: Jossey-Bass.

Newmann, F., Bryk, A., & Nagaoka, J. (2001). *Authentic intellectual work and standardized tests: Conflict or coexistence?* Chicago: Consortium on Chicago School Research.

Newmann, F., Secada, W., & Wehlage, G. (1995). *A guide to authentic instruction and assessment: Visions, standards and scoring*. Madison: Wisconsin Center for Educational Research.

New York State Education Department. (1991). *A new compact for learning*. Albany, NY: Author.

New York State Education Department. (1996a). *Learning standards for social studies*. Albany, NY: Author.

New York State Education Department. (1996b). *Social studies resource guide*. Albany, NY: Author.

New York State Education Department. (1999). *Social studies resource guide with core curriculum*. Albany, NY: Author.

Nickell, P. (1992). "Doing the stuff of social studies": A conversation with Grant Wiggins. *Social Education, 56*(2), 91–94.

Nisbett, R., & Ross, L. (1980). *Human inference: Strategies and shortcomings of social judgment*. Englewood Cliffs, NJ: Prentice Hall.

Noble, A., & Smith, M. L. (1994). Old and new beliefs about measurement-driven reform: "Build it and they will come." *Educational Policy, 8*(2), 111–136.

Novick, P. (1988). *That noble dream: The "objectivity question" and the American historical profession*. Cambridge, UK: Cambridge University Press.

Novick, R. (1996). Actual schools, possible practices: New developments in professional development. *Education Policy Analysis Archives, 4*(14). Available online at http://epaa.asu.edu/epaa/v4n14.html

Nuthall, G., & Alton-Lee, A. (1995). Assessing classroom learning: How students use their knowledge and experience to answer classroom achievement test questions in science and social studies. *American Educational Research Journal, 32*(1), 185–223.

O'Day, J., & Smith, M. (1993). Systemic reform and educational opportunity. In S. Fuhrman (Ed.), *Designing coherent education policy: Improving the system* (pp. 250–312). San Francisco: Jossey-Bass.

Ohanian, S. (1999). *One size fits few: The folly of educational standards*. Portsmouth, NH: Heinemann.

Onosko, J. (1991). Barriers to the promotion of higher-order thinking in social studies. *Theory and Research in Social Education, 19*(4), 341–366.

Onosko, J., & Stevenson, R. (1991). Effective staff development practices for higher order thinking. In A. Costa (Ed.), *Developing minds: A resource book for teaching thinking* (pp. 27–30). Alexandria, VA: ASCD.

Orland, L. (2001). Reading a mentoring situation: One aspect of learning to mentor. *Teaching and Teacher Education, 17*(1), 75–88.

O'Sullivan, R. (1991). Teachers' perceptions of the effects of testing on classroom practices. In R. Stake (Ed.), *Advances in program evaluation* (Vol. 1B, pp. 145–161). Greenwich, CT: JAI.

Pajares, M. (1992). Teachers' beliefs and educational research: Cleaning up a messy construct. *Review of Educational Research, 62*, 307–332.

Paxton, R. (1997). "Someone with a life wrote it": The effects of a visible author on high school history students. *Journal of Educational Psychology, 89*(2), 235–250.

Peel, E. (1967). Some problems in the psychology of history teaching. In W. Burston & O. Thompson (Eds.), *Studies in the nature and teaching of history* (pp. 159–190). New York: Humanities Press.

Pellegrino, J. (1992). Commentary: Understanding what we measure and measuring what we understand. In B. Gifford & M. O'Connor (Eds.), *Changing assessments: Alternative views of aptitude, achievement, and instruction* (pp. 275–294). Boston: Kluwer.

Penyak, L., & Duray, P. (1999). Oral history and problematic questions promote issues-centered education. *The Social Studies, 90*(2), 68–71.

Philips, D. (1995). The good, the bad, and the ugly: The many faces of constructivism. *Educational Researcher, 24*(7), 5–12.

Piaget, J. (1962). *Play, dreams, and imitation in childhood*. New York: W. W. Norton.

Piaget, J. (2001). *Studies in reflecting abstraction*. (R. Campbell, Ed. & Trans.). Philadelphia: Psychology Press.

Poetter, T., McKamey, C., Ritter, C., & Tisdel, P. (1999). Emerging profiles of teacher-mentors as researchers: Benefits of shared inquiry. *Action in Teacher Education, 21*(3), 102–126.

Popham, W. J., Cruse, K., Rankin, S., Sandifer, P., & Williams, P. (1985). Measurement-driven instruction: It's on the road. *Phi Delta Kappan, 66*(9), 628–634.

Popham, W. J., (1987). The merits of measurement-driven instruction. *Phi Delta Kappan, 68,* 679–689.

Popham, W. J. (1998). Farewell, curriculum: Confessions of an assessment convert. *Phi Delta Kappan,* 380–384.

Popham, W. J. (1999). Where large scale assessment is heading and why it shouldn't. *Educational Measurement: Issues and Practice, 18,* 13–17.

Porter, A. (1989). External standards and good teaching: The pros and cons of telling teachers what to do. *Educational Evaluation and Policy Analysis, 11*(4), 343–356.

Porter, A., Floden, R., Freeman, D., Schmidt, W., & Schwille, J. (1988). Content determinants in elementary school mathematics. In D. Grouws, T. Cooney, & D. Jones (Eds.), *Effective mathematics teaching.* Reston, VA: National Council of Teachers of Mathematics.

Powell, A., Farrar, E., & Cohen, D. (1985). *The shopping mall high school.* Boston: Houghton-Mifflin.

Prawat, R. (1989). Teaching for understanding: Three key attributes. *Teaching and Teacher Education, 5,* 315–328.

Provenzo, E., & McCloskey, G. (1996). *Schoolteachers and schooling: Ethoses in conflict.* Norwood, NJ: Ablex.

Queen, J. A., Algozzine, B., & Eaddy, M. (1996). The success of 4 × 4 block scheduling in social studies. *The Social Studies, 87,* 279–253.

Ravitch, D. (1995). *National standards in American education: A citizen's guide.* Washington, DC: Brookings Institution.

Ravitch, D., & Finn, C. (1987). *What do our 17 year olds know?* New York: Harper & Row.

Resnick, L. (1987). *Education and learning to think.* Washington, DC: National Academy Press.

Rettig, M., & Canady, R. (Eds.). (1996). *Teaching in the block: Strategies for engaging active learners.* Princeton, NJ: Eye on Education.

Riley, K., Wilson, E., & Fogg, T. (2000). Transforming the spirit of teaching through wise practice: Observations of two Alabama social studies teachers. *Social Education, 64*(6), 361–363.

Rogers, P. (1987). The past as a frame of reference. In C. Portal (Ed.), *The history curriculum for teachers* (pp. 3–21). London: Falmer.

Rogers, V., & Stevenson, C. (1988). How do we know what kids are learning in school? *Educational Leadership, 45,* 68–75.

Romanowski, M. (1996). Issues and influences that shape the teaching of U.S. history. In J. Brophy (Ed.), *Advances in research on teaching* (Vol. 6, pp. 291–312). Greenwich, CT: JAI Press.

Romberg, T., Zarinnia, A., & Williams, S. (1989). The influence of mandated testing on mathematics instruction. Madison: University of Wisconsin, National Center for Research in Mathematical Sciences Education.

Rosenholtz, S. (1991). *Teacher's workplace: The social organization of schools.* New York: Teachers College Press.

Rosenshine, B., & Stevens, R. (1986). Teaching functions. In M. C. Wittrock (Ed.), *Handbook of research on teaching* (3rd ed., pp. 376–391). New York: Macmillan.

Rossi, J. (1995). In-depth study in an issues-oriented social studies classroom. *Theory and Research in Social Education, 23*(2), 88–120.

Rossi, J., & Pace, C. (1998). Issues-centered instruction with low achieving high school students: The dilemma of two teachers. *Theory and Research in Social Education, 26*(3), 380–409.

Rothman, R. (1995). *Measuring up: Standards, assessment, and school reform.* San Francisco: Jossey-Bass.

Rowan, B. (1990). Commitment and control: Alternative strategies for the organizational design of school. In C. Cazden (Ed.), *Review of research in education* (Vol. 16, pp. 353–389). Washington, DC: American Educational Research Association.

Rust, F. (1999). Professional conversations: New teachers explore teaching through conversation, story, and narrative. *Teaching and Teacher Education, 15,* 367–380.

Rutter, R. (1986). Profile of the profession. *Social Education, 50*(4), 252–255.

Sacks, P. (1999). *Standardized minds: The high price of America's testing culture and what we can do to change it*. Cambridge, MA: Perseus.

Salmon-Cox, L. (1981). Teachers and standardized achievement tests: What's really happening? *Phi Delta Kappan, 62*, 631–634.

Sanchez, T. (1997). The social studies teacher's lament: How powerful is the textbook in dealing with knowledge of ethnic diversity and attitude change? *Urban Education, 32*(1), 63–80.

Santayana, G. (1968). *The birth of reason and other essays*. New York: Columbia University Press.

Sarason, S. (1982). *The culture of school and the problem of change* (2nd ed.). Boston: Allyn and Bacon.

Schwab, J. (1978). The practical: Translation into curriculum. In I. Westbury & I. Wilkof (Eds.), *Science, curriculum, and liberal education* (pp. 365–383). Chicago: University of Chicago Press.

Sedlak, M., Wheeler, C., Pullin, D., & Cusick, P. (1986). *Selling students short: Classroom bargains and academic reform in the American high school*. New York: Teachers College Press.

Segall, A. (2002). *Disturbing practice: Reading teacher education as text*. New York: Peter Lang.

Seixas, P. (1993a). The community of inquiry as a basis for knowledge and learning: The case of history. *American Educational Research Journal, 30*(2), 305–324.

Seixas, P. (1993b). Historical understanding among adolescents in a multicultural setting. *Curriculum Inquiry, 23*(3), 301–327.

Seixas, P. (1994). Students' understanding of historical significance. *Theory and Research in Social Education, 22*(3), 281–304.

Seixas, P. (1996). Conceptualizing the growth of historical understanding. In D. Olson & N. Torrance (Eds.), *The handbook of education and human development* (pp. 765–783). Cambridge, MA: Blackwell.

Seixas, P. (1997). Mapping the terrain of historical significance. *Social Education, 61*(1), 22–27.

Seixas, P. (1999). Beyond content and pedagogy: In search of a way to talk about history education. *Journal of Curriculum Studies, 31*(3), 317–337.

Sewall, G. (1988). American history textbooks: Where do we go from here? *Phi Delta Kappan, 64*, 113–118.

Shanker, A. (1995). The case for high stakes and real consequences. In D. Ravitch (Ed.), *Debating the future of American education: Do we need national standards and assessments?* (pp. 145–153). Washington, DC: Brookings Institution.

Shaughnessy, J., & Haladyna, T. (1985). Research on student attitude toward social studies. *Social Education, 49*(8), 692–695.

Shaver, J. (1979). The usefulness of educational research in curricular/instructional decision-making in social studies. *Theory and Research in Social Education, 7*(3), 21–46.

Shaver, J., Davis, O. L., & Helburn, S. (1979). The status of social studies education: Impressions from three NSF studies. *Social Education*, 150–153.

Shemilt, D. (1980). *Evaluation study: Schools council history 13–16 project*. Edinburgh: Holmes McDougall.

Shemilt, D. (1987). Adolescent ideas about evidence and methodology in history. In C. Portal (Ed.), *The history curriculum for teachers* (pp. 62–99). London: Falmer.

Shemilt, D. (2000). The caliph's coin: The currency of narrative frameworks in history teaching. In P. Stearns, P. Seixas, & S. Wineburg (Eds.), *Knowing, teaching, and learning history* (pp. 83–101). New York: New York University Press.

Shermis, S. S., & Barth, J. (1982). Teaching for passive citizenship: A critique of philosophical assumptions. *Theory and Research in Social Education, 10*(4), 17–37.

Shulman, L. (1983). Autonomy and obligation. In L. Shulman & G. Sykes (Eds.), *Handbook of Teaching and Policy* (pp. 484–504). New York: Longman.

Shulman, L. (1986). Those who understand: Knowledge growth in teaching. *Educational Researcher, 15*(2), 4–14.

Shulman, L. (1987). Knowledge and teaching: Foundations of the new reform. *Harvard Educational Review, 57*(1), 1–22.

Sizer, T. (1984). *Horace's compromise: The dilemma of the American high school*. Boston: Houghton Mifflin.

Skinner, B. F. (1974). *About behaviorism*. New York: Knopf.

Slavin, R. (1993). Ability grouping in the middle grades: Achievement effects and alternatives. *Elementary School Journal, 93*, 535–552.

Slavin, R. (1996). Research on cooperative learning and achievement: What we know, what we need to know. *Contemporary Educational Psychology, 21*(1), 43–69.

Sleeper, M. (1973). The uses of history in adolescence. *Youth & Society, 4*(3), 259–274.

Smith, J., & Niemi, R. (2001). Learning history in school: The impact of course work and instructional practices on achievement. *Theory and Research in Social Education, 29*(1), 18–42.

Smith, M., & O'Day, J. (1991). Systemic school reform. In S. Fuhrman & B. Malen (Eds.), *The politics of curriculum and testing* (pp. 233–267). New York: Falmer.

Smith, M. L. (1991). Put to the test: The effects of external testing on teachers. *Educational Researcher, 20*(5), 8–11.

Smith, R. (2000). The influence of teacher background on the inclusion of multicultural education: A case study of two contrasts. *Urban Review, 32*(2), 155–176.

Smylie, M. (1995). Teacher learning in the workplace; Implications for school reform. In T. Guskey & M. Huberman (Eds.), *Professional development in education: New paradigms and practices* (pp. 92–113). New York: Teachers College Press.

Spillane, J. (1993). *Interactive policy-making: State instructional policy and the role of the school district*. Unpublished PhD, Michigan State University, East Lansing.

Spinder, J., & Biott, C. (2000). Target setting in the induction of newly qualified teachers: Emerging colleagueship in a context of performance management. *Educational Research, 42*(3), 275–285.

Spoehr, K., & Spoehr, L. (1994). Learning to think historically. *Educational Psychologist, 29*(2), 71–77.

Stake, R. (1991). The teacher, standardized testing, and prospects of revolution. *Phi Delta Kappan, 73*(3), 243–247.

Stake, R., & Easley, J. (1978). *Case studies in science education*. Urbana: University of Illinois.

Stake, R., & Rugg, D. (1991). Impact on the classroom. In R. E. Stake (Ed.), *Advances in program evaluation* (Vol. 1, pp. xix–xxii). Greenwich, CT: JAI Press.

Stern, S. (1994). Beyond the rhetoric: An historian's view of the "national" standards for United States history. *Journal of Education, 176*(3), 61–71.

Stevenson, R. (1990). Engagement and cognitive challenge in thoughtful social studies classes: A study of student perspectives. *Journal of Curriculum Studies, 22*(4), 329–341.

Stodolsky, S., & Grossman, P. (1995). The impact of subject matter on curricular activity: An analysis of five academic subjects. *American Educational Research Journal, 32*(2), 227–249.

Sturtevant, E. (1996). Lifetime influences on the literacy-related instructional beliefs of experienced high school history teachers: Two comparative case studies. *Journal of Literacy Research, 28*(2), 227–257.

Sykes, G., & Darling-Hammond, L. (Eds.). (1999). *Teaching as the learning profession: Handbook of policy and practice*. San Francisco: Jossey-Bass.

Tauer, S. (1998). The mentor-protege relationship and its impact on the experienced teacher. *Teaching and Teacher Education, 14*(2), 205–218.

Thornton, S. (1988). Curriculum consonance in United States history classrooms. *Journal of Curriculum and Supervision, 3*, 308–320.

Thornton, S. (1991). Teacher as curricular-instructional gatekeeper in the social studies. In J. Shaver (Ed.), *Handbook of research on social studies teaching and learning* (pp. 237–248). New York: Macmillan.

Toenjes, L., & Dworkin, A. G. (2002). Are increasing test scores in Texas really a myth, or is Haney's myth a myth? *Educational Policy Analysis Archives, 10*(17). Available online at http://epaa.asu.edu/epaa/v10n17.html

Tyack, D., & Cuban, L. (1995). *Tinkering toward utopia*. Cambridge, MA: Harvard University Press.

Tyson-Bernstein, H. (1988). *A conspiracy of good intentions: America's textbook fiasco*. Washington, DC: Council for Basic Education.

Van Sertima, I. (1976). *They came before Columbus: The African presence in ancient America*. New York: Random House.

VanSledright, B. (1997). And Santayana lives on: Students' views on the purposes for studying American history. *Journal of Curriculum Studies, 29*(5), 529–557.

VanSledright, B. (1995a). "I don't remember—the ideas are all jumbled in my head." Eighth graders' reconstructions of colonial American history. *Journal of Curriculum and Supervision, 10*(4), 317–345.

VanSledright, B. (1995b). The teaching-learning interaction in American history: A study of two teachers and their fifth graders. *Journal of Social Studies Research, 19*(1), 3–23.

VanSledright, B. (1996a). Closing the gap between school and disciplinary history? Historian as high school history teacher. In J. Brophy (Ed.), *Advances in research on teaching* (Vol. 6, pp. 257–289). Greenwich, CT: JAI.

VanSledright, B. (1996b). Studying colonization in eighth grade: What can it teach us about the learning context of current reforms? *Theory and Research in Social Education, 24*(2), 107–145.

VanSledright, B. (1998). On the importance of historical positionality to thinking about and teaching history. *International Journal of Social Education, 12*(2), 1–18.

VanSledright, B., & Brophy, J. (1992). Storytelling, imagination, and fanciful elaboration in children's historical reconstructions. *American Educational Research Journal, 29*(4), 837–859.

VanSledright, B., & Brophy, J. (1995). "Storytellers," "scientists," and "reformers" in the teaching of U.S. history to fifth graders. *Advances in Research on Teaching, 5*, 195–243.

VanSledright, B., & Grant, S. G. (1991). Surviving its own rhetoric: Building a conversational community within the social studies. *Theory and Research in Social Education, 19*(3), 283–304.

VanSledright, B., & Kelly, C. (1995). *Learning to read American history: How do multiple text sources influence historical literacy in fifth grade?* Paper presented at the American Educational Research Association, San Francisco, CA.

Verducci, S. (2000). A conceptual history of empathy and a question it raises for moral education. *Educational Theory, 50*(1), 63–80.

Vinson, K. (1998). The "traditions" revisited: Instructional approaches and high school social studies teachers. *Theory and Research in Social Education, 26*(1), 50–82.

Voss, J. F. & Wiley, J. (2000). A case study of developing historical understanding via instruction: The importance of integrating text components and constructing arguments. In P. N. Stearns, P. Seixas, & S. Wineburg (Eds.), *Knowing, teaching, and learning history: National and international perspectives* (pp. 375–389). New York: New York University Press.

Vygotsky, L. (1962). *Thought and language.* Cambridge, MA: MIT Press.

Vygotsky, L. (1978). *Mind in society: The development of higher psychological processes.* Cambridge, MA: Harvard University Press.

Wade, R. (1993). Content analysis of social studies textbooks: A review of ten years of research. *Theory and Research in Social Education, 21*(2), 232–256.

Wahlgren, E. (1986). *The Vikings and America.* New York: Thames and Hudson.

Warren, D. (Ed.). (1989). *American teachers: Histories of a profession at work.* New York: Macmillan.

Wells, G. (1986). *The meaning makers: Children learning language and using language to learn.* Portsmouth, NH: Heinemann.

Wertsch, J. (1994). Struggling with the past: Some dynamics of historical representation. In M. Carretero & J. Voss (Eds.), *Cognitive and instructional processes in history and the social sciences* (pp. 323–338). Hillsdale, NJ: Lawrence Erlbaum Associates.

Whelan, M. (1997). Social studies for social reform: Charles Beard's vision of history and social studies education. *Theory and Research in Social Education, 25*(3), 288–315.

White, H. (1987). *The content of the form: Narrative discourse and historical representation.* Baltimore, MD: Johns Hopkins University Press.

Wiggins, G. (1989). The futility of trying to teach everything of importance. *Educational Leadership, 47*, 44–59.

Wiggins, G. (1993). *Assessing student performance: Exploring the purpose and limits of testing.* San Francisco: Jossey-Bass.

Wiggins, G. (1995). Curricular coherence and assessment: Making sure that the effect matches the intent. In J. Beane (Ed.), *Toward a coherent curriculum* (pp. 101–119). Alexandria, VA: ASCD.

Wiggins, G. (1998). *Educative assessment*. San Francisco: Jossey-Bass.

Wiggins, G., & McTighe, J. (1998). *Understanding by design*. Alexandria, VA: ASCD.

Wilen, W., & White, J. (1991). Interaction and discourse in social studies classrooms. In J. Shaver (Ed.), *Handbook of research on social studies teaching and learning* (pp. 483–495). New York: Macmillan.

Wilson, S., & Floden, R. (2001). Hedging bets: Standards-based reform in classrooms. In S. Fuhrman (Ed.), From the capitol to the classroom: Standards-based reform in the states (pp. 193–216). Chicago: University of Chicago Press.

Wilson, S., & Sykes, G. (1989). Toward better teacher preparation and certification. In P. Gagnon (Ed.), *Historical literacy: The case for history in American education* (pp. 268–286). New York: Macmillan.

Wilson, S., & Wineburg, S. (1988). Peering at history through different lenses: The role of disciplinary perspectives in teaching history. *Teachers College Record, 89*(4), 525–539.

Wilson, S., & Wineburg, S. (1993). Wrinkles in time and place: Using performance assessments to understand the knowledge of history teachers. *American Educational Research Association, 30*, 729–769.

Wineburg, S. (1991). On the reading of historical texts: Notes on the breach between school and academy. *American Educational Research Journal, 28*(3), 495–520.

Wineburg, S., Mosborg, S., & Porat, D. (2000). What can *Forrest Gump* tell us about students' historical understanding? *Social Education, 65*(1), 55–58.

Wineburg, S., & Wilson, S. (1991). Subject matter knowledge in the teaching of history. In J. Brophy (Ed.), *Advances in research on teaching* (Vol. 3, pp. 305–347). Greenwich, CT: JAI.

Yeager, E., & Davis, O. L. (1996). Classroom teachers' thinking about historical texts. *Theory and Research in Social Education, 24*(2), 146–166.

Yeager, E., & Wilson, E. (1997). Teaching historical thinking in the social studies methods course: A case study. *The Social Studies, 88*, 121–126.

Yeh, S. (2001). Tests worth testing to: Constructing state-mandated tests that emphasize critical thinking. *Educational Researcher, 30*(9), 12–17.

Young, K., & Leinhardt, G. (1998). Writing from primary sources: A way of knowing in history. *Written Communication, 15*(1), 25–68.

Zancanella, D. (1992). The influence of state-mandated testing on teachers of literature. *Educational Evaluation and Policy Analysis, 14*(3), 283–295.

Zeichner, K. (1986). Content and contexts: Neglected elements in studies of student teaching as an occasion for learning to teach. *Journal of Education for Teaching, 12*, 5–24.

Author Index

Note: *n* indicates footnote.

A

Abate, S., 196
Adams, D., 195
Adler, S., 181
Airasian, P., 137, 140, 141
Algozzine, B., 196
Alton-Lee, A., 86, 92, 102, 105, 131
Alvermann, D., 175
Amrein, A., 131, 142, 193, 194
Anders, S., 157, 203
Anderson, C., 154
Anderson, J., 85
Angell, A., 158
Angus, D., 188
Anyon, J., 175
Apple, M., 51, 185, 210
Appleby, J., 14, 126, 161
Armento, B., 174
Avery, P., 106, 146, 154

B

Baker, D., 196
Baker, E., 146
Ball, D., 174
Ball, S., 176
Banks, J., 67, 68
Barnes, C., 113, 114

Barton, K., 39, 58, 60, 63, 64, 67, 71, 75, 80, 84, 86, 88, 94*n*, 95–96, 100, 101, 103, 123, 159
Barton, P., 144
Barr, R., 49
Barth, J., 27, 49, 158
Beacham, M., 157, 203
Beals, M., 14
Beard, C., 51
Beck, I., 58, 100, 175
Beatty, A., 90, 92
Becker, C., 32–33
Bedwell, L., 40
Bennett, C., 30, 32
Berkin, C., 16*n*
Berliner, D., 131, 142, 145, 193, 194
Bickmore, K., 31, 33, 203
Biddle, B., 145
Biott, C., 198
Blackwell, V., 190
Bodnar, J., 96
Bolman, L., 162
Boorstin, D., 8*n*
Booth, M., 98, 99
Borko, H., 201–202
Bornstien, H., 189
Brinkley, A., 16*n*
Bowe, R., 176
Bradley Commission, 37, 38, 39, 176

Subject Index